gospel demands it, and the world needs it. Leading us through Newbigin's many works, Goheen shows how it is possible."

—**Steve Bevans, SVD**, Catholic Theological Union

"Goheen effectively captures Newbigin as a passionate thinker, communicator, and leader. The fact that Newbigin continues to be read and discussed two decades after his death testifies to the continuing force of his vision, ideas, and convictions. Goheen mines Newbigin's voluminous writings and presents the major themes that compose his dynamic ecclesiology, which is rooted in his vision of God's mission to the world. The biblical narrative—the election of Israel, the incarnation, Christ's death and resurrection, the commissioning of the disciples to follow Jesus Christ in his mission to the world, living toward the eschaton—invites the participation of all disciples. In each generation the church must discover its vocation, under the lordship of Christ, as a witness sent into the world. The many years Goheen has invested in thorough study of the Newbigin literary oeuvre yields rich insights in this book."

—**Wilbert R. Shenk**, Fuller Graduate School of Intercultural Studies

"Goheen is a superb interpreter of Newbigin. In this inspiring and highly readable book, Goheen invites us to rediscover Newbigin's missional ecclesiology for this generation. This book makes a convincing case that Newbigin's responses to crucial questions—What is the gospel? What must we be as God's people? How should the church encounter Western culture?—speak to the church today more than ever. I appeal to pastors, students, teachers, and local church leaders: read this book! It will shape your understanding of the church's missional vocation in the world."

—**Dean Flemming**, MidAmerica Nazarene University

The Church and Its Vocation

LESSLIE NEWBIGIN'S MISSIONARY ECCLESIOLOGY

MICHAEL W. GOHEEN

Foreword by N. T. Wright

Baker Academic

a division of Baker Publishing Group
Grand Rapids, Michigan

Published by Baker Academic
a division of Baker Publishing Group
PO Box 6287, Grand Rapids, MI 49516-6287
www.bakeracademic.com

Printed in the United States of America

Library of Congress Cataloging-in-Publication Data
Names: Goheen, Michael W., 1955– author.
Title: The church and its vocation : Lesslie Newbigin's missionary ecclesiology / Michael W. Goheen.
Description: Grand Rapids, MI : Baker Academic, [2018] | Includes bibliographical references and index.
Identifiers: LCCN 2018020575 | ISBN 9781540960474 (pbk.)
Subjects: LCSH: Missions—Theory. | Newbigin, Lesslie.
Classification: LCC BV2063 .G567 2018 | DDC 207/.2—dc23
LC record available at https://lccn.loc.gov/2018020575

18 19 20 21 22 23 24   7 6 5 4 3 2 1

To Marnie, Erin, Ben, Brittany, and Brielle

with affection and gratitude

Contents

Foreword

N. T. WRIGHT

Like many, I have personal reasons to be grateful to God for Lesslie Newbigin. I don't remember which occasion it was when I first met him, but he was already a legend in his own lifetime; I was like a teenager suddenly meeting a rock star. He had, after all, been a missionary in India, working through all the issues of missionary theology and praxis, and had been secretary of the body that drew up the founding charters of the famous ecumenical experiment we know as the Church of South India. I think Lesslie quietly relished the fact that he, a lifelong Presbyterian, was called to be a bishop: God's sense of humor, he might have said, or (perhaps better) the way in which the sovereign grace of God overrules our small human attempts at organization. He had been involved in the founding of the World Council of Churches (in the heady days after the Second World War when people were looking for signs of new hope) and had sat around the table with Karl Barth and others. And, being Lesslie, he was completely unaffected by it all. Quite short in stature, but with a strikingly handsome face and a quiet composure and poise, he was the very antithesis of the highly strung, self-promoting rock star. He gave every impression, not that he had gotten life figured out, but that he knew God had it figured out and that he was totally content just to trust him.

Mike Goheen, in this fine study that opens up the heart and breadth of Lesslie's thought, has told the story of how I had invited Lesslie to preach in Worcester College Chapel, Oxford, and how his mere arrival that evening transformed my mood from one of nervous anticipation of the new academic term to one of readiness for the challenges and possibilities that would come. I remember telling that story to a friend who had worked in India, in the area where Lesslie had served as bishop. My friend at once told me that in that part of India one could go from town to town and admire a school, a hospital, a church building, only to be told, "Bishop Newbigin encouraged us to build this, and told us who we should employ to get it done." Lesslie was, in other words, a walking model of the theological truth that lay behind all he did: a quiet confidence in the sovereignty and loving purposes of God, not such as might make you sit back and shrug your shoulders, but such as would make you think that it was therefore going to be a good idea to discern your own vocation within that purpose and steadily set about whatever tasks such a vocation might entail.

This same doctrine of divine sovereignty undergirded Lesslie's sense (strongly reinforced by his reading of Michael Polanyi) that if all truth was God's truth, then there was no area of life over which human research could claim absolute rights; in other words, there was no such thing as neutrality or "objectivity," no such thing as a God's-eye view of reality available to us. All the truth we see, in whatever sphere, comes with strings attached: world-view strings having to do with our own motivations and mind-sets, and not least with our wider culture. In the wrong hands, this might have meant the collapse of all truth statements into a subjective morass. But with Lesslie's strong view of the world as God's creation and all human vocations as located within God's purposes, it meant that all human research would ultimately belong within the celebration of God's good creation and the humble obedience to his redeeming purposes. I well remember the anger expressed by one chemistry professor who heard Lesslie preach on that occasion in Worcester College Chapel and felt that his own professional integrity as an "objective" scientist was being undermined. Interestingly, it was his fellow scientists, atheists all, who put him right. Yes, the experiments can be repeated on the other side of the world; but, excuse me, why were we doing *these* experiments in the first place? It doesn't take long to get back to the culture-conditioned human motivations behind all our apparently "neutral" observations. That is important, as Lesslie saw very well, for our reading of the Gospels as history, as part of God's true history: skeptical historiography put on a pose of neutral objectivity that needed to be unmasked. Lesslie helped many of us not only to glimpse a bigger vision of God and God's creation but also to reflect on the epistemology required for that glimpse to become a grasp.

Within all that, Lesslie taught a generation of us that a primary task of the Christian in any culture was *engagement*. He had, after all, sat on the floor of his local ashram with Hindu teachers, getting inside their worldview, not in order to work toward some fashionable relativistic synthesis, but to discern (much like Paul in Athens) points of contact and points of radical disagreement. If all truth was God's truth, then one might well expect many happy surprises as well as many moments of courteous challenge. This was quite different, in the 1980s, from what many Christians (British Christians at least) had supposed, poised as we were between a liberal "affirmation" and a conservative "rejection" of this or that aspect of "culture." Indeed, Lesslie taught us what he himself had discovered on his return to live in Britain after so many years in India: to look at British culture itself with a critical discernment, to stop taking things for granted, and to inquire of this or that cultural development whether it was honoring to God the Creator. Lesslie, after all, had not come back to Britain to retire: he just translated his missionary vocation into a sequence of different modes.

What was more, Lesslie had been through a period of radical exploration and had come out the other side. He had, by his own admission, walked down the path toward a more liberal or relativistic view of gospel and culture, had seen where it led, and had firmly turned around again—not, being Lesslie, to any kind of closed-in conservatism, but to the larger world, the fresh outside air, the fully biblical vision of the creation and redemption of the world. I remember being at one or two conferences with him in the early 1990s where some young would-be radicals were trying to argue for relativistic positions and Lesslie, kindly and courteously, would argue a biblical case for the massive and all-embracing truth of the gospel: for, in the phrase he made his own, the gospel as "public truth." (This is all the more important given the way in which some followers of Karl Barth appear to argue for a distinct sphere of Christian "truth.") He carried conviction as few others could have done. This was reinforced, in terms of his rhetorical style, by his unnerving ability, being almost blind, to give a perfect lecture, laying out a large theme with its many interlocking parts and bringing it all in to land just under the hour without a glance at notes or a watch. He was the kind of consummate professional who made it all look easy.

I was especially fortunate to have met Lesslie and been captivated by his vision of Jesus and the kingdom just before I set about writing my own big book *Jesus and the Victory of God*. Many strands come together in a project like that, but Lesslie's vision, expounded and also exemplified, helped give me the courage to shape the argument. But that wasn't the end of it. The year after it was published I was startled to pick up the phone one day and hear Lesslie's voice on the other end. Being far too blind to be able to read for himself, he made a virtue of necessity—perhaps I should say a seminar of necessity—by calling a team of students from King's College in London to come and read to him. They had been reading *Jesus and the Victory of God* out loud, footnotes and all; and he was phoning to tell me which chapter they had just finished and how excited they had been by it. I was overwhelmed with gratitude, especially since the debt was much more in the other direction. Lesslie was, after all—as Mike's book bears out again and again—a *biblical* theologian of the church's mission. It was that deep, lifelong engagement with Scripture that undergirded all he did. The phone call was then followed up with letters; unable to see, Lesslie would use an old typewriter and bash away at where he remembered the keys ought to be, producing masterpieces of impressionistic writing whose overall impact was of the excitement still motivating this old man, increasingly frail in physique, to relish Scripture, to celebrate God's kingdom, and to encourage relative youngsters like myself in our work.

It was only later, after Lesslie's death, that I began to discover more of his earlier writings. We had all read *Foolishness to the Greeks*; indeed, it was like a second Bible to some of us. But there was so much more. Lesslie had thought his way into, and then through, most if not all of the great theological issues of the day, reflecting on them with his own mixture of prayerful humility and missionary strategy. Because his life didn't fit into the normal academic pattern, I suspect that many of his profound and original books have mostly been ignored by professors who review books by other professors and engage with them in their footnotes. I hope that this book will go a long way toward turning that around. I have often reflected that, like some musical composers, Lesslie may in fact have his greatest impact generations after his death, and my prayer is that Mike's work will play a role in that process. Certainly, as I reflect on the beliefs about the church's vocation that I have come to hold over the years, and then as I look at the vast sweep of Lesslie's work surveyed here in *The Church and Its Vocation*, I begin to realize that at my best I have simply been thinking Lesslie's thoughts after him. I thank God for Lesslie Newbigin and for books like this present one that introduce him powerfully to a new generation.

Preface

It is a delight to return to the subject of Lesslie Newbigin's missionary ecclesiology. It was the theme of my doctoral dissertation almost two decades ago. I spent a number of years reading all of Newbigin's writings chronologically more than once while attempting to understand his historical context. I also tried to read the books he read. It was a rich exercise. And I have my wife, Marnie, to thank for it. She kept me from pursuing a more thematic dissertation and encouraged me to soak in Newbigin so I could be discipled by him through his life and writing. The resulting published dissertation was well over 250,000 words. No doubt the length should have been trimmed, the focus sharpened, and the argument made much tighter. Someone once suggested to me in jest that it should have been titled *Everything You Wanted to Know about Newbigin but Were Afraid to Ask*. One of my promoters, George Vandervelde, insisted on excluding a long chapter on a missionary encounter with world religions that would have made it even longer. But I have heard from many since then that the abundance of material on Newbigin in his historical context has been helpful in a variety of ways. And so, in spite of its sprawling nature, it seems to have served purposes I did not originally intend.

In the two decades since my dissertation was published, I have had opportunity to immerse myself even more in Newbigin's insights and have gained a clearer understanding of his thought. This has come for a number of reasons. First, I have taught and lectured on this material in a variety of institutions and venues within North America and throughout the world. The questions and discussions, perhaps especially coming from those outside the West, have sharpened my thinking on the subject and made me all the more aware of its relevance. I write this preface on an overnight flight home from Brazil, where I have just finished presenting much of the material in this book over the past three weeks to students, pastors, and scholars from various confessional backgrounds in four different cities. Those rich interactions have convinced me that with the spread of Western globalization as a missionary religion into all the urban parts of the world, Newbigin's insights continue to be relevant and important—and will be for the foreseeable future.

Moreover, I have had opportunity to wrestle with Newbigin's teaching on a missionary church as I have worked in more than one local congregation in a part-time pastoral capacity with fellow pastors to implement his insights. I have also had the occasion to read a number of dissertations and other secondary literature on Newbigin as well as more of his unpublished archived material that was unavailable to me twenty years ago. And finally, the process of reworking theological education in Phoenix has been heavily dependent on my immersion in Newbigin's work. The close relationships I have developed there with pastors who have wrestled to work out the material of this book, along with the attempt to design and implement a missional curriculum, have deepened my understanding of various areas of Newbigin's work. Through all of this, my thinking on his missionary ecclesiology has become clearer and more focused.

This book is the first of two that are planned. In this first volume I sketch Newbigin's missionary ecclesiology in a relatively brief and systematic way within the context of the central dynamic of his thought. In the second book Tim Sheridan and I will trace Newbigin's ecclesiological heirs—missional church, emerging and emergent church, deep church, and center church—in light of Newbigin's missionary ecclesiology. The two books began as one, but it became clear that we needed more space on Newbigin to accomplish our goal of evaluating other ecclesial movements in light of his work.

And so this book sketches Newbigin's missionary ecclesiology in a systematic way within the central dynamic of his theological vision. It is meant to be a more popular summary for a wide readership. To keep its lines of argument clear I will not interact extensively with other authors, nor will I deal much with historical background or engage some of the controversial issues raised by his thought. For those who are interested, I footnote where you can go to further pursue these kinds of things. I have also totally reworked my website www.missionworldview.com and have added many more resources, including many of my articles on Newbigin, both published and unpublished.

A couple of other explanatory notes may be helpful. First, in the last couple of decades the term "missional" has become a common word to distinguish the identity and nature of the church beyond an understanding of mission as cross-cultural or as an activity of the church. I have embraced the word "missional" in my writing and continue to use it even though it sometimes falls prey to being used in ways that are trendy or superficial. In this book I stick with Newbigin's original language of a *missionary* church. And second, much of Newbigin's writing was done before our culture became sensitive to the sexist overtones in the exclusive use of masculine pronouns. Rather than engage in the creative and sometimes tricky project of "correcting" his work, I have kept intact his original language.

I thank Thomas West for providing me with electronic copies of numerous documents from the Newbigin archives in Selly Oak. As I was finishing the last chapter, a new website with much of Newbigin's work appeared online: http://newbiginresources.org/. This is a happy development. I only wish it had appeared months earlier; it would have made my job much easier. But it raises an issue about pagination: some of the unpublished documents I quote appear on that website. The page numbers of those online documents sometimes differ from those of the archived originals from which I worked.

I am thankful for Jim Kinney's patience; this book, originally a joint project with Tim Sheridan on Newbigin and his theological heirs, is years overdue. When I signed the contract I had no idea that so much of my time would be given in the next five years to developing some creative initiatives in theological education. So this book has had to wait. I am also thankful for my colleagues in leadership in Phoenix—Tyler Johnson, Chris Gonzalez, and Jim Mullins—who have encouraged me, as Missional Training Center has become more established, to return to making writing a priority. I also thank two of my sons-in-law, Mark Glanville and Dave Groen, who read portions of this book and gave helpful feedback.

I dedicate this book to my wife, Marnie, and our four adult children, Erin, Ben, Brittany, and Brielle. They have been on this "Newbigin journey" with me for over two decades. They have all read and engaged Newbigin's writing to some degree. My last memory of Newbigin is of him sitting at a table in a restaurant telling jokes to my wife and my kids, who were between eleven and seventeen at the time. My oldest two, Erin and Ben, were paranymphs at my doctoral dissertation defense at the University of Utrecht almost two decades ago when they were in their late teens. I am thankful that all of them, along with their spouses, continue to live out—as academics, pastors, musicians, and parents—much of what I have written in this book. Marnie encouraged me to study Newbigin's life carefully, which has borne more fruit than either of us could have imagined.

Michael W. Goheen
Vancouver, BC

Introduction

Ecclesiology is first of all about the church's identity—who we are and who we serve. And if the biblical story is not the place where our identity is forged, then by default this place will be somewhere else, almost certainly in our cultural story and social location. That will mean we are no longer the people we are called to be and will be serving the wrong master. So the choice for the church in every age will always be, Will our identity be shaped by Scripture or by our culture—by the biblical story or the cultural story? This is why ecclesiology is so important: it demands that we return to the Bible to find out who we are and whom we are meant to serve.

Consider the case of the German church under Nazism. The Protestant "German Christians" embraced the nationalism and racism of the Nazi Party. Roman Catholics, originally more suspicious of German Socialism, dropped their resistance and became complicit with the same German gods when Hitler described Christianity as the foundation of German values. There was resistance to the Nazi program from some, such as the Confessing Church, and this resistance grew as the true colors of Nazi ideology were exposed. But generally a good majority of the church had forgotten who they were and who they were supposed to be serving. They were shaped by the German story of National Socialism, and they served the gods of racism and national- ism. Think also of the South African church under apartheid or of the church in Russia and Eastern Europe under Communism. These are all rather glaring examples of churches that have lost their way. Their identity and, conse- quently, the gods they served were determined by the reigning idolatrous story and ideologies of the culture in which they were set. But sometimes mistaken identity and false gods, even if they are dangerous, do not seem to be so apparent—at least not until we gain some historical distance.

Ecclesiology is not simply an academic exercise to get our doctrine of the church correct for the sake of orthodox theology. It is the hard work of returning to the Scriptures and asking the deepest foundational questions: Who are we? What is our role in the biblical story? What is our vocation? What does it mean to be the faithful people of God? How are we called to serve God's purposes? How do we fulfill that calling at our particular time and in our particular context? How is that context forming us in ways contrary to our identity? It is not saying too much to insist that ecclesiological reflection is a matter of life and death for the church.

Imagine a Christian entering Germany or South Africa or Russia and finding the church in that place utterly compromised to the reigning public doctrine of its day. If that person were to challenge the church to reflect deeply on who they were and whom they were serving, it would not be an invitation to a leisurely academic theological exercise. It would be an urgent matter with the goal of restoring the church to the vocation God had given them in the scriptural story. Ecclesiology would not be just a head of doctrine in systematic theology but a pressing imperative to get the church back on track. This is how we need to understand Lesslie Newbigin.

Newbigin returned to Britain with new eyes after almost four decades of missionary service in India. He found a church that had been accommodated to the modern scientific worldview. Many had lost confidence in the gospel and had tailored their own ecclesial identity to fit the reigning idolatrous ideology of the day. The church was content to be relegated to the private realm of life, far removed from having any influence over the majority of human life. They allowed the gospel and the biblical story to be confined to the status of subjective values and personal preferences. Europe had become a pagan society shaped by an idolatrous public doctrine. It had reconfigured the gospel and the church, and the church—tragically—instead of resisting had simply capitulated. For Newbigin, ecclesiology was thus a pressing imperative, an urgent task that might enable the church to extract itself from captivity to the powers of Western culture.

Ecclesiology for Newbigin was about much more than simply the internal life of the institutional church. It went much deeper than worship, preaching, sacraments, leadership, church order, ecclesial structures, and the like. It was a matter of recovering our missionary identity. And reclaiming our missionary identity was not simply about doing more evangelism, or a more extensive engagement with social and political issues in the public life, or even increased programs of mercy and justice. It was much deeper than all of this.

A concern for this depth dimension led to the rise of the Gospel and Our Culture movement in Britain. While this movement started off as preparation for a conference designed to address many social, political, economic, and cultural issues of the day, Newbigin saw that the discussion had to go deeper and address the "underlying issues."[1] How the church should respond to these issues went beyond social ethics. It was a matter of retrieving the comprehensive and public truth of the gospel, the Bible as the true interpretation of universal history, the role of the people of God in embodying and telling that story, and a proper understanding of and missionary relationship between God's people and their culture. All of this must undergird faithful social engagement. And it was precisely because Newbigin did probe deeper that his little book *The Other Side of 1984*, drafted for the conference, dropped like a bombshell in the midst of the British church and has had ripple effects around the world.

To be sure, Newbigin never discarded the traditional concerns of ecclesiology—worship and liturgy, preaching and teaching, leadership and church order. To the contrary, he wanted to see each of these areas of the internal life of the church serve the vocation and role God had given the people of God. Neither did he neglect the traditional concerns of mission—evangelism and church planting, mercy and justice, social ethics and political engagement. Rather, he wanted to place them within a broader vision of the missionary vocation of the church. Ecclesiology was relating our identity to all these things and reshaping them in light of the role that God called his people to play in the biblical drama.

It is this combination of characteristics that makes Newbigin's missionary ecclesiology still so important for our day. First, he is driven not by any academic agenda but by the urgency of recovering our true identity so that we may truly serve God's purpose. Second, he drives much deeper than most ecclesiological reflection by laying bare the foundational issues involved in determining the role of God's people in the biblical story. Third, he does not disregard centuries of reflection on the church and on mission but reframes them in a missionary ecclesiology.

This book is a basic and popular introduction to Newbigin's missionary ecclesiology. But as will quickly become evident, his ecclesiology involves much more than is normally associated with that word. Probing ecclesiology means asking foundational questions: What is the gospel? What is the Bible? What is the Christian faith? As we inquire more deeply into Newbigin's

---

1. Lesslie Newbigin, *Unfinished Agenda: An Updated Autobiography* (Edinburgh: Saint Andrew Press, 1993), 252.

missionary ecclesiology, we begin to see a central dynamic that is shaping his thought. It is a dynamic driven by his understanding of the gospel and, we might even say, a dynamic that leads us to the very heart of the Christian faith. So this book will articulate Newbigin's missionary ecclesiology but in the process will also uncover the core dynamic that shapes his understanding of the Christian faith and his theological vision.

Newbigin's Missionary Ecclesiology

The twentieth century witnessed a growing interest in ecclesiology. Yale historian Jaroslav Pelikan states, "The doctrine of the church became, as it had never quite been before, the bearer of the whole Christian message for the twentieth century, as well as the recapitulation of the entire doctrinal tradition from preceding centuries."[2] We are well into the twenty-first century, and interest in ecclesiology shows no signs of letting up. Every imaginable adjective has been used to describe ever-new visions of the church.

Jürgen Moltmann puts his finger on one of the primary reasons ecclesiology has become such an urgent issue. The church for many years took its bearings from the *corpus Christianum*. Its identity and vocation were defined by its location and its role within the culture and society of the Christian West. But today we can no longer think of the West as Christian. It is becoming increasingly secularized, and any Christian influence on the West is disintegrating. In this new situation it is essential that the church reflect anew on its identity. From whence will fresh ecclesiological reflection take its cue?

From mission, Moltmann believes. The disintegration of Christendom means the church must embrace their new missionary situation and recover their "missionary initiative and their own particular missionary charge."[3] This new missionary setting may then be a source of ecclesiological renewal. And so, says Moltmann, "One of the strongest impulses toward the renewal of the theological concept of the church comes from the theology of mission."[4] Yet the problem remains that "up to now the European churches have found it hard to discover Europe as a missionary field or to see themselves as

2. Jaroslav Pelikan, *The Christian Tradition: A History of the Development of Doctrine*, vol. 5, *Christian Doctrine and Modern Culture (Since 1700)* (Chicago: University of Chicago Press, 1989), 282.
3. Jürgen Moltmann, *The Church in the Power of the Spirit*, trans. Margaret Kohl (1977; repr., Minneapolis: Fortress, 1993), 8.
4. Moltmann, *Church in the Power of the Spirit*, 7.

missionary churches."[5] It is difficult for the church to reimagine its identity because it has been shaped for so long by its role and place in a Christian culture.

But if we are to be true to Scripture, then a "theological interpretation of the churches today must absorb these germs of a missionary church in the decay of the *corpus Christianum*. What we have to learn from them is not that the church 'has' a mission, but the very reverse: that the mission of Christ creates its own church. Mission does not come from the church; it is from mission and in the light of mission that the church has to be understood."[6] Ecclesiology will have to reflect on its identity and calling, not in light of its social and cultural role in Europe but in terms of God's mission narrated in Scripture. "To grasp the missionary church theologically in a world-wide context means understanding it in the context of the *missio Dei*. . . . If the church sees itself to be sent in the same framework as the Father's sending of the Son and the Holy Spirit, then it also sees itself in the framework of God's history with the world and discovers its place and function within this history."[7] The church's identity must be shaped by understanding its place in God's mission and purpose for the world.

This shifts ecclesiological reflection from issues concerning the inner institutional life of the church to its role in the midst of world history. A question then arises: What does this new approach to ecclesiology do with centuries of reflection on the church that considered the church primarily as an institution? Hendrikus Berkhof—another theologian who, like Newbigin and Moltmann, believes mission must be a source to revitalize ecclesiology—addresses that question. There is a "necessity of re-studying ecclesiology," he says, "in fact all of theology, from the standpoint of the [church's] relationship to the world."[8] He sets out to rethink ecclesiology from the standpoint of mission.

Traditionally, ecclesiological reflection has been tied to the study of the institutional church—that is, to preaching and teaching, sacraments and worship, leadership and church order. Berkhof divides his doctrine of the church into three main parts: institution, community, and mission. The church as institution is concerned with a totality of activities organized to be a means of grace. He treats the traditional themes of instruction, baptism, preaching, the Lord's Supper, leadership, and the gathering, among others. The church

---

5. Moltmann, *Church in the Power of the Spirit*, 8.
6. Moltmann, *Church in the Power of the Spirit*, 10.
7. Moltmann, *Church in the Power of the Spirit*, 10–11.
8. Hendrikus Berkhof, *Christian Faith: An Introduction to the Study of the Faith*, trans. Sierd Woudstra (Grand Rapids: Eerdmans, 1979), 411.

as community deals with the totality of personal relationships within the fellowship of congregations. And finally, he considers the church as mission: here Berkhof treats the role of the church in the midst of the world in all the ways it functions as salt and light. While the institutional church had been the primary focus of ecclesiology from the early days of the church, the church as community had developed since the Reformation. As for the church as mission, only since World War II had this notion slowly begun to take hold under the influence of people such as Hendrik Kraemer.[9]

The order of Berkhof's ecclesiology—treating the church first as institution, then as community, and finally as mission—is important. The section on the church's mission in the world comes last and begins in this way: "As the institute mediates Christ to the congregation, so the congregation in turn mediates him to the world. In this chain the world comes last, yet it is the goal that gives meaning and purpose to the preceding links. Everything that has come before serves this goal."[10] All that is done in the gathering of congregations—the means of grace, leadership, spiritual gifts, and relationships—forms God's people for their missionary calling in the midst of the world. "Around the institution a congregation is being gathered, which subsequently is scattered among the peoples of the world as God's people. Whatever comes before, this final development is the goal. But without all the preceding the latter lacks roots, drive, and force."[11] The church as institution and community serves the church's mission in the world.

Defining the relationship of the church in terms of its calling in the world raises an urgent issue: What is the relationship of the church to the culture in which it is set? As Berkhof speaks of it, once we have established "the fact of the church's orientation to the world, we now face the question of the how."[12] Our missional identity not only establishes that the church is called for the sake of the world; it also must ask what that looks like. More specifically, an urgent *ecclesiological* question is, What is the relationship of the church to culture?

Berkhof argues that the only faithful stance includes both "antithesis toward" and "solidarity with."[13] There must be solidarity with our culture as well as separation from its idolatry. The church may betray its identity in

9. Kraemer probably influenced Newbigin more than any other person. When I first met Newbigin at his home in London, he showed me a picture of Kraemer he kept on his shelf. He asked me whether I knew who it was, and I said I did. He then spent quite a bit of time talking about Kraemer's influence on his thinking.

10. Berkhof, *Christian Faith*, 410.

11. Berkhof, *Christian Faith*, 411.

12. Berkhof, *Christian Faith*, 413.

13. Berkhof, *Christian Faith*, 415.

two ways. The first is "churchism" or "sacralization." This is when the church forgets its solidarity with its culture and "turns in upon herself as a bulwark in an evil world or, less aggressively, as an introverted, self-sufficient group, which is content with her own rites, language and connections." The second is "worldliness" or "secularism." Here the church abandons its antithesis toward culture and becomes "as much as possible assimilated and conformed to the world." In both cases, the church "does essentially the same thing: she avoids the clash and the offense."[14] A true encounter with culture demands identification and rejection, yes and no, participation and withdrawal. Loss of either one is a recipe for unfaithfulness.

Reference to Moltmann and Berkhof opens the way to understand Newbigin's missionary ecclesiology and what will follow in this book. Like Moltmann, Newbigin believes that the church may only be understood in terms of *God's mission unfolded in the biblical story* and its role in that history. It is not culture that gives the church its marching orders but God and what he is doing for the sake of the whole world. For Newbigin this means reading the Bible as the story of God's mighty deeds to restore the whole creation with Jesus as the center point of that story. The church finds its identity by participating in what he is doing in redemptive history according to his command and invitation. Thus we begin in chapters 1 and 2 with Newbigin's understanding of the Bible as universal history and the gospel of the kingdom as the center point and clue to interpreting the whole story. It is in this context that we may understand the proper identity of the church.

Like Berkhof, Newbigin believes that ecclesiology means looking at the vocation of the church in the world but also at the inner institutional and communal life of the church. Thus, chapters 3 and 4 take up the church's calling in the world and the importance of its communal life together. Both are important for the missionary church. But also, like Berkhof, defining the church in the midst of the world leads to the burning question of the relationship of the church to its culture. If the church's identity is established by its relationship to the world, it is necessary to understand how the church relates to its cultural context precisely because another vision of life prevails there. And so in chapters 5 and 6 we will turn to an important aspect of Newbigin's missionary ecclesiology—a missionary encounter with culture. Finally, in the last chapter I will offer some reflections on the significance of Newbigin's missionary ecclesiology for today.

14. Berkhof, *Christian Faith*, 421.

The Central Dynamic of Newbigin's Thought

As we approach Newbigin's missionary ecclesiology, we have to reset our minds to think beyond the "churchly" issues we normally associate with ecclesiology. To penetrate to his understanding of the church, we will need to accompany him as he asks deeper and more foundational questions about the gospel, Scripture, and even the nature of the Christian faith. When one follows Newbigin along this path, a central dynamic of his thought becomes clear. Although he never called it this, I call it his "gospel dynamic." By "dynamic" I mean a basic, powerful force that drives his thought. But I also want to communicate the idea, as the word "dynamic" is used in psychology, that this basic force is an interactive combination of factors: the gospel, the biblical story, the mission of the church, and a missionary encounter with culture. This dynamic can be briefly sketched as follows.

Newbigin believes that all thought must begin with the gospel—that is, the central events of the biblical story associated with Jesus Christ: his life, death, resurrection, ascension, and outpouring of the Spirit. The good news is that in Jesus, God is acting through these events to bring the kingdom of God into the midst of history. Jesus does not need to stop and define the kingdom because the Jews are already primed and ready for its arrival. They know that the kingdom is the climactic moment toward which the whole Bible had been moving; it is the goal of universal history, the cosmic renewal of the whole creation from the power and effects of sin. The good news is that the end of universal history is now present in the middle of history in Jesus and by the Spirit.

The good news of the kingdom necessarily sets us in the middle of a story that claims to be the true story of the world. The gospel is a message about the *end* of universal history—the restoration of creation from sin. The biblical story *begins* with the creation of the whole world. Thus, the gospel places us between creation and consummation, the beginning and end of cosmic history. Moreover, the good news is the climactic moment of a long story of what God the Creator is doing in and with the nation of Israel to direct history to its goal. Thus, the gospel requires us to read the Bible as a cosmic story that begins in creation and ends with the renewal of creation. But it is also a story of what God is doing through Israel, Jesus, and the church. The gospel demands we see the Bible as a true story of God's redemptive work that gives us the meaning of history.

A central thread of this story is God's chosen people. The biblical story is a narrative of God's dealing with an elect people in whom and through whom he will accomplish his purpose for the world. They are to be a people who bear in their lives the goal of universal history: the reconciliation and renewal God intends for all. They are a people who are blessed; they are being restored to the original blessing of what it means to be truly human. They are also a people who are to be a blessing; they are chosen for the sake of the world to be a means of blessing to all. They are first of all the place where God brings about his purpose. Then they are a channel of God's renewing work to the world. It is this outward orientation—"for the sake of the world"—that makes God's people missional by their very nature. Their identity is found in the role they play in universal history.

This people is set in the midst of the world to be a sign and preview of where God is taking all of history. They do not exist in a religious vacuum but live out their calling in the midst of a world that serves other gods. After Jesus, God's people are sent to live out their vocation in the midst of all the cultures of the world. Thus, the church will always embody and announce the gospel within some cultural context. From the beginning, the primary threat to Israel's vocation was the idolatry of the nations around them. The problem only becomes more intense as the church is sent as a nongeographical and multiethnic people to live as part of all the cultures of the world. Thus, the embodiment of God's purposes for creation will always involve a missionary encounter with the cultures of the world.

This is the fourfold dynamic that drives Newbigin's thought: gospel, story, missional people, and missionary encounter with culture. These are not four discrete pieces of his theological vision. Rather, they are closely intertwined, and each requires the others in order to be properly understood. Put another way, if we start with the gospel, we find ourselves in the middle of the Bible as one story whose central thread is the missional vocation of God's people, a people who necessarily live out their calling in a missionary encounter with culture. This dynamic expresses something intrinsic to the Christian faith. It also shows how central a missionary ecclesiology is to Scripture. In the chapters that follow, we will find ourselves face-to-face with this "gospel dynamic" of gospel, biblical story, missionary church, and missionary encounter with culture.

Why Newbigin?

I have found that, even though Newbigin was one of the most influential Christian leaders and thinkers in the twentieth century—perhaps reaching the pinnacle of his global influence in the 1980s—many people still don't really know him. And so a legitimate question might be, Why Newbigin?[15] My first response would be that I have studied Newbigin all my life and been deeply shaped by his thought. But that can't stand as the only reason. I would then point to a large number of other people who have been deeply impacted by this thinking.[16] But the larger question is why Newbigin had this kind of influence.

When introducing Newbigin to deliver the Hickman Lectures at Duke Divinity School in 1994, American church historian Geoffrey Wainwright remarked that when the history of the church in the twentieth century comes to be written—if the church historians know their job—Newbigin will have to be considered one of the top ten or twelve theological figures of the century. In Wainwright's book about Newbigin, he honors Newbigin's significant contribution by portraying him in patristic terms as a "Father of the Church."[17] Wainwright offers five reasons he deserves such a designation: Newbigin's broad range of ministry was constantly nourished by Holy Scripture; he carried out his work with a commitment to the early ecumenical creeds; he always worked to build up the church as a visible social community; he exercised a comprehensive ministry; and "there was the sheer stature of Newbigin as a man of God."[18] Those are words of high praise! And these reasons alone would be sufficient to justify a focus on Newbigin. But I want to add a further response to the question of why Newbigin.

Alan Neely comments that Newbigin's ministry experience has been "scarcely paralleled."[19] Newbigin spent almost forty years in India as a missionary. As one reads about his work in India, the sheer range of his ministry is remarkable.[20] This breadth of experience provides a rich resource for theological reflection. His ministry runs the gamut from street evangelism to becoming the patron saint of and advocate for a leper community to deep theological discussions on the Hindu Upanishads and the Gospel of John with

15. See Michael W. Goheen, "The Legacy of Lesslie Newbigin for Mission in the 21st Century," *Trinity Journal for Theology and Ministry* 4, no. 2 (2010): 8–21 (special issue, "The Gospel in the Public Square: Essays by and in Honor of Lesslie Newbigin").

16. For a sampling of testimonies to his influence on the centenary of his birth, see Fellowship of Saint Thomas, "Lesslie Newbigin Centenary," www.fost.org.uk/bigincont.htm.

17. Geoffrey Wainwright, *Lesslie Newbigin: A Theological Life* (New York: Oxford University Press, 2000), v; see also 390–93.

18. Wainwright, *Lesslie Newbigin*, 392.

19. Alan Neely, review of *Unfinished Agenda: An Autobiography*, by Lesslie Newbigin, *Faith and Mission* 4, no. 1 (Fall 1986): 106.

20. See Lesslie Newbigin, *A South India Diary* (London: SCM, 1951); American edition: *That All May Be One: A South India Diary—the Story of an Experiment in Christian Unity* (New York: Association Press, 1952). This book offers a window into the pastoral life of Newbigin in his early years as a missionary. See also Newbigin, *Unfinished Agenda*.

learned Hindu monks to spending days evangelizing primitive cave dwellers on the furthest margins of Indian society to a powerful bishopric in one of the most significant cities in India. He was also a significant ecumenical figure who led the International Missionary Council, edited the most important missions journal of the time, and took a high position of leadership within the World Council of Churches. He was deeply involved in many theological struggles of the ecumenical tradition during the twentieth century, always maintaining a deeply orthodox Christian position through it all. During this time he traveled and spent significant time in Asia, Africa, the Pacific, the Caribbean, and Latin America. This, together with his lengthy ministry in India, allowed him to experience the global church on a scale that few people ever have. Upon his return from India he taught mission theology at a graduate level at Selly Oaks College and pastored a small inner-city church in the poor and multiracial context of Winson Green. He was the elected moderator of the United Reformed Church, and he also launched the Gospel and Our Culture movement, which for many people worldwide raised the question of the gospel and Western culture and ultimately had a far-reaching impact. This brief overview indicates something of the breadth and wealth of Newbigin's ministry experience that funded his ecclesiological reflection.

Wainwright notes the wide-ranging nature of his ministry in another way—in terms of the many roles he played throughout his life: confident believer, direct evangelist, ecumenical advocate, pastoral bishop, missionary strategist, religious interlocutor, social visionary, liturgical preacher, scriptural teacher, and Christian apologist. Each of these could be explored both in Newbigin's writings, as Wainwright himself does, and also in terms of his ministry experience. And it would all underline the truth of Neely's assessment that few people have paralleled Newbigin's experience.

With his broad and diverse ministry, Newbigin combined deep theological reflection on what he was doing. He was a doer—that is clear—but he was also a thinker. He reflected often and deeply on his ministry praxis in the light of Scripture. Wainwright comments that one of the reasons he dares to designate Newbigin as a "Father of the Church" is that he combined rich ministry experience with profound theological reflection. He describes it: "Right practice demands, of course, critical and constructive reflection, and the best Christian theology takes place in the interplay between reflection and practice."[21] And this is what Newbigin embodies—the wide-ranging experience and the accompanying deep theological reflection of the early church fathers. And, to our benefit, he often put his reflection into writing,

21. Wainwright, *Lesslie Newbigin*, v.

leaving behind scores of books, journal articles, book reviews, speeches, sermons, and Bible studies.[22]

There are a number of characteristics of Newbigin's theological reflection that make his writing relevant and helpful even now, two decades after his death. He was able to drive to the foundational and fundamental issues that were at stake. His thinking consistently started and continued in light of the gospel as he thought from the ground up to the various issues he engaged. He never ignored theology, tradition, or confessions—nor did he allow these to replace the gospel or the Bible's teaching as the final authority. He was a good biblical exegete who returned to the fountain of the Scriptures again and again. For example, on an overnight flight from Bombay to Rome to speak on the mission of the church in the contemporary world, he spent the whole flight reading through the entire New Testament and noting every reference to the word "world."[23] Nourished by the Scriptures and guided by the creeds and confessions of the church, he maintained an orthodoxy that shaped his engagement with many theological as well as social, political, educational, and economic themes.

Moreover, this theological reflection was always in service of the church. He could not have been further from an ivory-tower academic shielded from the messiness of church life. The problems the church was facing in its mission set the agenda for Newbigin's theology. The majority of his writings were occasional and contextual, shaped by the burning issues and needs of the day. His theology was a dialogue between Scripture and the urgent concerns of the church. But surprisingly, as one reads his work decades later, it doesn't feel outdated. One might think that the seeming ad hoc nature of his theology would lead to rapid irrelevance. But such is not the case. Wilbert Shenk commented to me that his students are always surprised by the freshness of Newbigin's writing and its "contemporary quality" that resonates with their experience decades later.[24] I have found the same thing with my students. This is largely because of what has already been mentioned above: Newbigin treated an issue by driving to its heart and shining the light of Scripture on it. While the issues may change, the theological struggle with foundational issues remains relevant and alive.

Furthermore, Newbigin's theological work is characterized by a clarity of thought and of communication that is rare. "Throughout his life, his analytic penetration, his conceptual power, and his mental agility ensured the

22. The bibliography assembled at the end of my dissertation runs more than 8,000 words and includes just over 350 entries. There is much more in several Newbigin archives.

23. Newbigin, *Unfinished Agenda*, 144.

24. Personal communication via telephone, July 27, 2017.

intellectual quality of his practical wisdom."[25] But the intellectual quality of his theology is coupled with an ability to speak and write with unusual clarity. He was able, often, to make very complex and difficult issues understandable. Tim Stafford compares Newbigin to C. S. Lewis, "who seems to know everything, and write about it with effortless erudition."[26]

In the context of this book, a response to the question of why Newbigin must be the important role he played in the development of a missionary ecclesiology in the twentieth century.[27] This is clear in two books Newbigin authored in the 1950s. Both books played an important role in articulating a consensus on the missionary ecclesiology at the time but also in contributing to its ongoing development. In 1952 a new framework for the missionary church was formulated at the important meeting of the International Missionary Council in Willingen, Germany. There the missionary nature of the church was sharply articulated in the context of the mission of the Triune God. Newbigin played a significant role in formulating the final statement of the conference. The next year Newbigin wrote *The Household of God: Lectures on the Nature of the Church*, based on his Kerr Lectures at Trinity College, Glasgow. He believed the ecumenical movement lacked an adequate ecclesiology, and this was his attempt to provide one. Many continue to believe this is one of his most important books. Then in 1958 he wrote *One Gospel, One Body, One World*, about which David Bosch comments, "It summarized a consensus that had now been reached."[28] That consensus was (1) the church is mission; (2) the home base is everywhere; and (3) mission in partnership. Newbigin's later books popularized this ecclesiological consensus and expanded its reach, especially as he posed the question of what this ecclesiology would look like in Western culture. Today it is widely recognized that Newbigin's missionary ecclesiology is the source and inspiration of many ecclesiological movements in North America.

A final response to the question of why Newbigin is to underline Wainwright's comment about the sheer stature of Newbigin as a man of God. In our culture, theological reflection is often judged only by academic standards, and a person's godliness and character is considered irrelevant. However, I believe the latter to be a critical and essential dimension to good theologizing.

25. Wainwright, *Lesslie Newbigin*, vi.
26. Tim Stafford, "God's Missionary to Us," *Christianity Today*, December 9, 1996, 28.
27. See Michael W. Goheen, "Historical Perspectives on the Missional Church Movement: Probing Lesslie Newbigin's Formative Influence," *Trinity Journal for Theology and Ministry* 4, no. 2 (2010): 62–84 (special issue, "The Gospel in the Public Square: Essays by and in Honor of Lesslie Newbigin").
28. David Bosch, *Transforming Mission: Paradigm Shifts in the Theology of Mission* (Maryknoll, NY: Orbis, 1991), 370.

Newbigin's devotional life was deeply rooted in Christ, and his life displayed a joy and humility that was deeply attractive. In a time when academic life, book publishing, and lecture circuits have become an opportunity for celebrity status and for various other self-serving benefits, Newbigin's life stands as an example of self-giving and humble service for the sake of the church as well as for those outside the church. His life was a model to be emulated. I find Stafford's words about Newbigin to the point: "He does not act like a great man. In fact, it is not entirely clear that he realizes he is a great man. If he does, he does not seem to consider it important."[29] This humble service to the church and the world, but first of all to his Lord, gives weight to Newbigin's words. We are wise to attend to them.

29. Stafford, "God's Missionary to Us," 33.

1

The Biblical Story
as Universal History

To rightly approach Lesslie Newbigin's missionary ecclesiology, we must begin where he always began: with Jesus Christ revealed in the gospel.[1] "If it is really true that God has done what the Gospel tells us that he has done . . . it must, it necessarily must become the starting point and controlling reality of all thought."[2] Anyone who would consider Newbigin's understanding of any issue, including ecclesiology, must begin with Jesus Christ as he is revealed in the gospel.

Near the end of his life Newbigin lamented that in the ecumenical tradition "we have used the word 'gospel' without giving as much attention as we need to the question of what exactly we mean by that word."[3] Certainly the

1. See Michael W. Goheen, *"As the Father Has Sent Me, I Am Sending You": J. E. Lesslie Newbigin's Missionary Ecclesiology* (Zoetermeer: Boekencentrum, 2000), https://dspace.library.uu.nl/handle/1874/597; Michael W. Goheen, "'As the Father Has Sent Me, I Am Sending You': Lesslie Newbigin's Missionary Ecclesiology," *International Review of Mission* 91, no. 362 (July 2002): 354–69. A word of warning regarding the online version of my dissertation: when the dissertation was transferred electronically with formatting done for the page size common in North America to the European size, the pagination was altered. I will reference the original book pages, but unfortunately these will not correspond to the electronic online version. Therefore, I will also refer to chapters and section numbers for easier reference.

2. Lesslie Newbigin, "The Gospel and Modern Western Culture," unpublished speech, Newbigin Archives, University of Birmingham (n.d.), 13. See Lesslie Newbigin, *The Gospel in a Pluralist Society* (Grand Rapids: Eerdmans, 1989), 86.

3. Lesslie Newbigin, *Signs amid the Rubble: The Purposes of God in Human History*, ed. Geoffrey Wainwright (Grand Rapids: Eerdmans, 2003), 113.

ecumenical tradition is not the only Christian body to be guilty of this charge; the evangelical tradition is likewise culpable. And this is no small oversight. The way we implicitly understand the gospel has enormous implications for the way we comprehend the whole Christian faith. This includes our conception of the church and its mission. Moreover, when we do not attend to what we mean by the word "gospel," its content is filled, by default, with meaning more derived from our theological traditions than from what Jesus meant when he proclaimed the good news of the kingdom or from Paul's restatement of the gospel of Jesus in light of the crucifixion and resurrection.

Jesus and the Biblical Story

The gospel can only be understood in terms of a reciprocal relationship between the central events of the life, death, and resurrection of Jesus Christ and the whole of the biblical story.[4] Newbigin expresses it thus: "The reading of the Bible involves a continual twofold movement: we have to understand Jesus in the context of the whole story, and we have to understand the whole story in the light of Jesus."[5] This means we need constantly to move back and forth between two mutually dependent approaches to open up the content of the gospel. On the one hand, we begin with Jesus Christ and his life, death, resurrection, ascension, and gift of the Spirit as the *clue* to faithfully understanding and reading the biblical story. On the other hand, we articulate the biblical story as the *context* for rightly understanding Jesus Christ and the central redemptive-historical events surrounding his advent in history.

Newbigin's own approach proceeds in this way. In his 1948 talk to the Amsterdam Assembly of the World Council of Churches, Newbigin poses the question, "What is the Gospel?" which he answers by quoting Jesus's announcement in Mark 1:14: "In the New Testament the earliest and simplest statement of the Gospel is 'the time is fulfilled and the Kingdom of God is at hand.'"[6] To properly understand this announcement of good news, one must look both to what comes before in the Old Testament writings and to

4. For an articulation of Newbigin's understanding of the gospel as revelation, see Krish Kandiah, "Toward a Theology of Evangelism for Late-Modern Cultures: A Critical Dialogue with Lesslie Newbigin's Doctrine of Revelation" (PhD diss., University of London, 2005), chap. 2.

5. Lesslie Newbigin, *Proper Confidence: Faith, Doubt, and Certainty in Christian Discipleship* (Grand Rapids: Eerdmans, 1995), 88; see Lesslie Newbigin, "Biblical Authority," unpublished article, Newbigin Archives, University of Birmingham (1997), 2.

6. Lesslie Newbigin, "The Duty and Authority of the Church to Preach the Gospel," in *The Church's Witness to God's Design*, ed. Lesslie Newbigin and Hendrik Kraemer, Amsterdam Assembly Series 2 (New York: Harper Brothers, 1948), 23.

what follows in the New Testament record. He then proceeds in his talk to outline this narrative context in terms of five headings: creation, fall, election, redemption, and consummation. Similarly, in his William Belden Lectures at Harvard fourteen years later, he says:

> As a starting point for this study, I take the words with which, according to our most ancient records, Jesus opened his public ministry. "After John was arrested," so the gospel of Mark tells us, "Jesus came into Galilee, preaching the gospel of God, and saying, 'The time is fulfilled and the Kingdom of God is at hand; repent and believe the gospel'"—believe, that is to say, this piece of good news which is now announced. What is the good news? It is that the time is fulfilled and the Kingdom of God is at hand.[7]

We must look backward and forward to ask *what* is being fulfilled and *how* it is being fulfilled. We first inquire into the background of the coming of Christ: the Old Testament. This is made up of three "presuppositions of Christ's revelation": creation, sin, and election.[8] Then, second, we go to the New Testament record, which announces the present arrival and the future consummation of the kingdom of God as the end of universal history.[9]

In both cases Newbigin begins with Jesus's announcement of the good news of the coming of the kingdom: "the centre of his teaching was himself, the claim, that is to say, that in him the Kingdom of God had come."[10] This announcement of something that is happening demands a response—either faith and full allegiance or unbelief and rejection. But what was the meaning of this remarkable announcement? The kingdom of God breaking into the world in Jesus is about the goal of cosmic history. That goal is about the renewal of creation, which stands at the beginning of universal history. To embrace the good news in faith is to be invited into the Bible as a story of cosmic history. And so, moreover, the kingdom of God can only be understood in terms of the content of that story: creation, sin, election, redemption present in the work of Christ and the Holy Spirit, and consummation. This narrative content sets the context for understanding the good news.

This biblical narrative is a story of cosmic history. And that insight, expressed and stressed by Newbigin repeatedly, has significant implications for the gospel and for the mission of God's people. In one remarkable statement,

---

7. Lesslie Newbigin, *A Faith for This One World?* (London: SCM, 1961), 60.
8. Newbigin, *Faith for This One World?*, 56–83.
9. Newbigin, *Faith for This One World?*, 84–105.
10. Newbigin, *Faith for This One World?*, 58.

Newbigin summarizes a number of themes that lie at the heart of his understanding of the Christian faith:

> If we take the Bible in its canonical wholeness, as we must, then it is best understood as history. It is universal, cosmic history. It interprets the entire story of all things from creation to consummation, and the story of the human race within creation, and within the human race the story of the people called by God to be the bearers of the meaning of the whole, and—at the very centre—the story of the One in whom God's purpose was decisively revealed by being decisively effected. It is obviously a different story from the stories that the world tells about itself.[11]

In this statement there are four important interrelated themes that will set the agenda for the remaining chapters of this book. First, the Bible is universal history that narrates the true story of the whole world from creation to consummation. Second, a central thread in the biblical narrative is that God has chosen a people to be the bearers of the end and meaning of this story. Third, at the center of the story, Jesus reveals and accomplishes the end and therefore the purpose of universal history. Fourth, this cosmic story is comprehensive and so is incompatible with all other cultural stories. Biblical story, election of a people to mission, the gospel of Jesus, and a missionary encounter with culture—these four themes form the heart of Newbigin's thought. And in this framework we see just what he means by a missionary church and just how central the people of God are to his understanding of the Christian faith.

The Bible Is a Story

For Newbigin, the essential form of the Bible is a narrative: "It is essentially a story that claims to be *the* story, the true story both of the cosmos and of human life within the cosmos."[12] When he refers to the essential form of Scripture as a narrative, Newbigin is not referring to a literary genre. The Bible is in the form of a story, but it "contains, indeed, much else: prayer, poetry, legislation, ethical teaching, and so on. But essentially it is a story."[13] The overarching structure of the Bible is a historical narrative into which all

11. Lesslie Newbigin, "The Bible: Good News for Secularised People" (keynote address, Europe and Middle East Regional Conference, Eisenach, Germany, April 1991), Newbigin Archives, University of Birmingham, 6.

12. Lesslie Newbigin, *Truth and Authority in Modernity* (Valley Forge, PA: Trinity Press International, 1996), 38.

13. Lesslie Newbigin, *The Open Secret: An Introduction to the Theology of Mission*, rev. ed. (Grand Rapids: Eerdmans, 1995), 81.

other literary genres may be fitted. This all-encompassing story is indeed narrated in the historical books of the Bible, and the historical literary genre plays its own unique role in the canon, alongside the other literary genres, in forming God's people into a faithful community. Yet story forms the all-embracing framework and context into which all the books of the Bible find their place. The narrative of God's redemptive work is like the skeleton of a body, which gives the basic shape, while the various books are like the organs and body parts, which find their place and play their unique role within that fundamental structure.

By "narrative" we are speaking of the movement of history toward a goal that discloses the meaning of the whole. Specifically, it is a revelatory record of God's actions in history whereby he leads the world to its ultimate purpose. "Revelation is not the communication of a body of timeless truths which one has only to receive in order to know the whole mind of God. Revelation is rather the disclosure of the direction in which God is leading the world and his family."[14]

The category of narrative has overarching significance for Newbigin. He speaks of the "great divide" among religions.[15] The very nature of religion is that it is concerned with that which is ultimate or that which finally unifies, controls, and gives meaning to everything. It is a claim to ultimacy: it claims to make sense of reality as a whole. Ultimate truth can be found in one of two ways, and this is what leads to the great divide. One can find unchanging truth in something that lies behind and includes all reality. This truth is all-encompassing and therefore gives unity and meaning to all multiplicity. This is the way of Eastern religions—for example, Brahman in Hinduism. Or one can find it in a universal story that has an end yet to come. This is the way of Judaism, Islam, humanism, and the Christian faith. The first finds unity and meaning in some eternal and unchanging being, and the second finds it in a comprehensive historical narrative. For Newbigin, the Christian faith finds ultimate truth in a story that is centered in Jesus Christ. "To speak of the finality of Christ is to speak of the Gospel as the clue to history."[16] Thus the basic structure of the Bible and the Christian faith is universal history, and "the deepest meaning of history lies in the fact that in it God, who *is*, is wrestling with the estranged and rebellious wills of men, until his own perfect love is embodied and reflected in a redeemed and restored creation."[17]

14. Lesslie Newbigin, *The Good Shepherd: Meditations on Christian Ministry in Today's World* (Grand Rapids: Eerdmans, 1977), 117.

15. Lesslie Newbigin, *The Finality of Christ* (London: SCM, 1969), 65–69.

16. Newbigin, *Finality of Christ*, 65.

17. Newbigin, *Finality of Christ*, 69.

To speak of a narrative, therefore, goes to the very nature of the kind of religion Christianity is. It is a narrative that unifies and gives meaning to everything. There is no more foundational or ultimate category for the Christian faith than a narrative centered in Jesus Christ.

The Bible's narrative form is that of a historical record of the mighty acts of God. It is first a historical record: the story of the Bible is concerned with *events that happened in history.* "In contrast to the great religions of Asia, the classical world view, and the view that has controlled European thought since the 18th century, the Bible affirms that history is the sphere where we make contact with reality."[18] The Bible is concerned with events in history, things that happened and are part of the same narrative fabric that records the world's other historical events. This fundamentally historical component is not negotiable. The whole Christian faith would fall to the ground if it were not the case that the life, death, and resurrection of Jesus were real, historical events.[19]

Newbigin warns against the way "narrative" is sometimes used in theological discourse to speak of a story that orders and shapes the life of the Christian community but is little concerned with history. Specifically, he departs at this point from postliberals such as Hans Frei and George Lindbeck, from whom he learned much about the way the Bible functions as a master narrative to form a community. "When the word *narrative* is used in theological discourse, it is sometimes with the implication that the historical truth of the narrative is not important. . . . It is of the essence of the Christian faith that this story is the true story." He asks, "How do we understand the meaning of 'true' in this context?" If we follow the lead of the Bible itself, then "true" means a narrative account of "things that really happened."[20]

The historical nature of the biblical story must be protected on two sides from the encroaching power of the Enlightenment in the Christian community. On the one side, the liberal tradition has reduced the story to a record of the religious experience of an ancient Near Eastern people. The "happenedness" of most of the narrative is suspect at best. The narrative of the Enlightenment is assumed to be true and used to judge the historical veracity of the biblical account. When judged by the central criterion of the Enlightenment story—scientific knowledge—most of the narrative is dismissed as a sort of religious experience. On the other side, the evangelical tradition has reduced the Bible to propositional truth. There is a long, powerfully

18. Newbigin, "Biblical Authority," 2.
19. See Newbigin, *Gospel in a Pluralist Society,* 66.
20. Newbigin, *Truth and Authority,* 40–41.

entrenched tradition that arose in the middle of the twentieth century with theologians, such as Carl F. H. Henry, who rightly want to protect Scripture as truth from liberal higher criticism. In an attempt to hold on to the universal truth of the Scriptures, the Bible is molded into a book of timeless and eternal propositional truths about God and the world. The Enlightenment notion of truth is seized in order to protect the truth of Scripture. This is an extremely important point for Newbigin, and so we need to delve a little more deeply into the source of this problem.

For the Bible, the source of ultimately reliable truth is a narrative series of historical events that disclose God's purpose for the world. Alternatively, the Greco-Roman stream within Western culture relocates that source of ultimate truth to unchanging ideas that stand above history. This has a pagan source in Plato and Aristotle. While this Greek tradition has played an important role throughout Western history, the influence of Augustine's *City of God* kept this tradition from becoming dominant for a thousand years. Augustine's narrative of the coming of the city of God did not eliminate the Greek pagan approach but kept it at bay. However, we see a shift beginning in the late Middle Ages that culminated in the Enlightenment, wherein this Greek approach moves to an ascendant position in the wake of the scientific revolution. "The Enlightenment . . . was—from one point of view—a shift in the location of reliable truth from the story told in the Bible to the eternal truths of reason, of which the mathematical physics of Newton offered the supreme model."[21]

When this shift takes place, the truth of what God and the world are like appears to be best expressed in timeless theological statements. Perhaps these eternal truths are illustrated by stories, but the deepest truth is found in timeless propositions. Newbigin quotes the first statement of the Westminster Confession of Faith that God is "infinite in being and perfection, a most pure spirit, invisible, without body, parts or passion, immutable, immense, eternal, incomprehensible, almighty, most wise, most holy, most free, most absolute" and then comments that "we are in a world different from the Bible."[22] He is not disputing the truth *content* of this confession; rather, it is the *form* of this articulation that does not follow the pedagogy of the Bible. It shows more dependency on Aristotle than on the Old Testament. The very way truth is expressed in the Bible is in a historical story. Truth comes as a narrative that reveals God through his mighty deeds and invites us to know him; it is a story in which God's redemptive work in history reveals his purpose and calls us

---

21. Newbigin, *Proper Confidence*, 73.
22. Westminster Confession of Faith 2.1, quoted in Newbigin, *Open Secret*, 82.

to find our place. "The Bible does not tell stories that illustrate something true apart from the story. The Bible tells a story that is *the* story, the story of which our human life is a part."[23] All theological formulations, including evangelical ones that claim to be expressions of eternal truth, are really "attempts we make at particular moments in the story to grasp and state how things are in terms of our experience at that point. They are all provisional and relative to time and place, as we recognize when as twentieth-century people we read the seventeenth-century language of the Westminster Confession." These formulations may be more or less faithful to the story, but in either case they are second-order activities. Newbigin is surely on target in this critique of some species of evangelicalism. He concludes, "The reality with which we have to deal is the story—the story that begins before the creation of the world, ends beyond the end of the world, and leads through the narrow road that is marked by the names of Abraham, Isaac, and Jacob, Moses, Amos, Paul, and, name above every name, Jesus."[24]

The story the Bible tells with these historical names and events is not simply one species of religious experience expressed in myths that arise out of an ancient Near Eastern people. Rather, what makes the biblical record unique is that it deals with nothing less than *the mighty acts of God*. This is not a mere record of an ancient tribe's religious experiences but what the one living God is doing for the salvation of the world in and through a certain people. "It is history in the sense that it tells of things that really happened, the same things as those of which pagan historians wrote. *But it was told as the narrative of the mighty acts of God.*"[25] The events are selected, recorded, organized, and interpreted because they testify to events in which God discloses the origin, meaning, and ultimate goal of history—a redeemed and restored creation. Since these are the mighty acts of God, the story the Bible tells is true for all people throughout their whole lives at all times. This is God's story.

The Biblical Story Is Universal History

What exactly is the status of this biblical narrative in Newbigin's understanding? This is an important question since many answers are given or, more likely, assumed in various theological circles. And the answer we give to that question will impact our view of church and mission.

23. Newbigin, *Open Secret*, 82.
24. Newbigin, *Open Secret*, 83.
25. Newbigin, *Truth and Authority*, 67 (my emphasis).

We have already noted several options that Newbigin would reject. Narrative cannot be reduced simply to a literary genre. Nor can narrative be reduced to either the mythological story of a premodern ancient Near Eastern people, as in the liberal tradition, or even the true myth of the postliberal tradition. And there are other understandings of the notion of "narrative" that Newbigin would reject. Two common misunderstandings are that story has to do with either a way of interpreting Scripture (redemptive-historical or narrative hermeneutic) or an approach to theology (biblical or narrative or redemptive-historical theology). No doubt these are implications of the biblical story, but narrative cannot be reduced to hermeneutics or theology.

The very nature of Scripture is that it is the true story of the world and that it provides the all-encompassing framework for or the overarching umbrella under which *any* kind of second-order theological reflection must be done. For Newbigin story cannot be reduced to theology; it is much bigger and more significant than that. It is the true story of the whole world. To be fully human as God intends is to be part of the biblical story that finds its center in Jesus Christ.[26]

We can put it another way to show just what an astonishing claim Newbigin is making here. The claim that the Bible tells the true story of the whole world is nothing less than *the very nature of the Christian faith*. It is not a literary genre, a hermeneutic, or a way of doing theology. It is what the Christian faith *is*—the whole point of Christianity. "The Christian faith *is* a particular way of understanding history as a whole which finds in the story about Jesus its decisive clue."[27] "Christian faith *is itself* an interpretation of history."[28]

One of the primary ways that Newbigin made this point was to speak of the Bible in terms of universal or cosmic history. The Bible "sets before us a vision of cosmic history from the creation of the world to its consummation, of the nations which make up the one human family, and—of course—of one nation chosen to be the bearer of the meaning of history for the sake of all, and of one man called to be the bearer of that meaning for the nation. The Bible *is* universal history."[29] The Bible is "cosmic history," the "entire story of all things," a story that moves "from creation to consummation,"

26. See Lesslie Newbigin, *A Word in Season: Perspectives on Christian World Missions* (Grand Rapids: Eerdmans, 1994), 118.

27. Lesslie Newbigin, "The Centrality of Jesus for History," in *Incarnation and Myth: The Debate Continued*, ed. Michael Goulder (Grand Rapids: Eerdmans, 1979), 200 (my emphasis). Newbigin says elsewhere that "the Christian faith is a faith regarding the meaning and end of the human story as a whole" (*Open Secret*, 89).

28. Newbigin, *Finality of Christ*, 55 (my emphasis).

29. Newbigin, *Gospel in a Pluralist Society*, 89.

the "story of the human race within creation."[30] It doesn't get much more comprehensive than that. And it is a bold claim!

Newbigin often summarizes a conversation he had with his Hindu friend Chaturvedi Badrinath, a scholar of the world's religions, to make his point. He believes that, sadly, Badrinath understands the nature of the Scriptures better than many Christians, even while Badrinath himself thinks the Christian claim to be absurd.

> I can't understand why you missionaries present the Bible to us in India as a book of religion. It is not a book of religion—and anyway we have plenty of books of religion in India. We don't need any more! I find in your Bible a unique interpretation of universal history, the history of the whole creation and the history of the human race. And therefore a unique interpretation of the human person as a responsible actor in history. That is unique. There is nothing else in the whole religious literature of the world to put alongside it.[31]

This is a story that encompasses the entire creation and all the nations of the world along with every part of their cultural lives. It is a story of the purposeful activity of God, who is Creator, Ruler, Sustainer, Redeemer, and Judge of the entire universe. But that purpose is found in a small ancient Near Eastern nation and in a first-century Jewish man because that is where God was at work revealing and accomplishing his purpose. This is the "scandal of particularity"[32] and certainly is a "tremendously bold claim,"[33] a "stupendous claim" that is nothing short of "astounding."[34] No wonder Badrinath thought the claim to be absurd!

The Biblical Story Will Clash with Other Cultural Stories

This claim that the Bible is the true story of the world immediately raises the problem of other stories that make the same claim. The church always lives in a cultural context that has a different story to tell about the world. The way we understand human life depends on what story we believe is true. In our contemporary culture, the Bible is contested by the humanist story. Both

30. Newbigin, "The Bible: Good News for Secularised People," 6.
31. Lesslie Newbigin, *A Walk through the Bible* (Louisville: Westminster John Knox, 1999), 4.
32. Newbigin, *Open Secret*, 66–67.
33. Lesslie Newbigin, "Why Study the Old Testament?," *National Christian Council Review* 74 (1954): 75.
34. Newbigin, *Proper Confidence*, 77.

stories are comprehensive and claim to be true. Both stories invite hearers to find their place in the story and so claim the ultimate allegiance of those who hear them. The Bible never stands in a cultural vacuum but is always in a context where it is challenged by an alternative and rival story.[35]

The problem in Western culture is that the biblical story has been tailored to fit into the more comprehensive cultural story. The fact-value dichotomy that plagues the West has forced the Bible into the inferior realm of religious values. The Western story of progress by way of science, technology, and the construction of a rational society is assumed to be the true story of the world. The problem for Newbigin is not so much that this is what contemporary Western non-Christians believe. That is normal and properly basic. This is how stories function: when one embraces a story, everything else must fit into it. And so Western folk who indwell the humanist story should make the Bible fit their story; they will reject its claim and see it as just another religious book that belongs in the private realm of religion. The problem is that *Christians* who have embraced Christ have allowed themselves to be drawn into the Western story as their ultimate allegiance and, like their unbelieving neighbors, have made peace with the relegation of their Christian faith to the realm of values. This is nothing short of sheer syncretism. It is a misunderstanding of the nature of Scripture and is the church's abandonment of its vocation to live in the midst of history as a witness to the true story of the world. "To be human is to be a part of a story, and to be fully human as God intends is to be part of the true story and to understand its beginning and its ending. The true story is one of which the central clues are given in the Bible, and the hinge of the story on which all its meaning turns is the incarnation, death, and resurrection of Jesus Christ. That is the message we are entrusted with, and we owe it to all people to share it."[36]

This explains two important phrases that are associated with Newbigin's later work in Western culture: gospel as public truth and gospel as missionary encounter. He spent much of his energy seeking to foster a missionary encounter between the gospel and Western culture. A missionary encounter is a clash between two equally ultimate and comprehensive stories. These two stories are "different and incompatible" such that if the church lives fully in the biblical story, it will inevitably clash with the cultural story, the received dogma that controls the public life of society. It is only as the church understands the gospel and the biblical story as public truth—truth for all

---

35. Newbigin, *Gospel in a Pluralist Society*, 15–16.
36. Newbigin, *Word in Season*, 118.

nations, all peoples, and all of cultural life—that it will be equipped for its missionary encounter.

We will return in chapter 6 to the Western story and a missionary encounter. But it is important at this stage to note the way Newbigin always pleaded for an understanding of Scripture as story, not as mere theology done within the academic setting but as a matter of life and death for the Christian church. If the church did not embrace the Bible as one story and as their story, it would inevitably succumb to another—and that is unfaithful compromise and syncretism. As he puts it, "If this biblical story is not the one that really controls our thinking then inevitably we shall be swept into the story that the world tells about itself. We shall become increasingly indistinguishable from the pagan world of which we are a part."[37]

So the implications of this confession of scriptural authority for the church and its mission are significant. This is not simply a matter of getting our doctrine of Scripture correct for the sake of orthodoxy. It is a matter of faithfulness to our missional calling—our very being! "I do not believe that we can speak effectively of the Gospel as a word addressed to our culture unless we recover a sense of the Scriptures as a canonical whole, as the story which provides the true context for our understanding of the meaning of our lives—both personal and public."[38] Here are the three important dimensions of biblical authority that need to be recovered if the church is to be faithful to its missionary vocation: the Bible is a *story*; it is a *true* story; and it is a *comprehensive* story with authority over every nation and over the whole of human life. The Bible is the true story of the whole world. We are set in the midst of the world to witness to God's comprehensive purpose. Until the consummation, he has "entrusted to us the task of making His victory known and effective in every nation and in every sphere of life."[39]

The Biblical Story Reveals God's Purpose

The Bible tells us the true story of the world because it reveals God's purpose for the entire creation. For Newbigin the oft-used word "purpose" carries significant weight. He often elaborates this in terms of knowing the meaning of the world because you know the origin and goal of history. The Bible is

37. Newbigin, "Biblical Authority," 2.

38. Lesslie Newbigin, "Response to 'Word of God?,' John Coventry, SJ," *Gospel and Our Culture Newsletter* 10 (1991): 2.

39. Lesslie Newbigin, "The Present Christ and the Coming Christ," *Ecumenical Review* 6, no. 1 (1954): 123.

cosmic history because it begins with the *origin* of the whole world in creation; there, God reveals his purpose for the creation and for humankind. The Bible finds its *goal* in the renewal of whole creation; there, the purpose for the world is disclosed. The story of God's dealings with Israel and the church, and ultimately in Jesus Christ, discloses the *meaning* of the creation and of human life. Israel is chosen to bear and embody the meaning of the whole, Jesus fully reveals and accomplishes it, and the church is sent to make it known among the nations. It is a universal story revealed in a particular nation, a particular man, and a particular community. God's work in Israel, in Jesus, and in the church moves toward the renewal of all creation as the goal of history.

God's Purpose Is the Cosmic Renewal of Creation

The biblical narrative reveals the purpose of God for the world. Newbigin describes that purpose as "cosmic renewal or restoration . . . a divine act by which all created things are to be renewed."[40] This cosmic renewal is characterized both by its *cosmic breadth* and by its *restorative essence*. Salvation is as wide as creation, and it is the restoration of the sin-corrupted creation back to its original purpose. That is the goal of universal history.

The cosmic scope of salvation is the restoration of the entirety of human life in the midst of the nonhuman creation. The renewal of human life involves four dimensions of restoration: of the broken harmony between God and humanity, among human beings in their various relationships, between humanity and the nonhuman creation, and within each human being. The recovery of the original shalom in these relationships is the "very essence" of salvation;[41] God's purpose for his creation at the beginning becomes the goal of redemptive history. "The salvation of which the Gospel speaks and which is determinative of the nature and function of the Church is as the very word itself should teach us—a making whole, a healing. It is the summing-up of all things in Christ. It embraces within its scope the restoration of harmony between man and God, between man and man, and between man and nature for which all things were at the first created. It is the restoration of the whole creation."[42]

Even though he has not developed a robust doctrine of creation—something desperately needed today in North America[43]—it remains true that throughout

40. Newbigin, *Signs amid the Rubble*, 28.
41. Lesslie Newbigin, *Household of God: Lectures on the Nature of the Church* (New York: Friendship Press, 1954), 161.
42. Newbigin, *Household of God*, 159.
43. The best place to find such a robust doctrine of creation is in Albert M. Wolters, *Creation Regained: Biblical Basics for a Reformational Worldview* (Grand Rapids: Eerdmans, 2005), chap. 2.

his writings Newbigin continually makes the connection between creation and salvation: salvation is the restoration of the creation from sin and its curse. Simply, salvation is "the restoration of creation to its original purpose by the purging away of sin."[44]

The first chapters of Genesis describe the creation of humans and their fall into sin in terms of the four relationships just mentioned: with God, with one another, with the nonhuman creation, and within themselves.[45] Sin has brought about a radical contradiction and disharmony in each of those relationships. "Salvation means that man is released from bondage, and that the contradictions of which we have spoken are overcome. . . . It means 'wholeness.' It means the healing of that which is wounded, the mending of that which is broken, the setting free of that which is bound."[46] The plotline of the biblical story with its ultimate goal of cosmic restoration is made clear in the movement of creation, sin, and salvation. Genesis shows us God's original purpose for humanity and the creation and its corruption by sin; the biblical story narrates God's restoration of that purpose lost by sin and its curse. "What is given to us in these chapters of Genesis . . . is the truth about man expressed in pictures—the truth of his creation, of his nature, and of his sin. . . . What God has given to us in the Bible is the revelation of the nature which God has given to man, of the manner in which sin has corrupted that nature, and of the salvation which God has provided for us."[47]

Newbigin contrasts this goal with two erroneous positions within the liberal and evangelical traditions of the church: the Western history of progress that afflicts the liberal tradition and the individual, otherworldly salvation that corrupts the evangelical tradition. The "Christianized form of the idea of progress" found in liberalism has a vision for the purpose of history as a whole: the restoration of society. However, this restoration looks more like the paradise of the Enlightenment dream. It eliminates restoration as an act of God at the end of history and sees history as a gradual and incremental movement toward cosmic and corporate harmony. And this position has no place for the individual when the end arrives. The liberal tradition has departed from the biblical story by simply domesticating it to the Western story of progress.

The second position is the knee-jerk response of the evangelical tradition to these distortions: salvation is God's work of snatching individuals from this corrupted world into another world. In this vision there is a place for the

44. Lesslie Newbigin, *Sin and Salvation* (Philadelphia: Westminster, 1956), 124.
45. Newbigin, *Sin and Salvation*, 11–15, 21–22.
46. Newbigin, *Sin and Salvation*, 14.
47. Newbigin, *Sin and Salvation*, 22.

individual, but history is relegated to the margins. This view of the end is indebted to the pagan Greek worldview. Unfortunately, this individualistic and otherworldly salvation continues to ravage the evangelical community, and it continues to have a devastating effect on the mission of the church. We must reject this, Newbigin rightly believes, as an utter misunderstanding of the biblical nature of salvation.

> The emphasis of the New Testament teaching about last things is not upon our escaping out of this world into another one, but upon Christ's return-ing to this world in glory . . . to reign . . . over a renewed and transformed creation.[48]

> The end of the story is not escape into another world. It is the triumph of God in this world—a triumph that lies on the other side of death. . . . It is life beyond death—not the immortality of the souls liberated from this world but the resurrection of the body and the re-creation of all things.[49]

God's Purpose and the Logic of Election

The Bible is a story of universal history that is moving toward the goal of cosmic renewal. How does God reveal and accomplish this universal pur-pose? The answer is, perhaps somewhat surprisingly, through the logic of election[50]—the calling of a particular people through whom God will disclose and bring about his universal purpose for the world.

No doubt to give election such a prominent place in the biblical story would occasion surprise and objections.[51] Newbigin states two such objections as metaphysical and ethical. The metaphysical difficulty is that it is self-evident that God is present always and everywhere, and therefore to speak of him as acting in a particular series of events in one nation at one point in history is ridiculous and even scandalous. This is the "scandal of particularity."[52] The ethical difficulty is that such a choice of a particular people for special favor would be discriminatory and arbitrary. It is the random action of a despot

48. Lesslie Newbigin, *Behold, I Make All Things New* (Madras: Christian Literature Society, 1968), 22.

49. Lesslie Newbigin, "The Bible Study Lectures," in *Digest of the Proceedings of the Ninth Meet-ing of the Consultation on Church Union (COCU)*, ed. Paul A. Crow (Princeton: COCU, 1970), 220. See Newbigin, *Sin and Salvation*, 122–23.

50. See Newbigin, *Gospel in a Pluralist Society*, 80.

51. See George Hunsberger, *Bearing the Witness of the Spirit: Lesslie Newbigin's Theology of Cul-tural Plurality* (Grand Rapids: Eerdmans, 1998), for an articulation of the importance of election in the thought of Lesslie Newbigin.

52. Newbigin, *Open Secret*, 66–67.

but not a benevolent God who has created and loves all people.[53] This is the "scandal of divine election."[54]

These two objections arise because those who make them misunderstand two things: salvation and election. And so Newbigin attempts to rehabilitate a doctrine of election in keeping with Scripture and to demonstrate the integral logic of election to the salvation that is the goal of the biblical story. He believes that "the principle of election is the only principle congruous with the nature of God's redemptive purpose"[55] and that "God's way of universal salvation . . . *must* be accomplished by the way of election."[56] As we see how Newbigin articulates salvation and election, the objections above lose their force.

The problem is when we view salvation as individualistic and spiritualistic. It is misunderstood as a spiritualized one-to-one relationship of the human soul with God. However, in Scripture, salvation is social and cosmic: it is about knitting together the human race again in reconciliation with God, with each other, and with the nonhuman creation. It is a restoration of the harmony and shalom of the creation, of the way God made humanity and the world at the beginning. Newbigin describes salvation this way:

> God, according to the Bible, is concerned with the redemption of the whole human race and of the whole created world. The goal of His purpose is not a collection of individual spirits abstracted one by one from their involvement in the world of matter and in the human community and set in a new and purely spiritual relation to Himself. Such a thought is irreconcilable with the biblical view of God, of man, and of the world. The redemption with which He is concerned is both social and cosmic, and therefore the way of its working involves at every point the re-creation of true human relationships and of true relationship between man and the rest of the created order.[57]

It is "in the context of this biblical conception of the nature and scope of salvation that we are to understand . . . the doctrine of election." If salvation is conceived of "as ultimately a matter of the relationship between each individual soul and God, then the whole idea of divine election appears as a piece of arbitrary favoritism, typical of an irresponsible potentate but unworthy of the God and Father of our Lord Jesus Christ." This is a misunderstanding of salvation that corrupts election. "But once it is understood that salvation is

53. Newbigin, *Faith for This One World?*, 78.
54. Newbigin, *Faith for This One World?*, 82.
55. Newbigin, *Household of God*, 111.
56. Newbigin, *Open Secret*, 71 (my emphasis).
57. Newbigin, *Household of God*, 109.

corporate and cosmic, and that therefore the means which God employs for our salvation must be congruous with that end, it becomes clear that God must deal with us according to the principle of election."[58]

The only way of proceeding in revealing and accomplishing the cosmic and corporate salvation of the end is by choosing a community to be the nucleus of his renewing work. God begins with some community, knits them back together, and restores the creational relationships fractured in the fall. He begins with a reconciled community and then incorporates others from outside into this community. In short, God's people have been chosen to be reconciled to God, to each other, and to the nonhuman creation and to draw others into that reconciliation. God's people are to be "his reconciled and reconciling people." And the election of this kind of people is the "only principle congruous with the nature of God's redemptive activity."[59] In election we see that God moves along the channels he cut at creation to accomplish his universal purpose.

So it is a misunderstanding of salvation that leads to objections to election. However, a misunderstanding of the nature of election itself also contributes to the problem. Too often election is understood strictly in terms of its benefits and the blessing of God's salvation. Election, in this misunderstanding, is only for privilege and not for responsibility; election is so that the people of God might enjoy salvation, not be a means of salvation for the world. Election is about being a reconciled community but not a reconciling community. In short, "the missionary character of the doctrine of election is forgotten."[60]

A missionary doctrine of election understands that God's choice of a people is not simply for their own sake but also for the sake of the world. "The chosen people are chosen for the sake of the world. The mission of the Church is the clue to the meaning and the end of world history. But the Church does not exist for itself, it exists for the sake of fulfilling God's purpose for the world."[61] Thus, to be elect in Christ means to be incorporated into his mission to the world and to bear God's reconciling purpose for his whole world.[62]

We can capture both the missionary nature of the doctrine of election and the "inner necessity"[63] of election for God's universal purpose in two phrases: the elect community *makes known* God's universal purpose as a reconciled people, and the elect community *brings about* God's universal purpose as a

58. Newbigin, *Household of God*, 110.
59. Newbigin, *Household of God*, 111.
60. Newbigin, *Household of God*, 111.
61. Newbigin, *Faith for This One World?*, 81.
62. Newbigin, *Gospel in a Pluralist Society*, 27.
63. Newbigin, "Duty and Authority," 29.

reconciling people. On the one hand, God's people become the starting point of God's redemptive purposes by being the reconciled community God is creating. It makes known in the midst of the world where God is taking universal history: it is a clue to cosmic history. On the other hand, it offers the invitation to others to join in the reconciled community that will one day fill the earth. It is a reconciled community that is making known God's universal purpose and a reconciling community that is bringing it about.

From this we can see that it is precisely in election that God discloses and will one day bring about his universal purposes: he travels a particular road to arrive at a universal destination. "From the beginning of the Bible to its end we are presented with the story of a universal purpose carried out through a continuous series of particular choices. . . . This is the pattern throughout the Bible. The key to the relation between the universal and particular is God's way of election. The one (or the few) is chosen for the sake of the many; the particular is chosen for the sake of the universal."[64]

Newbigin speaks of election as a series of choices or the "process of narrowing."[65] The missional thrust of Scripture can be seen in terms of election and the "three Israels"[66]—Old Testament Israel, Jesus, and the church. In the Old Testament story, God chooses Abraham and a nation that will come from him to bear the blessing for all nations. Israel is called to be a sign and instrument of God's redemptive purpose for all humanity, but they fail in their calling. And so God judges Israel, and "from the beginning there is a process of elimination. . . . There is a covenant between God and Israel, and those who flout the terms of the covenant are no part of the chosen people." There is a narrowing until, at the cross, "He alone on that day is Israel." Jesus fulfills the purpose of election, faithfully doing what Israel did not do—disclosing and effecting God's renewal for the whole world. "But this is not the end of the story of Israel. It is the beginning of the story of the true Israel."[67] For Newbigin, "Jesus does not found a new people of God, a new society," but restores Israel to their calling. His mission is to Israel, and he appoints twelve as a representative number to make known the beginnings of the true Israel. Following the cross and resurrection and the mighty event of Pentecost, the way is clear for all nations: "Now at last the ancient promise that Israel shall be a light to the Gentiles and salvation to the ends of the earth is to be

---

64. Newbigin, *Open Secret*, 68.

65. Newbigin, *Open Secret*, 31.

66. Lesslie Newbigin, "Canon and Mission," unpublished notes, Newbigin Archives, University of Birmingham (n.d.), 2.

67. Lesslie Newbigin, *The Reunion of the Church: A Defence of the South India Scheme* (London: SCM, 1948), 30.

fulfilled." The "Church is the Israel of God, not a newly founded society."[68] Gentiles are incorporated into the true Israel that is gathered, renewed, and sent by Christ. They are like branches engrafted into an olive tree. "There is only one Israel of God, one olive tree of God's planting."[69]

This brief summary shows how God's universal purpose is carried out through a continuous series of particular choices. The election of Israel, Jesus, and the church is a central theme in the biblical story. In this particular nation, this particular man, and this particular community God is revealing and accomplishing his universal purpose for the world. Their election means blessing for all nations. This makes mission a central theme in the biblical story. Thus, the Bible "is not a repository of the occasional 'missionary text' but is from Genesis to Revelation the essential missionary text."[70] To read the story aright is to read it along its missionary grain.

God's Purpose Is Personal and Invitational

The story of the Bible reveals God's purpose as the renewal of the entire creation and whole life of humankind returning to its original created design. "Purpose is a personal word. It implies a mind which has a purpose real in the mind though not yet realized in the world of objects; it can only be known by listening to the person whose purpose it is."[71] Creation has a purpose because a personal God has created and designed it so. And he is working to realize his purpose in history. That means there is only one way to know what his purpose is—listen to him if and how he chooses to reveal it.

One of the things Newbigin targets here is the way the enthronement of scientific reason has taken over Western epistemology, either effectively denying the possibility of revelation or distorting the nature of revelation. True knowledge comes in modernity only by way of analysis. Scientific knowledge is impersonal; it employs methodological analysis to examine an object. Newbigin does not dismiss scientific knowledge in its place. There is a proper competence for scientific analysis at lower levels of explanation that can give us knowledge—physical, chemical, biological, mechanical, sociological, and more. There is a proper, God-given autonomy of various areas of creation, which allows for scientific examination. Analysis is good in its place. However, this way of knowing is not appropriate for knowing other

---

68. Newbigin, *Reunion of the Church*, 31.
69. Newbigin, *Reunion of the Church*, 32.
70. Newbigin, "Canon and Mission," 1.
71. Lesslie Newbigin, "Can the West Be Converted?," *International Bulletin of Missionary Research* 11 (1985): 6.

persons and certainly not for knowing God or his purpose. If one wants to know the purpose of any person, listening is in order, not analysis.

Martin Buber's book *I and Thou* captures the problem for Newbigin. Buber distinguishes between two kinds of knowledge. I-It knowledge is appropriate to the scientific examination of things. In this kind of knowledge, the knower is a masterful actor, free to interrogate and examine the object in order to gain knowledge. The other, I-Thou knowledge, is appropriate to the knowing of other persons. Here it is not appropriate to interrogate and examine the person as an object. Rather, the posture of humble and submissive listening is appropriate. Any epistemology that precludes this kind of listening effectively shuts itself off at the start from knowing God's purpose for the world.

Newbigin is concerned that often the church reads the Bible through a lens fashioned by the dominance of science in our culture. He is concerned that much biblical scholarship succumbs to I-It knowledge and remakes the Bible exclusively into an object to be examined rather than a word to be heard. Not only in the academy but also in the pew, we hear the Bible as information that informs the mind rather than a personal revelation that invites our loving response. I-It knowledge is inappropriate to the Scriptures, wherein God reveals himself and his purpose; it invites our submissive listening in order that we might know him and participate in his purpose for the world. If the nature of the world is personal, then the only way to know it is by an attentive posture of listening to the One whose nature and purpose are disclosed in the Scriptures.

The fact that the revelation of God is personal means more: God is revealing not simply his purpose but also himself. The biblical story would be misunderstood if it were taken to mean that God simply communicates information about his plan for the creation that might otherwise not be known. Rather, in the narrative disclosure of God's purpose, there is revelation of God himself. Revelation is "the self-communication of the one whose purpose the story embodies."[72]

This makes clear why the Bible must come to us as a narrative of God's mighty acts in history. "I would want to speak of the Bible as that body of literature which—primarily but not only in narrative form—renders accessible to us the character and actions and purpose of God."[73] Note the three words Newbigin uses: "purpose," "character," and "actions." The biblical

---

72. Newbigin, "Centrality of Jesus," 205.
73. Lesslie Newbigin, *Foolishness to the Greeks: The Gospel and Western Culture* (Grand Rapids: Eerdmans, 1986), 59.

narrative is one of God's actions in the world, his mighty deeds of creating, ruling, sustaining, judging, and redeeming. As one attends to those mighty works, one comes to know his purpose and his character. God himself and his purpose can only be known by attending to his creating and redeeming actions as narrated in the biblical story.

Story is the only way to know another person. "When you read a good novel you come to know the hero of the story as if you had actually met him. No description of him, for example in an obituary notice, can be a substitute for this. It is as you watch him dealing with actual situations and people that you come to know him. So it is, I think, in reading the Bible. As you read and re-read and go on reading, you come to know God. He is the one whose nature the Bible discloses. You come to know him personally."[74] Since the Bible narrates the mighty acts of God in creation and restoration, it reveals his character as well as his purpose for the whole of creation.

This personal revelation is also invitational. The Scriptures are not a "series of propositions" to be examined; rather, they are the "appeal of a personal love which seeks not to coerce submission but to evoke love."[75] We dare not reduce the word "revelation" to "information." Revelation does not simply mean that God has informed us about the meaning and end of universal history or simply told us something about himself or even explained to us what he has done in the world. "Revelation is indeed this, but it is this only because it is something much more. The revelation of which we speak in the Christian tradition is more than the communication of information; it is the giving of an invitation. It is more than an unfolding of the purpose, which was otherwise hidden in the mind of God but is now made known to us through God's revealing acts; it is also a summons, a call, an invitation."[76]

So the revelation of God's purpose is not just personal; it is also invitational. The invitation is threefold: to enter into a personal relationship with God, to participate in his purpose for the world, and to join the community in which this personal communion and comprehensive mission is a reality. "It is clear that we are here moving away from a view of revelation as the impartation of information, to one which sees it as the revealing of a purpose and the establishing of a personal relation."[77] This is especially seen in what

74. Newbigin, "The Bible: Good News for Secularised People," 7. See also Newbigin, *Gospel in a Pluralist Society*, 99.

75. Lesslie Newbigin, "The Bible and Our Contemporary Mission," *Clergy Review* 69, no. 1 (1984): 16.

76. Newbigin, *Proper Confidence*, 65.

77. Lesslie Newbigin, "Revelation," unpublished paper (1936), 24.

Newbigin referred to as two of the most important words in the Gospels: "follow me" (Mark 1:17).[78]

All that we have observed about the personal and invitational nature of the biblical story is beautifully illustrated in John 15:15: "I no longer call you servants, for a servant does not know his master's business. Instead, I have called you friends, for everything that I learned from my Father I have made known to you." Newbigin calls this verse the "clearest indication of the nature of Scriptural authority."[79] Here we have Jesus, who embodies the fullest revelation of the character and purpose of God. He reveals the Father and his purpose to his little community of disciples and calls them into intimate fellowship with himself. He calls them his friends. They are not servants who are asked to carry out some assorted tasks. Rather, they are friends because Jesus tells them what the Father is doing. They are let in on the big story and personally invited as a community of friends to participate in what he is doing. This invitation calls them to faith, love, and obedience. It is a summons to be with him and know him, to love him as a friend, and to join him in his mission.

The call of Scripture is an invitation into a personal relationship as well as to costly participation in his comprehensive purposes for the world. In other words, it is to know Jesus and seek his kingdom. A problem arises when we detach Jesus from the kingdom.[80] Newbigin believed that Jesus and kingdom had become disconnected in the twentieth-century church. Evangelicals emphasized the person of Jesus in their gospel but neglected the kingdom that he proclaimed. So the invitation was reduced to a personal relationship. The ecumenical tradition emphasized the breadth of the kingdom mission and therefore involvement in the social, economic, political, and cultural issues. But it neglected the person of Jesus. Mission became simply another social program or political movement. For Newbigin, the gospel is an invitation to believe, follow, love, and obey Jesus, and that means entry into his kingdom-community and costly participation in his comprehensive mission.

Behind these words is a long history of Newbigin's reflection on the notion of conversion. He focused his attention on the nature of conversion during

78. Newbigin speaks of the words "follow me" as "the central keyword" and "the most fundamental in the sayings of Jesus" (*Gospel in a Pluralist Society*, 240). See also Newbigin, "How Should We Understand Sacraments and Ministry?" (paper for the Anglican-Reformed International Commission meeting, London, 1983), 8.

79. Newbigin, *Proper Confidence*, 90.

80. Lesslie Newbigin, *Mission in Christ's Way: Bible Studies* (Geneva: WCC Publications, 1987), 7–10.

the 1960s, when this topic was a pressing issue in missiological circles. The pietistic and evangelical tradition emphasized the personal dimension of individuals coming to know God through faith. The ecumenical tradition was concerned with the social dimensions of conversion, the costly engagement in the public square with the economic, social, and political powers. The Eastern Orthodox tradition was dissatisfied with both because the church was neglected: conversion meant incorporation into the church. Newbigin saw strong biblical warrant for all three concerns. For him the invitation is personal: we are called to believe, to love, to follow Jesus, to enter into a relationship with him, and to offer our allegiance to him. The invitation is also costly: we are summoned to join Jesus in his mission to the world, to exhibit a comprehensive and costly obedience that challenges the powers that stand in opposition to his kingdom. Finally, the invitation is communal: it is an invitation to be baptized and to join the community that is following Jesus and knows him, that is participating in his mission and exhibiting a costly obedience across the spectrum of human life. This is the invitation that is issued to all people in the gospel.

The Cosmic-Communal-Personal Logic of the Biblical Story

We see in the unfolding of this chapter the narrative and theological logic that Newbigin believes the gospel and biblical story itself demands: cosmic, communal, personal. The Bible tells the story of the cosmic renewal of all of human life in the context of the nonhuman creation. At the center of this cosmic story is a chosen community called to embody the end of the story. All people are personally invited into and within that community to participate in the cosmic salvation of the biblical story and to play their role as part of the community to make it known. And faithfulness to the biblical story means that one moves precisely in that order: cosmic, communal, personal.

What is at stake is that the very nature of the Christian faith may be misunderstood by reducing salvation to the individual and making that the starting point for understanding the Bible, salvation, and mission.

> In distinction from a great deal of Christian writing which takes the individual person as its starting point for the understanding of salvation and then extrapolates from that to the wider issues of social, political, and economic life, I am suggesting that, with the Bible as our guide, we should proceed in the opposite direction, that we begin with the Bible as the unique interpretation of human and cosmic history and move from that starting

point to an understanding of what the Bible shows us of the meaning of personal life.[81]

It is clear that, for Newbigin, this move from the cosmic to the individual moves through the communal. It is instructive to note where Newbigin makes this statement and the logic of his argument preceding it. His words come at the opening of a chapter on mission in which he will stress that the new being of God's people is the primary way the gospel is made known. The chapters that precede this statement and give it context hammer home two points: the Bible tells the story of universal history, and the election of a community is at the center of the story and the clue to understanding it. The logic of Newbigin's thought is clear: the Bible is a cosmic story of God's mighty deeds in history whose meaning has been disclosed and accomplished in Christ; at the center of the narrative is a chosen community that bears the goal of the story; every person is invited to find their place in the story as part of God's people. To rightly understand mission we need to follow this biblical logic.

Conclusion

In approaching Newbigin's missional ecclesiology, it is essential to understand the Bible as the true story of the world. The very nature and mission of the church is inextricably tied to this: "The business of the church is to tell and to embody a story, the story of God's mighty acts in creation and redemption and of God's promises concerning what will be in the end. The church affirms the truth of this story by celebrating it, interpreting it, and enacting it in the life of the contemporary world." The missionary church is to do this in a world where there are idolatrous and competing stories that are diminishing and destroying the lives of people. The biblical story is true, and to understand the world through a different story is quite simply to misunderstand it. "The church's affirmation is that the story it tells, embodies, and enacts is the true story and that others are to be evaluated in reference to it. . . . [It] is the true interpretation of all human and cosmic history and to understand history otherwise is to misunderstand it, therefore misunderstanding the human situation here and now."[82] The missionary nature of the church is found in the fact that "God has entrusted to it this story and that there is no other body that will tell it."[83] As the church

81. Newbigin, *Gospel in a Pluralist Society*, 128.
82. Newbigin, *Proper Confidence*, 76–77.
83. Newbigin, *Proper Confidence*, 78.

incarnates and announces this story centered in Jesus, it invites all people to return to what it truly means to be human by joining the new humanity that will one day fill the earth. The mission of the church is a summons to all people "to respond to a word of calling by believing and acting, specifically, by becoming part of the community which is already committed to the service of the Builder."[84]

---

84. Newbigin, *Proper Confidence*, 66.

2

The Good News
of the Kingdom and the
Missionary Church

Our starting point to understand Lesslie Newbigin's missionary ecclesiology is the gospel of Jesus Christ.[1] But what is the gospel? Our answer to that question will always be given in terms of the context in which we place the central events of the life, death, and resurrection of Jesus Christ. That broader context is what gives meaning to those events. Often the larger context is assumed with little conscious reflection. For example, sometimes the gospel is placed in the context of individual testimonies of salvation or evangelistic presentations that follow the logic of individual sin, Christ as substitute, and the need for faith. Then the meaning of the Christ-event is simply as the means of personal salvation. Other times the work of Christ is understood within the context of a systematic theology, usually standing between sin (treated individually) and salvation (treated as the benefits of Christ applied to individuals). Again in this case the work of Christ is a matter of individual salvation. Newbigin would not doubt that there is some truth in this. He would, however, insist that this is an entirely too reductionistic view of the gospel. It has been uprooted from its biblical context and placed within another.

1. Lesslie Newbigin, *Proper Confidence: Faith, Doubt, and Certainty in Christian Discipleship* (Grand Rapids: Eerdmans, 1995), 96, 100.

For Newbigin the gospel must be placed first and foremost within the setting of the cosmic history narrated in Scripture. Understanding the nature of the biblical story puts us in a place to more carefully answer the question, What is the gospel? The Bible is a unified narrative of God's mighty deeds in history that moves toward the ultimate goal of the cosmic renewal. The gospel stands at the center of this story. "The Gospel of God, with which both Testaments are concerned . . . refers to the beginning and the end of all things and therefore to the real meaning of all that happens."[2] In this light we can offer a preliminary definition of Newbigin's understanding of the good news of the kingdom: *The good news is a message about the fullest revelation and the final accomplishment of the end of universal history—the comprehensive restoration of all creation and the whole of human life in the kingdom of God—present and coming in history in Jesus Christ and by the Spirit's power.* In this chapter we will unpack this loaded definition of the gospel and its significance for a missionary ecclesiology.

Jesus and the Good News of the Kingdom

Anyone who would define the gospel must make a decision about where to begin.[3] In his various discussions of the gospel, Newbigin almost always begins in the same place: with the first announcement made by Jesus, at the outset of his public ministry, about the kingdom of God: "Jesus went into Galilee, proclaiming the good news of God. 'The time has come,' he said. 'The kingdom of God has come near. Repent and believe the good news!'" (Mark 1:14–15). The good news is the announcement of the arrival of the kingdom: "The original preaching of the Gospel on the lips of Jesus was—precisely— the announcement of the coming of the kingdom."[4] What is the kingdom of God? To answer that question, we have to first look at the background of the Old Testament story. That will tell us *what* is being fulfilled. But we then have to look forward into the New Testament witness. That will tell us *how* it is being fulfilled.[5] Taken together, these will allow us to understand what the kingdom of God is and how it is being fulfilled in Jesus.

2. Lesslie Newbigin, *Trinitarian Doctrine for Today's Mission* (1963; repr., Carlisle, UK: Paternoster, 1998), 26.

3. For example, Greg Gilbert starts with (a rather selective reading of) Romans 1–4 in *What Is the Gospel?* (Wheaton: Crossway, 2010); Scot McKnight begins with 1 Corinthians 15:1–9 in *The King Jesus Gospel: The Original Good News Revisited* (Grand Rapids: Zondervan, 2016). Their starting point impacts their articulation of the content of the gospel.

4. Lesslie Newbigin, *The Good Shepherd: Meditations on Christian Ministry in Today's World* (Grand Rapids: Eerdmans, 1977), 67.

5. Lesslie Newbigin, *A Faith for This One World?* (London: SCM, 1961), 60–61.

Looking Back at the Old Testament Story

The Old Testament is a redemptive-historical story. It is a story of God's mighty acts that move toward the healing of the world from sin and the restoration of God's sovereign rule over all things. Behind the announcement of the kingdom is this "Old Testament belief in a cosmic renewal or restoration." Jesus steps into the redemptive story of the Old Testament and "carries forward these prophetic and apocalyptic hopes of the Hebrews which began with the ardent but humble hope of the restoration of the kingdom of David and led up to the growing hopes of a restoration of God's rightful sovereignty over the whole world."[6] Jesus proclaims that cosmic renewal is now breaking into the middle of history in him. "The earliest and simplest statement of the Gospel is: 'The time is fulfilled and the Kingdom of God is at hand.' . . . The Gospel is the proclamation of a series of events in history which have been—from their first dawning—proclaimed to be decisive for human history and for every individual."[7] In Jesus, God accomplishes decisively and climactically the purpose toward which he had been working.

The Old Testament is universal history with cosmic renewal as the End.[8] The good news is the announcement that the End has arrived. Thus, the gospel is fundamentally an eschatological message.[9] Eschatology is not just what comes last chronologically but is the ultimate goal toward which all of history is moving. The good news is an announcement about this goal of history somehow being present in Jesus.

The end of universal history is what gives meaning to the creation and to human life. To be human is to live in some story that gives life meaning. The problem is that, while we are in the middle of history, it is impossible for us to know the End—that is, unless the one who rules history reveals it to us. One cannot know the meaning of history, or even whether there *is* meaning, until one has reached the end. "How do we know the meaning of the story as a whole? How do we know the meaning of the story while we are still in

---

6. Lesslie Newbigin, *Signs amid the Rubble: The Purposes of God in Human History*, ed. Geoffrey Wainwright (Grand Rapids: Eerdmans, 2003), 28.

7. Lesslie Newbigin, "The Duty and Authority of the Church to Preach the Gospel," in *The Church's Witness to God's Design*, ed. Lesslie Newbigin and Hendrik Kraemer, Amsterdam Assembly Series 2 (New York: Harper Brothers, 1948), 23.

8. Newbigin will sometimes capitalize the word "End" as a technical term to refer to the eschaton, and I will follow that practice in my own discussion. See, e.g., Lesslie Newbigin, *The Reunion of the Church: A Defence of the South India Scheme* (London: SCM, 1948), 73; Lesslie Newbigin, *The Household of God: Lectures on the Nature of the Church* (New York: Friendship Press, 1954), 19.

9. See Jürgen Schuster, *Christian Mission in Eschatological Perspective: Lesslie Newbigin's Contribution* (Nürnberg: VTR Publications, 2009), for an articulation of the importance of eschatology for Newbigin's view of mission.

the middle of it?"[10] Only if the Lord of history, the author of the story, has let us into the secret while we are still in the middle. And that is precisely what has happened: the author has let us into the secret! "The gospel is the announcement of the end of world history."[11] The goal of universal history has been fully revealed in the person and work of Jesus Christ. "The Christian faith is the faith that the point of the story has been disclosed: the 'end' has been revealed in the middle."[12]

Newbigin uses an evocative illustration to make his point. He asks us to imagine walking along a street and seeing a work of construction in progress. What kind of building is being constructed? An office? A house? A chapel? There are only two ways to find out: wait until the end or ask the architect who is building it. And then we must believe his word. Similarly, the only way to know the meaning of cosmic history is either to wait until the end—an option not available to us—or to trust the revelation of the one whose purpose it is: "The only way we can know that purpose is by a disclosure from the one whose purpose it is, a disclosure which we would have to take on trust."[13] The author and architect of cosmic history has disclosed his purpose. And he has done it not merely with information or words or promises; rather, it is in the life, death, and resurrection of Jesus. In Jesus, God's purpose for his whole creation has been revealed.

Two words are key to understanding the eschatological nature of the gospel: "reveal" and "accomplish." In Jesus, God both reveals and accomplishes the end of history. "God's purpose for the world is accomplished by the sending of His Son. . . . Jesus was sent once for all by the Father to reveal and establish His reign."[14] In his life, death, and resurrection, Jesus discloses and reveals the very nature of the kingdom of God. He shows us what it is like—what is coming on that final day. We see in Jesus a preview of the coming attraction; we receive windows to peer into a future world yet to come. In the healings we see that there is no disease in the new creation; in the exorcisms we see that Satan is cast out of the new creation; in the calming of the sea we see that the curse is lifted from the nonhuman creation. In Jesus we come

10. Lesslie Newbigin, "The Bible: Good News for Secularised People" (keynote address, Europe and Middle East Regional Conference, Eisenach, Germany, April 1991), Newbigin Archives, University of Birmingham, 6.

11. Lesslie Newbigin, "The Life and Mission of the Church," in *We Were Brought Together*, ed. David M. Taylor (Sydney: Australian Council for the World Council of Churches, 1960), 61.

12. Lesslie Newbigin, *A Word in Season: Perspectives on Christian World Missions* (Grand Rapids: Eerdmans, 1994), 110.

13. Newbigin, *Proper Confidence*, 57–58.

14. Lesslie Newbigin, "The Life and Mission of the Church," in *The Life and Mission of the Church*, ed. C. I. Itty (Bangalore, India: Student Christian Movement of India, 1958), 6.

to know the goal that defines history and human life. But he does more than simply reveal it to us; he also accomplishes and establishes God's reign in the midst of history. "The Gospel announces an accomplished redemption."[15] It is now present in the world, and with its advent we are assured that one day it will come fully. The new creation is not just a promise; it has been accomplished. It is here now and it will certainly come. Jesus stands "at the very centre of the story [as] the One in whom God's purpose was decisively revealed by being decisively effected."[16] These two words—"reveal" and "accomplish"—provide a helpful lens on the good news of the kingdom.[17]

Looking Forward at the New Testament Witness

When we turn to the New Testament witness, what is immediately clear is that history has not come to a close: the End is present in the middle, but clearly it has not arrived in fullness. The cosmic renewal of the kingdom is both a present and a future reality; it is somehow now and not yet. "The kingdom is both present and future. It is present in that, through the total work of Jesus, we are given here and now the foretaste, the first-fruit, the *arrabon* of its grace and peace. It is future in that the story of which our lives are a part, the story of creation and of the human family is . . . a movement directed toward a real goal, a real event in which it becomes clear that something has been accomplished."[18]

What does it mean that the kingdom as the goal of universal history has arrived and is present now? It means that God's power to heal the creation has entered history in the person of Jesus Christ and by the work of the Spirit. In Jesus, new powers are present—the powers of the coming age that will one day finally sum up all things.

> The central proclamation of the New Testament is that in Christ the new age has already dawned. In the words of the very first proclamation of the gospel, "The Kingdom of God has come near." In Christ the powers of the new age are at work. The domain of Heaven has touched that of earth and God's rule is actually being exercised in the world through Jesus. Those who accept Him come within the sphere of operations of the powers of

15. Newbigin, "Duty and Authority," 31.
16. Lesslie Newbigin, "The Bible: Good News for Secularised People," 6.
17. God's purpose is "revealed and effected" in the historic event of Jesus Christ; see Lesslie Newbigin, *The Open Secret: An Introduction to the Theology of Mission*, rev. ed. (Grand Rapids: Eerdmans, 1995), 177.
18. Lesslie Newbigin, "The Kingdom of God and Our Hopes for the Future," in *The Kingdom of God and Human Society*, ed. R. S. Barbour (Edinburgh: T&T Clark, 1993), 12.

the kingdom: they may in fact be said to have been translated out of the present age into the new age which is to come. The new age is no longer something in the distant future. It is already present proleptically. Christians have already, as it is said, tasted the powers of the age to come.[19]

Two things can be further mentioned about the coming of the powers of the kingdom (and we will return to both in more detail later). First, the new powers are the work of the Holy Spirit. The Spirit brings the new world of the kingdom of God into the midst of the old world. Second, the imagery of foretaste, deposit, and firstfruits captures something of how the kingdom may be present and yet have a future realization. Newbigin uses this imagery both for the Spirit and for the church.

To say that the kingdom is both present and future is certainly not novel and is well within mainstream New Testament scholarship on the eschatological message of Jesus. The question is what it means exactly to say the kingdom is both present and future. Newbigin's characteristic answer is that the kingdom is hidden in the present but will be made manifest in the future. This is "not the difference between the incomplete and the complete; it is the difference between hidden and manifest."[20] In the present it is hidden and veiled: it is not a demonstration of power and manifest victory that is obvious to the naked eye of unconverted people. It is not a matter of the kingdom being partially here and awaiting a more complete arrival. Rather, it is hidden in the sense that it comes in the way of weakness and suffering.

This gives us a lens to understand the relationship of the kingdom to history. It is a relationship neither of total continuity nor of total discontinuity. The kingdom is not simply future and so unrelated to present history. Nor is it collapsed into history so that history is a smooth, progressive, and gradual arrival of the kingdom. The presence of the kingdom creates crisis and conflict as it encounters the powers that oppose the kingdom. History is thus characterized by a conflict and struggle between the powers of the kingdom and those of this world. This produces suffering for those who take the side of the kingdom.

It seems that Newbigin has affirmed two quite paradoxical things about the coming of the kingdom in the present. On the one hand, the powers of the age to come have broken into history. God's power to heal and renew is present in the work of the Spirit and is now at work in the world. On the other hand, the kingdom arrives in weakness and suffering. Power and

---

19. Newbigin, *Signs amid the Rubble*, 27.
20. Lesslie Newbigin, *The Gospel in a Pluralist Society* (Grand Rapids: Eerdmans, 1989), 105.

weakness—these seem to stand in tension. To this Newbigin answers that this is precisely the "double character"[21] of the kingdom until Christ returns. God's power to heal and renew all of human life is now present, and therefore we see the mighty works of God in the ministry of Jesus and the church as signs of this restoration. But since the advent of the kingdom is a comprehensive salvation, on the other hand, we see a conflict between the powers. An antithetical encounter between the powers of the kingdom and powers of the present age is necessarily engaged. The mission of Jesus and the church is then in the way of suffering. Only when Christ returns will the victory of the kingdom be made manifest. But until that day the kingdom is characterized by a double character: power and weakness, victory and defeat, mighty works and suffering, faith and hope. Both are manifest in the mission of Jesus; if either is lost, the mission of the church will be distorted either by a triumphalist activism or by a defeatist quietism.

We await the final coming of the kingdom when what is hidden will be revealed and be fully manifest for every eye to see. But why is the final victory and demonstration of God's power held off? Newbigin always answers the same way: the precise meaning of this gap is mission to the nations.[22]

> What has been done for the whole world must be made known to the whole world, so that the whole world may be brought under the obedience to the Gospel, and may be healed in the salvation which God has wrought for it. It is for this that the end is held back. The end has been revealed once for all; it must now be made known to all that all may believe. The decisive victory has been won over the world; the remaining centers of enemy resistance must now be destroyed. That is the meaning of the time still given to us. It is the time for bringing all men and all nations to the obedience of the faith. It is for no other purpose that the end is delayed.[23]

It is precisely the hidden and veiled nature of the kingdom that allows people to hear the good news, to repent, and to be converted. If the kingdom were made manifest in its awesome power, then history would have arrived at its goal; there would be no room for repentance. "The unveiling of the glory of God's kingdom in all its terrible majesty could leave no further room for the free acceptance in faith which Jesus called for. Only when that glory was veiled in the lowliness of the incarnation could it call out freely given

---

21. Newbigin, *Gospel in a Pluralist Society*, 107.
22. Newbigin, *Gospel in a Pluralist Society*, 106.
23. Newbigin, *Household of God*, 157–58.

repentance and faith."[24] And so Jesus manifests the kingdom in his life and deeds; he prays that the kingdom might come; and he proclaims the kingdom, inviting listeners to enter the sphere of the operation of its powers. And the church follows in the way of Jesus.

The Kingdom Comes in the Person and Work of Jesus

The good news is about the restoration of the creation that lies at the End bursting into the middle of history. It enters history both through Jesus and by the Spirit. The kingdom comes through the cluster of redemptive events in Jesus Christ: his life, death, resurrection, and ascension, and his gift of the Spirit. Newbigin often grouped all of these events together and referred to them in various ways—the "Christ-event" or the "total fact of Christ" or the "total event of Christ."[25] By this he means to make clear that the whole person and work of Christ from incarnation to Pentecost is an integrated singular event of salvation in which each individual moment has its necessary and meaningful place in the whole. Each is uniquely significant as part of the one revelation and accomplishment of the kingdom of God.

This last statement is important. When we consider any aspect of the person and work of Jesus—his ministry, death, resurrection, ascension, gift of the Spirit—we may not abstract them from the biblical story. The Bible is narrating the coming of cosmic salvation, and the message of the gospel is that it arrived in Jesus. The question is, What is the significance of each of these historical moments in the Christ-event for the coming of the kingdom?

Jesus's Life and Ministry

First, the kingdom of God arrives in the life and ministry of Jesus. At the beginning of his ministry, the Spirit is poured out on Jesus. The Spirit is an eschatological gift promised by the prophets for the last days.[26] If the Spirit is present, then the last days or the kingdom has dawned in Jesus. "But if it is by the Spirit of God that I drive out demons, then the kingdom of God has come upon you" (Matt. 12:28). Jesus carries out his kingdom ministry in the power of the Spirit. This ministry is carried out in a threefold way: Jesus embodies the presence of the kingdom in his own life; Jesus does the mighty works of the kingdom—works of healing and deliverance—that are windows into the very

---

24. Newbigin, *Gospel in a Pluralist Society*, 108; see Newbigin, *Household of God*, 126.

25. Newbigin, *Faith for This One World?*, 57.

26. Lesslie Newbigin, *The Holy Spirit and the Church* (Madras: Christian Literature Society, 1972), 4. In several places he quotes Luke 4:18 to connect the eschatological Spirit with Jesus (e.g., Newbigin, *Faith for This One World?*, 85).

nature of the coming age; and Jesus announces the kingdom and teaches about it with his words.[27] This ministry is carried out in a life of prayer that God's kingdom would be fully manifest one day, and until that day he prays that eyes would be open to the kingdom and that people would believe. But Jesus's ministry is not carried out in triumphant power; rather, the kingdom comes in seeming weakness and suffering as he absorbs the full force of evil in himself.

Jesus's Death and Resurrection

Second, the kingdom of God arrives in the death of Jesus on the cross and in his resurrection. These two events stand together as the hinge and turning point that give cosmic history its meaning and direction.[28] "At the centre of history, which is both the history of man and the history of nature, stands the pivotal, critical once-for-all event of the death and resurrection of Jesus. By this event the human situation is irreversibly changed."[29] These two events constitute the hinge of universal history: in the death of Jesus, there is the end of the old, and in the resurrection, the beginning of the new. In the crucifixion of Jesus, God accomplishes the victory over sin and death and all that has corrupted and enslaved the creation. In the resurrection of Jesus, the new creation that will one day fill the earth begins. The death and resurrection of Jesus are cosmic events.

The Bible gives us many images to describe the decisive and cosmic event of the cross.

> Down the centuries, from the first witness until today, the church has sought and used innumerable symbols to express the inexpressible mystery of the event that is the center, the crisis of all cosmic history, the hinge upon which all happenings turn. Christ the sacrifice offered for our sin, Christ the substitute standing in our place, Christ the ransom paid for our redemption, Christ the conqueror casting out the prince of the world—these and other symbols have been used to point to the heart of the mystery. None can fully express it. It is that happening in which the reign of God is present.[30]

Several times Newbigin articulates the cross in terms of five images: the death of Jesus is a revelation of God's love for the world, a judgment on the

27. Lesslie Newbigin, "Holy Spirit: The Believers Strike Oil," *Reform*, May 1990, 6. Newbigin's own title in his notes is "Holy Spirit: Pledge of Glory."

28. Lesslie Newbigin, "This Is the Turning Point in History," *Reform*, April 1990, 4.

29. Lesslie Newbigin, "Bible Studies Given at the National Christian Council Triennial Assembly, Shillong," *National Council Review* 88 (1968): 9–10.

30. Newbigin, *Open Secret*, 50.

sin of the world, a ransom that pays the price to deliver the world, a sacrifice that takes the sin of the world on himself, and a victory over the sin and evil that rules the world.[31] But when we survey Newbigin's discussions of the cross, two images feature most prominently. And both have implications for the missionary church.

The first image is that of a victory: "It is there, on Calvary, that the kingdom, the kingly rule of God, won its decisive victory over all the powers that contradict it. . . . The cross is not a defeat reversed by the resurrection; it is a victory proclaimed (to chosen witnesses) by the resurrection."[32] The victory is sure but not obvious. And it is here that we see the paradoxical nature of the cross: in what looks like defeat lies the ultimate victory of God. "The centre of the revealed mystery of the reign of God is the Cross. There the power of God is revealed—but it is revealed as weakness. The glory of God is revealed—but it is revealed as humiliation. The victory of God is revealed—but it is revealed as defeat."[33] The church shares in this victory but also in the cross-shaped nature of Jesus's mission.

The second image of the cross is the archetypal image of the representative man who bears the destiny of the whole creation. The death of Jesus is the end of the old age dominated by evil; in the resurrection of Jesus the new creation is inaugurated. Since Jesus bears the destiny of the whole creation, this pattern is true for the whole cosmos, for the church and its mission, and for each person. This death-and-resurrection pattern unfolds in three historical stages. First, in the actual death and resurrection of Jesus evil is dealt with and the new creation begins. Then, the church shares in that pattern as it participates in the resurrection life of the new creation and makes it known through suffering in its conflict with evil.[34] Finally, the whole cosmos will one day partake in the judgment accomplished at the cross and the renewal begun in the resurrection.[35]

Jesus's Ascension

The third way the kingdom comes for Newbigin is in the ascension of Jesus. Newbigin mentions the ascension less than the other events. But the

31. Lesslie Newbigin, *Sin and Salvation* (Philadelphia: Westminster, 1956), 70–90; Newbigin, "This Is the Turning Point," 4.

32. Lesslie Newbigin, *Mission in Christ's Way: Bible Studies* (Geneva: WCC Publications, 1987), 6.

33. Newbigin, *Good Shepherd*, 64–65.

34. Newbigin, *Gospel in a Pluralist Society*, 107.

35. Newbigin, "Bible Studies"; Lesslie Newbigin, "The Bible Study Lectures," in *Digest of the Proceedings of the Ninth Meeting of the Consultation on Church Union (COCU)*, ed. Paul A. Crow (Princeton: COCU, 1970).

reality it points to—the sovereign rule of Christ over all things—is central to his understanding of the Christ-event. The resurrection means a new world has dawned in which Christ is enthroned as Lord of all—"the ruler and authority over all things."[36] The imagery of God's right hand pictures what is true of the new world dawning: the lordship of Jesus Christ over all creation. Newbigin points to Psalm 110:1, a text quoted twenty-two times in the New Testament: "The LORD says to my lord: 'Sit at my right hand until I make your enemies a footstool for your feet.'" This text, fulfilled in the ascension and exaltation of Jesus, expresses precisely the redemptive-historical time in which the church lives. On the one hand, Jesus has been vindicated and exalted. He is at the right hand of God, ruling all creation, and one day this comprehensive rule will be consummated. This is the good news—Christ is now Lord and one day will be fully revealed as Lord and Ruler of all—that must be proclaimed. On the other hand, it is a hidden authority. The powers of the world continue to resist this comprehensive rule of God. This means that time between the times will be characterized by an ultimate battle in which the church submits to the authority of Christ and proclaims his victory.[37] Yet the hidden nature of Christ's rule opens up the space for the good news to be proclaimed and for people to repent and acknowledge the rule of Christ. "The full revelation of God's kingdom must mean the obliteration of all that is opposed to it, and God in his mercy withholds that final revelation so that man may repent and believe. Until that day of Christ's coming in glory, His reign is to be known not by sight but by faith, not in full enjoyment but in foretaste, not in complete manifestation but in signs which point beyond themselves to a reality greater than themselves."[38]

The Kingdom Comes in the Work of the Spirit

The kingdom comes not only in Jesus but also by the work of the Spirit. In much theological work, the Spirit is confined to being the one who applies the work of Christ to individuals. Often both the work of Jesus and the work of the Spirit are shorn of their eschatological and communal context in Scripture. To rightly understand Newbigin's view of the Spirit, we have to place his work in four contexts: eschatological, missional, communal, and individual. The order is important: his thought moves from the broader context to the more narrow.

36. Newbigin, *Faith for This One World?*, 99.
37. Newbigin, *Household of God*, 158–59.
38. Newbigin, *Household of God*, 126.

The Spirit's Work as Eschatological

Newbigin understands the Spirit first and foremost in eschatological terms. The Spirit is primarily a gift of the last days; his arrival in the present means that the age to come has dawned in the midst of history. The cosmic salvation that is the goal of universal history is a work of the Spirit; the End is present with his presence. The promise of the Spirit in Isaiah, Ezekiel, and Joel as an eschatological gift sets the background for the Gospels.[39] The new era promised by the prophets is here: in the coming of Jesus, empowered by the Spirit, the last days have come. The kingdom is the work of the Spirit of God in Christ and in the apostolic community.[40]

Thus, the Spirit must be understood in eschatological perspective; the Spirit ushers in the end of history. With the coming of the Spirit, the last days are upon us. "The Spirit brings the reality of the new world to come into the midst of the old world that is. . . . [The Spirit is] the recognizable presence of a future that has been promised but is not yet in sight."[41] This eschatological future is made known first in the Spirit's work in Christ and then in the church. "From the very beginning of the New Testament, the coming of Jesus, his words and works are connected directly with the power of the Spirit."[42] The mission of Jesus continues as the Holy Spirit is given to the church. "The Church's mission is simply the continued ministry in the world of that same divine Spirit who was in Jesus. His presence in the world means that the new age of the Kingdom has really dawned."[43]

Three words describe the Spirit as an end-time gift: "deposit," "first-fruits," and "foretaste." Quite often Newbigin discusses these terms in an exposition of Acts 1.[44] A question about the kingdom (Acts 1:6) receives an answer about the Spirit (v. 8). "The question is about the Kingdom; the promise is about that which is the foretaste, the first-fruit, the *arrabon* of the Kingdom—namely the gift of the Spirit."[45] All three of these vivid images point to the double character of the Spirit's presence and the coming of the kingdom: the Spirit is a present reality but points to a future completion. A deposit is a down payment or pledge of actual money now; it is not simply a promissory note or an IOU but real money. But it promises

39. Lesslie Newbigin, *The Holy Spirit and the Church* (Madras: Christian Literature Society, 1972), 4.

40. Newbigin, *Faith for This One World?*, 84–85.

41. Newbigin, *Open Secret*, 63.

42. Newbigin, *Open Secret*, 57.

43. Newbigin, *Faith for This One World?*, 86.

44. Lesslie Newbigin, *Sign of the Kingdom* (Grand Rapids: Eerdmans, 1980), 33–43; Newbigin, *Household of God*, 155–59; Newbigin, *Mission in Christ's Way*, 15–21.

45. Newbigin, *Sign of the Kingdom*, 37.

that the rest of the purchase price will be paid in the future. A foretaste is an actual taste of the meal now, not simply the smell and promise of food. But it promises that the rest of the meal is coming. Firstfruits are an actual handful of grain or bunch of fruit held in one's hand, but they point us to the coming of the full harvest, assuring us that it will one day come. All these images point to a present experience and a future promise: the kingdom has arrived and is experienced in the work of the Spirit, but the fullness is a promised future.

The Spirit's Work as Missional

The eschatological nature of the Spirit is closely linked to his missionary nature. For Newbigin, eschatology and mission are closely intertwined; the holding back of the completion of the kingdom means mission to the world. Newbigin characterizes the time between the first coming of Jesus and his return in three ways: as a time when the kingdom has already arrived but is not fully present, as a time of mission characterized by a witness to the kingdom, and as the era of the Spirit. The Spirit is an earnest: this is the eschatological nature of his work. The Spirit is a witness: this is the missional nature of his work. "We may indicate the fundamental interconnection of the eschatological and missionary elements in the Church's nature in yet a third way, by reference to the doctrine of the Holy Spirit. . . . He spans, as it were, the gulf that yet yawns between the consummation for which we long and our actual life here."[46] The missionary movement of the Spirit's work is outward from the one (Jesus) to the many (all nations), from one place to the ends of the earth: "The new reality is let loose into the world in expanding and ever-widening circles as the gospel is carried out from Jerusalem to the ends of the earth."[47] The cosmic salvation accomplished in Christ moves outward to include more and more.

The Spirit's Work as Communal

The Spirit is not only eschatological and missional but also communal. The Spirit is given to a community, and mission incorporates the nations into this community. Newbigin refers to John 20:19–23 and to Acts 2:1–9 and says that in "both accounts we see that the gift of the Holy Spirit is to a company of people together and not to separate individuals."[48] Indeed, "in

---

46. Newbigin, *Household of God*, 161.
47. Newbigin, *Faith for This One World?*, 85.
48. Newbigin, *Holy Spirit and the Church*, 11.

the New Testament it is always to a community, to a group" that the Spirit is given.[49] The Spirit's ever-expanding witness to Christ's kingdom is borne by a community, and as people are converted they are baptized into the community of the Spirit.

The Spirit's Work in Individuals

Newbigin does not move from Christ to the application of Christ's work and the distribution of various salvific benefits to individuals. For Newbigin "all the benefits which Christ was sent to bring" enable people to be "restored to their true humanity because they are reconciled with their Maker."[50] And certainly the restoration of individuals to their full humanity in Christ is the Spirit's work and a sign of the presence of God's kingdom. However, the movement of Newbigin's thought on the Holy Spirit follows the Bible itself. It begins by placing both Jesus and the Spirit in eschatological context; the comprehensive salvation of the kingdom has arrived in their work. It moves then to mission as the movement of this end-time renewal outward into all the world. And this movement is through a chosen community that incorporates more and more people into that cosmic salvation. They then receive the many benefits accomplished by Christ. So to be sure, Christ's accomplished work brings many benefits to people by the work of the Spirit. Yet Newbigin keeps the eschatological, missional, and communal contexts of Scripture firmly in place when making infrequent reference to the Spirit's work in individuals.

A Chosen People Who Bear the Story

The purpose of cosmic history has been revealed and accomplished in Jesus Christ. The comprehensive salvation that will include all nations is now, by the Spirit, a present reality hastening toward its full realization. This good news must now go to the ends of the earth—to all people and all nations. This is first of all a work of the same Spirit at work in Jesus. However, the Spirit bears his witness to Christ and end-time salvation in and through a community. Jesus formed this community during his ministry and now sends them as a community to bear the witness of the Spirit to all nations. It is precisely this perspective that enables us to understand the missionary nature of the church.

---

49. Lesslie Newbigin, *Journey into Joy* (Grand Rapids: Eerdmans, 1972), 67.
50. Newbigin, "The Life and Mission of the Church," in *The Life and Mission of the Church*, 7.

Logic of Mission

"The logic of mission is this: the true meaning of the human story has been disclosed. Because it is the truth, it must be shared universally. It cannot be a private opinion. When we share it with all peoples, we give them the opportunity to know the truth about themselves, to know who they are because they can know the true story of which their lives are a part."[51] The historical logic of redemptive history is that, since Jesus has revealed and accomplished end-time salvation, this news must be made known to the ends of the earth. This movement to all peoples must be understood from two biblical standpoints: the Spirit and the church. On the one hand, the Spirit must be understood in terms of his role to witness to Christ and his salvation in ever-widening circles that move from one man and one place to many people in many lands. Mission is first a work of the Spirit. On the other hand, Jesus forms a community and sends them in the power of the Spirit to be witnesses to the good news to the ends of the earth. So this mission is a work of the church. It is precisely as we unfold both of these perspectives and the relation of the Spirit to the church that we come to understand more deeply Newbigin's missionary ecclesiology. But we must keep clearly before us what he has called the logic of mission: the End has arrived, and therefore it must now be made known to all.

Reconstituting God's Chosen People

"Jesus did not write a book," writes Newbigin. "He chose, called, and prepared a company of people, he entrusted to them his teaching, and he promised them the gift of the Spirit of God to guide them."[52] Central to the mission of Jesus is the gathering and formation of a community. This is fundamentally important for Newbigin. He says, "It is surely a fact of inexhaustible significance" that the Lord left behind a visible community and not a book.[53] It is "of the essence of the matter" that Jesus did not leave behind a verbatim record of what he said and did but created a community to be bound to him and be his witnesses in every nation.[54] This is the way Jesus planned for the good news, the arrival of the goal of universal history, to reach all peoples—through a community he formed.

The formation of a community is part of a long history. The Bible is a "sort of outline of world history," and "the central thread of the history is

51. Newbigin, *Gospel in a Pluralist Society*, 125.

52. Lesslie Newbigin, "Truth and Authority in Modernity," in *Faith and Modernity*, ed. Philip Sampson, Vinay Samuel, and Chris Sugden (Oxford: Regnum Books, 1994), 70.

53. Newbigin, *Household of God*, 20.

54. Lesslie Newbigin, "Christ and Cultures," *Scottish Journal of Theology* 31 (1978): 18.

the story of God's people."[55] We are reminded again of the "three Israels." God chooses Israel to bear his purpose for the world. The "whole core of biblical history is the story of a visible community to be God's own people, his royal priesthood on earth, the bearer of His light to the nations." This is Israel, one of the petty tribes of the Semitic world. The community Jesus leaves behind connects with that story: they are "recreated in Him."[56] Israel lost its way and did not heed God's call to be a royal priesthood and a light to the nations. And so "Christ accepted it as his vocation to recall Israel to its true vocation. He reconstituted the chosen people, choosing whom he would and appointing twelve to be the nucleus of a new Israel."[57]

This new Israel returns to its original vocation of being a light to the nations and a royal priesthood. But now the end of history is no longer simply a promise but an accomplished fact. The Spirit is now present. While still taking on the missional calling of making God's purpose known, the arrival of the kingdom brings significant change to the people of God.

The Overlap of the Ages

God's people have always been a missionary people—that is, from the beginning they were chosen to bear God's purpose for and be a light to the whole world. They have been blessed to be a blessing. But with the coming of Christ and the Spirit, the missionary nature of God's people needs to be reformulated. Eschatology deeply impacts ecclesiology. We can look at the impact of the coming of the kingdom on God's people in terms of three perspectives: the overlapping of the ages in the already–not yet era of redemptive history, the presence of Christ by the Holy Spirit in the midst of the church, and eschatological definitions of the church.

The role of God's people in redemptive history is one of continuity. It is determined by their election. They are to picture God's cosmic renewal in the midst of the world. However, the new era in redemptive history, a time marked out by the coming of the kingdom in Jesus and the Spirit, means discontinuity. What time is it in redemptive history? Newbigin answers that it is a time when the kingdom has come but not yet fully. Therefore, there is an overlapping of the old age and the age to come, a time when the powers of the new age are present but the powers of the old evil age remain. And the reason the end has been held off is so that the good news

---

55. Lesslie Newbigin, "Why Study the Old Testament?," *National Christian Council Review* 74 (1954): 75–76.

56. Newbigin, *Household of God*, 20–21.

57. Newbigin, *Faith for This One World?*, 77.

of the kingdom might go to all nations according to the original promise
to Abraham.

> The meaning of this "overlap of the ages" in which we live, the time be-
> tween the coming of Christ and His coming again, is that it is the time given
> for the witness of the apostolic Church to the ends of the earth. The end
> of all things, which has been revealed in Christ, is—so to say—held back
> until witness has been borne to the whole world concerning the judgment
> and salvation revealed in Christ. The implication of a true eschatological
> perspective will be missionary obedience, and the eschatology which does
> not issue in such obedience is a false eschatology.[58]

What makes this era unique is that it represents the culmination of the
biblical story. The biblical story is a journey with a universal destination:
salvation is for all nations in the context of the whole creation. Yet God has
traveled a particular path in Israel, narrowed to Christ, to arrive at this time.
But now that time has come! The full realization of the end has been held
off so that this good news might go to the whole world.

This understanding may be common. But we would err to miss the in-
credible significance of this insight. If the only reason for the delay of the
end is mission to all nations, as Newbigin maintains, then it is precisely this
that defines the people of God in this redemptive-historical era. Note the
strong statement: a true eschatological perspective will necessarily mean
missionary obedience; any eschatology that does not lead to mission is a
false eschatology.

So the coming of the kingdom defines the church in this way: they are a
people who live in the already–not yet era with the vocation of making the
end of history, accomplished in Christ and given in the Spirit, known to all
the nations and to the ends of the earth. But it is a community sent now to
the ends of the earth. This means that "Israel" is no longer a geographical and
ethnic community. Rather, they are nongeographical: they live in every nation
of the world. They are multiethnic: all nations are now incorporated into this
community. The eschatological and missionary nature of Israel transforms
them into a new kind of community.

Spirit and Church

Jesus forms a community and sends them to all nations to continue his
mission of making the kingdom known. He promises them the same Spirit

58. Newbigin, *Household of God*, 153–54.

that had empowered him in his mission. Newbigin presents the relationship between Jesus, the Spirit, and the church in two different ways. First, Jesus himself remains present in the midst of his church, making the End that he has ushered in visible in the midst of his people: "The coming of Jesus is the revelation of that end within the created order; in him the Creator who is both the beginning and the end was present among men, and by the operation of the Holy Spirit he is still present in the community of believers."[59] Jesus continues his mission by the work of the Spirit in the midst of the church. Second—and this is Newbigin's primary emphasis—Jesus sends the Spirit as the primary witness to his work. The Spirit works in and through the witness of the church as a witness to Jesus. And so mission is first of all the mission of the Spirit of God. "*His* mission. It is of greatest importance to recognize that it remains his mission."[60] This means that the first witness to Christ is the Spirit. This is even true of Jesus. The mighty works of Jesus are the work of the Spirit. And so as we follow in Christ's way, it is the Spirit who gives us power *and* it is the Spirit who is the first witness to Christ. It is not that mission first is the church's words and deeds, and for that task they ask for the Spirit's help. It is the work of the Spirit: "It is not the Church who bears witness and that the Spirit helps the church to do so. This kind of language completely misses the point. The point is that the Church is the place where the Spirit is present as witness. The witness is thus not an accomplishment of the Church but a promise to the Church."[61] As the church is faithful, it is the Spirit who acts and speaks. Newbigin insists, "It is impossible to stress too strongly that the beginning of mission is not an action of ours, but the presence of a new reality, the presence of the Spirit in power."[62]

What then is the relation of the church to the Spirit's witness? Newbigin answers that the relationship is threefold.[63] First, the church is the *locus* or the place of the Spirit's witness. The Spirit is the one who brings the eschatological life of the kingdom into the world. As the church shares in the Spirit, that new life is created in them. This new reality of the Spirit working in power in the "total life of the community" is the "central reality" of the church's mission.[64] "The whole meaning of this present age between Christ's coming and His coming again is that in it the powers of the age to come are at work now to draw all men into one in Christ. . . . The Church is not to be defined

59. Newbigin, *Faith for This One World?*, 99.
60. Newbigin, *Gospel in a Pluralist Society*, 117.
61. Newbigin, *Sign of the Kingdom*, 38.
62. Newbigin, *Gospel in a Pluralist Society*, 119.
63. Newbigin, *Faith for This One World?*, 87.
64. Newbigin, *Gospel in a Pluralist Society*, 137.

by what it is, but by that End to which it moves. And the power of that End now works in the church, the power of the Holy Spirit who is the earnest of the inheritance to be revealed."[65]

We remember that the End is cosmic renewal, the comprehensive salvation when men and women are restored again to their true humanity. This cosmic restoration has been revealed and accomplished in the work of Jesus Christ and is made present in the gift of the Spirit. This "salvation whose very essence is that it is corporate and cosmic, the restoration of the broken harmony between all men and between man and God and man and nature, must be communicated . . . in and by the actual development of a community which embodies—if only in foretaste—the restored harmony of which it speaks. A gospel of reconciliation can only be communicated by a reconciled fellowship."[66] The Spirit is at work within the ecclesial community to accomplish that End.

Second, the Spirit witnesses through the deeds and actions of the church to make known Christ and his kingdom. As the church reaches out to meet the world's needs, the Spirit witnesses to the coming kingdom. As the church does deeds of justice, mercy, compassion, and shalom, the Spirit witnesses in and through those deeds to the kingdom come in Jesus. As the church becomes deeply and lovingly involved in the sorrow and misery of the world, the Spirit points to Christ and his rule.

Finally, the Spirit witnesses to Christ and his rule in the evangelistic words of witness that the church speaks. Where the power of the Spirit is at work producing new life and deeds of justice, questions about this new reality will open opportunities for a verbal witness. In these words the Spirit witnesses to Christ.

It is precisely the witness of the Spirit to Christ that "constitutes the Church a witness to the kingdom" in its life, deeds, and words. Newbigin has much to say about this threefold witness of the church, and we will return to this in the next chapter.

Kingdom and Church

The church is an "eschatological reality"[67] and "can be rightly understood only in an eschatological perspective."[68] The church has begun to participate

65. Newbigin, *Household of God*, 19.
66. Newbigin, *Household of God*, 161.
67. Lesslie Newbigin, review of *God's Order: The Ephesian Letter and This Present Time*, by John A. MacKay, *Theology Today* 10 (1954): 546.
68. Newbigin, *Household of God*, 153.

in the kingdom salvation of the end of history given by the Spirit so that it might make known this good news to the ends of the earth. This missionary perspective shapes Newbigin's eschatological vision of the church.[69]

Newbigin employs three pictures of the church that express this eschatological perspective. Perhaps the most common image is actually a triad of images—namely, that the church is a firstfruit, instrument, and sign of the kingdom. It is first of all the firstfruit of the kingdom. Newbigin regularly substitutes "deposit" and "foretaste" here in the triad to get at the same reality. The church is a people that have already begun to taste of the kingdom life that God intends for humankind. They have a real experience of the salvation of the age to come as well as a hope for its full realization in the future. The church is also an instrument of the kingdom. The people of God are agents or instruments in the service of God's reign. God uses the church's costly engagement in the public life of culture as an instrument to bring about something of the justice, freedom, and peace of God's new creation. God uses evangelistic words to make known the good news of the kingdom. Finally, as the church tastes and embodies the life of God's kingdom and announces it and pursues its justice and peace in the world, it is a sign of the kingdom. "The point of a sign is to point to something that is real but not yet visible. . . . The Church is a sign of the Kingdom insofar as it is a foretaste. The Church is a sign that points people to a reality beyond what we can see."[70] This is the very identity and purpose of the church—to be a "pointing people," a sign pointing to a new reality present and coming in the midst of the world. "This Church then, this one new family created by God in Christ out of all the tribes and nations and peoples, is set in the midst of the world as the sign of that to which all creation, and all world history moves. It is the body of Christ, the new man, the second Adam, the new human race, growing up into its full stature and drawing into itself men of every kind."[71]

Newbigin employs a marvelous image to speak of the church as a people who reflect the kingdom in the midst of the world. When he and some pastoral companions would travel some distance by foot in India, they would often get up early, while it was still dark, to avoid the heat of the day. They would set off toward the east, but as they traveled, they might meet another

69. See George Vandervelde, "The Church as Missionary Community: The Church as Central Disclosure Point of the Kingdom," *Trinity Journal for Theology and Ministry* 4, no. 2 (Fall 2010): 112–29 (special issue, "The Gospel in the Public Square: Essays by and in Honor of Lesslie Newbigin").

70. Newbigin, *Word in Season*, 63.

71. Lesslie Newbigin, "The Mission and Unity of the Church" (Peter Ainslie Memorial Lecture, Grahamstown, South Africa, Rhodes University, October 17, 1960), 16–17.

party of people traveling west. Those folk might see a faint light on their faces. If they were to ask, "Where does that light come from?" the answer would be, "Turn around and look to the east." The sun was just coming up over the horizon, and a new day was dawning. One party reflected the light of that new day and invited others to turn to see it. The eastward travelers did not possess the light; they simply reflected the light of a new day. Newbigin says that the "church is that company which, going the opposite way to the majority . . . is given already the first glow of the light of a new day. It is that light that is the witness."[72]

A second image of the church that depicts its eschatological nature is of the church as "the provisional incorporation of humankind into Christ."[73] Jesus is the second Adam and the origin of the new humankind. In his death and resurrection he has ushered in the new creation. We are included in that new creation as we are incorporated into Christ by believing the gospel, by baptism into the visible body of God's people, and by the work of the Spirit.[74] Our incorporation into Christ means that we share in the victory of his crucifixion over evil and the new life of the resurrection. We are the first part of the harvest of the new humankind, but we do not yet fully manifest the new life of the kingdom—and so it is a provisional incorporation.

The notion that the church is the new humankind called out by God and belonging to the new creation leads to a third image: *ekklesia*. This is the common Greek word for "church" in the New Testament, but it is best translated "public assembly." The original meaning of this word is a public assembly to which all citizens of the city were summoned. The town clerk was the one who issued the call, and the public gathering of citizens who responded were the ones who discussed and settled affairs important for the city's life. As such, they were a representation of the whole city. In the New Testament, *ekklesia* is accompanied by the words "of God." The church is the public assembly of God. The one who calls out this public assembly is not the town clerk but God himself. In every place God calls forth his new humanity as a representative and public body to which he calls all people. The church is the firstfruit in each city of God's assembled new humanity.

---

72. Newbigin, *Mission in Christ's Way*, 21; see Newbigin, *Gospel in a Pluralist Society*, 120.

73. Lesslie Newbigin, "The Form and Structure of the Visible Unity of the Church," in *One in Christ* 13 (1977): 107–17.

74. Newbigin, *Household of God*, 147. He asks the question: How are we incorporated into Christ and into the eschatological events of his death and resurrection? The threefold answer he offers is the substance of the entire book. Protestants argue that it is by faith in the gospel that we are incorporated into Christ; Catholics say it is by baptism into the visible church; Pentecostals stress that it is by the work of the Spirit.

Ekklesia is the church's self-chosen name. By contrast, the enemies of the church employed other terms such as *heranos* and *thiasos*. These words interpreted the church not as the new humankind but as a private religious cult that offered personal and otherworldly salvation. These religious communities fit nicely in the private realm of life and did not challenge the public doctrine of the Roman Empire. The church refused to adopt this designation of a private religious fraternity. They saw themselves as the new humanity, called into the end-time kingdom by God and launched into the public life of the Roman Empire to challenge all competing allegiances.

Since the salvation of the kingdom is as wide as the creation, and since the church is the renewed humankind, the church may not be relegated to some private realm. It is a public body that must manifest the comprehensive and restorative salvation of the kingdom. This is what drove the church to adopt the title *ekklesia* and refuse any terms that gave it the identity of a private religious body. Newbigin's conclusion is that, sadly, today in the West, "church" usually means something closer to *heranos* and *thiasos* than to *ekklesia*. The church has forgotten its eschatological existence as the new humankind called out by God and has accepted the designation of private religious body concerned for personal and otherworldly salvation.

The Unity of the Church and Mission

It is precisely Newbigin's emphasis on the church as an eschatological and missionary body launched into the public life of the world that leads to his passionate concern for the unity of the church.[75] The unity of the church is shaped by the fact that the church is an eschatological reality. It has begun to participate in the End. The end of history is the summing up of all things in Christ; it will be a world reconciled and made one in Christ. If the church enjoys a foretaste of that coming world, then they will be one body that faithfully pictures the reconciled world that is coming. "The Church's unity is the sign and instrument of the salvation which Christ has wrought and whose end is the summing-up of all things in Christ."[76] The unity of the church is a preview of that day when the times will reach their fulfillment to bring unity to all things in heaven and on earth under Christ. "The quest

75. Michael W. Goheen, *"As the Father Has Sent Me, I Am Sending You": J. E. Lesslie Newbigin's Missionary Ecclesiology* (Zoetermeer: Boekencentrum, 2000), 200–218, 5.5.3. For an articulation of Newbigin's understanding of unity, see M. Scot Sherman, "Ut Omnes Unum Sint: The Case for Visible Church Reunion in the Ecclesiology of Bishop J. E. Lesslie Newbigin" (PhD diss., University of Wales, 2005).

76. Newbigin, *Household of God*, 171.

for unity is misunderstood if it is thought of in isolation from the fulfilment of God's purpose to 'unite all things in Christ, things in heaven and things on earth' (Eph. 1:10)."[77]

When it is a faithful foretaste and preview, the church witnesses to the good news of the new world that is coming that will be reconciled in unity in Christ. Newbigin often turned to the prayer of Jesus: "I pray also for those who will believe in me through their message, that all of them may be one, Father, just as you are in me and I am in you. May they also be in us so that the world may believe that you have sent me" (John 17:20–21). The unity of the church has a missionary purpose because it illustrates the End, a unity of humankind that transcends all usual human divisions and parties. It is a visible proof that Jesus is not simply one more name of a great religious leader. Rather, he is the Creator and Ruler of all and will one day reconcile all things to himself.[78] A reconciled church invites belief in the One at the center who draws humanity together from so many backgrounds and creates a community of love. "When the Church faces out toward the world it knows that it only exists as the first-fruits and the instrument of that reconciling work of Christ, and that division within its own life is a violent contradiction of its own fundamental nature."[79] Thus, the "unity of the Church" can only be understood "from a missionary point of view."[80]

Newbigin tells a story to illustrate that the world will only believe the gospel if the church is an embodiment of the gospel of reconciliation it proclaims:

> I have often stood at the door of a little church, with the Christian congregation seated on the ground in the middle and a great circle of Hindus and Muslims standing around. As I opened the Scripture and tried to preach the Word of God to them, I have always known that my words would only carry weight, would only be believed, if those standing around could recognize in those sitting in the middle that the promises of God were being fulfilled; if they could see that this new community in the village represented a new kind of body in which the old divisions of caste and education and temperament were being transcended in a new form of brotherhood. If they could not see anything of the kind, they would not be likely to believe.[81]

77. Lesslie Newbigin, "The Nature of the Unity We Seek: From the Church of South India," *Religion in Life* 26, no. 2 (1957): 187.

78. Lesslie Newbigin, *Is Christ Divided? A Plea for Christian Unity in a Revolutionary Age* (Grand Rapids: Eerdmans, 1961), 23.

79. Newbigin, *Household of God*, 9.

80. Newbigin, "Nature of the Unity We Seek," 187.

81. Newbigin, *Is Christ Divided?*, 24.

This is why Newbigin denounces disunity in such impassioned language, calling it "a direct and public contradiction of the Gospel,"[82] an "intolerable offence against the very nature of the church," "something illogical and incomprehensible,"[83] "a plain denial of the Gospel,"[84] a "public abdication of [the church's] right to preach the gospel to all nations,"[85] and an "intolerable scandal."[86] Those are strong words! Newbigin offers a vivid illustration of what he means by scandalous. He says that it may be unfortunate to have two rival temperance societies in the same town, but it is not scandalous. But a temperance society whose members are habitually drunk would be scandalous since their very inebriated existence contradicts their message. So it is for the church: disunity is scandalous because it contradicts the church's message—the good news that in Christ God is reconciling the world to himself.

So mission is dependent on unity, and unity is dependent on mission. When the church does not grasp its missionary vocation, it is little concerned about unity. Newbigin believed the only way to account for the "astounding complacency" toward a divided church that "so plainly and ostentatiously flouts the declared will of the Church's Lord" is the loss of a missionary understanding of the church.[87] "It is not possible to account for the contentment with the divisions of the Church except upon the basis of a loss of the conviction that the Church exists to bring all men to Christ. There is the closest possible connection between the acceptance of the missionary obligation and the acceptance of the obligation of unity. That which makes the Church one is what makes it a mission to the world."[88]

When Christians do take their missionary identity seriously and seek to live as a sign of the kingdom, their disunity becomes literally intolerable.[89] The problem of division is often the fact that we have lost our missionary consciousness. When we take mission seriously, we are forced to struggle toward unity. "I do not think that a resolute dealing with our divisions will come except in the context of a new acceptance on the part of all the Churches of the obligation to bring the Gospel to every creature; nor do I think that

---

82. Newbigin, *Is Christ Divided?*, 24.

83. Newbigin, *Reunion of the Church*, 23–24.

84. Newbigin, "The Mission and Unity of the Church," 17–18.

85. Newbigin, *Faith for This One World?*, 81.

86. Newbigin, *Household of God*, 9.

87. Newbigin, *Reunion of the Church*, 9.

88. Newbigin, *Reunion of the Church*, 11.

89. See Michael W. Goheen, "Mission and Unity: The Theological Dynamic of Comity," in *That the World May Believe: Essays on Mission and Unity in Honour of George Vandervelde*, ed. Michael W. Goheen and Margaret O'Gara (Lanham, MD: University Press of America, 2006), 83–91.

the world will believe that Gospel until it sees more evidence of its power to make us one. These two tasks—mission and unity—must be prosecuted together and in dissoluble relation one with the other."[90]

Thus, unity and mission belong together. They cannot be separated from each other because both belong to the very nature of the church. "The whole meaning of this present age between Christ's coming and His coming again is that in it the powers of the age to come are at work now to draw all men into one in Christ. When the Church ceases to be one, or ceases to be missionary, it contradicts its own nature."[91] Perhaps we might say that if one does not feel the passion of Newbigin for unity, one probably does not grasp very deeply his understanding of mission.

Conclusion

The church is rooted in the gospel. The good news is that in Christ and by the Spirit God has revealed and accomplished the cosmic renewal that lies at the end of history. The end of history has been held off so that this good news might reach all people and all nations to the very ends of the earth. In this time between the times, the Spirit gives this new eschatological life to the church to enable it to be a preview of the kingdom in the midst of all nations in its own life and to point to it in its words and deeds. Since the gospel is a gospel of the kingdom, the whole life of God's people bears witness to the reality that Jesus Christ is Lord to the glory of the Father. This is not simply one more task given to the church; it defines its very existence as missionary.

90. Newbigin, *Household of God*, 174.
91. Newbigin, *Household of God*, 19.

3

The Missionary Church and Its Vocation in the World

The end of universal history has been revealed and accomplished in the work of Jesus Christ. What must inevitably follow historically is the mission of the church: this good news must be made known to all peoples and to the ends of the earth. "The Church . . . is set by God in the midst of the world as the sign of that to which all creation and all world history moves."[1] This chapter is concerned with the question of how Newbigin understood the missionary vocation of the church in the midst of the world. In what ways was the church a sign set in the midst of the world to make known the goal of universal history? We begin this chapter with some foundational distinctions about the nature of mission that are important for Newbigin's missionary ecclesiology. Then we turn to five forms of witness that Newbigin especially emphasized.[2]

The Nature of Mission

Three helpful distinctions undergird Newbigin's understanding of the vocation of the church in the midst of the world: (1) God's mission and the

1. Lesslie Newbigin, "Mission and Unity of the Church" (Peter Ainslie Memorial Lecture, Grahamstown, South Africa, Rhodes University, October 17, 1960), 16–17.
2. Michael W. Goheen, *"As the Father Has Sent Me, I Am Sending You": J. E. Lesslie Newbigin's Missionary Ecclesiology* (Zoetermeer: Boekencentrum, 2000), 275–330 (chap. 7).

church's mission, (2) missionary dimension and missionary intention, and (3) mission and missions.

God's Mission and the Church's Mission

The first important distinction is between God's mission and the church's mission. We begin with Newbigin's affirmation that "the Church's mission to all the nations is a participation in the work of the triune God."[3] This statement was made in the early 1960s, about a decade after the emergence of the language of the *missio Dei*. Already there had been a major divergence between two major interpretations, and Newbigin was in the middle of these debates.

To understand the emergence of the *missio Dei*, it is important to understand the background of the nineteenth and early twentieth centuries: mission was considered to be primarily a work of the church. The optimism and anthropocentrism of the Enlightenment infected the missionary movement. This human-centered confidence was dealt a number of blows in the twentieth century that called for a new understanding of mission. It is in this context that the language of the mission of the Triune God emerged. This language makes clear in the strongest possible way four things: the church's mission must be distinguished from God's mission; God's mission has priority; it is the mission of the *Triune* God; and God's mission determines exactly the *what* and *how* of the church's mission. All this is true for Newbigin.

The theological framework of the *missio Dei* remains firmly in place today. There continues to be much reflection on a trinitarian understanding of the *missio Dei* as the framework for the missional church. Some of it appeals to Newbigin. And while there is much variety, some of it bears little resemblance to Newbigin's own understanding. So we must carefully articulate what Newbigin meant when he spoke of mission as participation in the mission of the Triune God.

Characteristics of Newbigin's Understanding of the *Missio Dei*

The first characteristic to note in Newbigin's understanding of the *missio Dei* is its strong Christocentrism. The starting point for thinking about the missionary nature of the church is Jesus Christ. He gathers and commissions the church, and mission is participation in and continuation of his mission. Newbigin penned the following words for the Willingen report and then quotes them to begin his own articulation of a theology of mission: "There is no participation

---

3. Lesslie Newbigin, *Trinitarian Doctrine for Today's Mission* (1963; repr., Carlisle, UK: Paternoster, 1998), 54.

in Christ without participation in His mission to the world. That by which the Church receives its existence is that by which it is also given its world-mission. 'As the Father hath sent Me, even so send I you.'"[4] A trinitarian understanding of God and his mission begins with Jesus. Two questions—Who is Jesus? and What was his mission?—lead to reflection on the triune nature of God.[5]

If our mission is to continue the mission of Jesus, then what is his mission? This was the question faced by the early church, and they responded by expounding the explicit trinitarian context of Jesus's mission. "The development of the doctrine of the Trinity in the early Church was only the making explicit of that which is from the beginning the presupposition and the context, the source and the goal of the mission of Jesus. It is in Trinitarian terms that we have to understand the nature and authority of the mission in which we are called to share."[6]

This is important. Trinitarian reflection is Christocentric and tied closely to the mission of Jesus—that is, it arises from the confession that Jesus is Lord and from the mission of the early church to express that confession in the pagan-classical world. And further, it develops as the church struggles to understand what it means to follow Jesus in mission. How are they to carry out their mission? Their answer is, in the way of Jesus. What is that way? This question gives rise to trinitarian reflection. The starting point is the sending of Jesus into the world.

In a skirmish with Konrad Raiser over a trinitarian understanding of the *missio Dei* within the ecumenical tradition, Newbigin again makes clear his starting point in Christ.[7] Raiser believes Newbigin's Christocentrism blurs a trinitarian understanding of God. Newbigin responds that "a Trinitarian perspective can be only an enlargement and development of a Christo-centric one and not an alternative set over against it, for the doctrine of the Trinity is the theological articulation of what it means to say that Jesus is the unique Word of God incarnate in world history."[8] This Christocentric starting point

---

4. Norman Goodall, ed., *Missions under the Cross: Addresses Delivered at the Enlarged Meeting of the Committee of the International Missionary Council at Willingen, in Germany, 1952; with Statements Issued by the Meeting* (London: Edinburgh House, 1953), 190; see Lesslie Newbigin, *The Open Secret: An Introduction to the Theology of Mission,* rev. ed. (Grand Rapids: Eerdmans, 1995), 1.

5. Newbigin, *Open Secret,* 15, 19, 20, 24, 28.

6. Lesslie Newbigin, "The Future of Missions and Missionaries," *Review and Expositor* 74, no. 2 (1977): 214.

7. For an analysis of that debate, see Michael W. Goheen, "The Future of Mission in the World Council of Churches: The Dialogue between Lesslie Newbigin and Konrad Raiser," *Mission Studies* 21, no. 1 (2004): 97–111.

8. Lesslie Newbigin, "Ecumenical Amnesia," *International Bulletin of Missionary Research* 18, no. 1 (1994): 2.

is fundamentally historical; it begins with Jesus of Nazareth—who he is and the nature of his mission.

A second characteristic of Newbigin's understanding of the mission of the Triune God is the immense space he gives to the work of the Spirit. Raiser and others may believe that Newbigin's Christocentrism has obscured the work of the Spirit, but such a judgment can be made only if one is not familiar with Newbigin's body of writing. Newbigin gives enormous space to the work of the Spirit because the Spirit is the primary actor in the mission of the church (as we have already seen in the preceding chapters).

The third point to note about Newbigin's understanding of God's mission is the clear narrative shape. The way Newbigin relates the various persons of the Trinity is in terms of the story of Scripture. It is impossible to read very far into Newbigin's work without recognizing that the overriding framework for everything is the biblical story. The work and mission of God narrated in the biblical story is fundamentally historical. The Triune God reveals himself in the context of his work in history to unfold his purpose to renew the creation. The strong historical feel of Newbigin contrasts with other trinitarian formulations that have a much more static, doctrinal, or metaphysical sense. It also contrasts with any kind of formulaic articulation of the *missio Dei*. For example, the statement that the Father sends the Son, the Son sends the Spirit, and the Father and Son send the church in the power of the Spirit certainly captures the Bible's teaching. However, if we unhinge that statement from the full narrative of Scripture, it becomes a wax nose that can be, and in fact has been, shaped in many ways. If that formulation is utilized, it must be as shorthand for the actual content of the biblical narrative. Any trinitarian understanding of the *missio Dei* that does not make redemptive history the primary context for the word "participation" or "sending" is not in line with Newbigin's understanding.

Finally—and closely related to the former point—Newbigin's understanding of the *missio Dei* is eschatological. The whole biblical story is moving toward the goal of salvation for all nations. The gospel announces that the end-time salvation has broken into the middle of history in Jesus Christ and the Holy Spirit. The consummation of the End is held off so that in these last days the gospel may go to the ends of the earth. The Spirit is given as an end-time gift that witnesses to the kingdom revealed and accomplished in Jesus. This brief statement again makes clear that the goal of the Father's work is the kingdom as the climax of history. In Jesus and by the work of the Spirit, that kingdom is now present. Newbigin's understanding of the *missio Dei* gives a prominent place to eschatology.

Mission in Christ's Way

"It seems to me to be of great importance to insist that mission is not first of all an action of ours. It is an action of God, the triune God. . . . This is the primal reality in missions; the rest is derivative."[9] How do we articulate the mission of the church as participation in the mission of the Triune God? We will expound it here in terms of mission in Christ's way, mission in the kingdom of the Father, and mission as bearing the witness of the Spirit.

"As the Father has sent me, I am sending you." With these words from John 20:21—a favorite verse for Newbigin—Jesus sends the church into the world to continue his mission. "This must determine the way we think about and carry out mission; it must be founded and modelled upon his. We are not authorized to do it in any other way."[10] How is the mission of the church modeled and founded on Jesus? Newbigin's answer is rich and can only be summarized briefly.

Mission in Christ's way is, first, to continue the ministry of the incarnate Jesus. This means we are to make known the kingdom of God. And we do it in the way that Christ did: by way of life, word, and deed. As Jesus formed and taught a community to bear witness to him, so that is essential to our own mission. Prayer and suffering marked the ministry of Jesus, and so it should characterize ours. And finally, Jesus carries out his mission in total dependence on the Father and in the power of the Spirit, so the church must follow in his way. This provides the impetus for the development of a trinitarian shape of mission; Jesus made known the kingdom of the Father in the power of the Spirit. This defines the church's mission: if we follow in the way of Jesus, our life will be fully trinitarian.

Continuing the mission of Jesus, second, is in the way of the cross and resurrection. The cross is a sign of the kingdom: it pictures the victory of God in seeming defeat, signifies the way of conflict and suffering, and shows us the way God identifies himself fully with the world and at the same time rejects the sin that distorts the world. Again and again Newbigin returns to the cross of Jesus to show that our mission is also in the way of the cross.

The mission of the church is also in the way of the resurrection. The resurrection is the dawning and inauguration of the new creation. We begin to share in the resurrection life of the Son. This means the renewing power of God is at work in the church bringing the new creation into the midst of history. Sharing in the resurrection life means also that we follow in the way

9. Lesslie Newbigin, *The Gospel in a Pluralist Society* (Grand Rapids: Eerdmans, 1989), 134–35.
10. Lesslie Newbigin, *Mission in Christ's Way: Bible Studies* (Geneva: WCC Publications, 1987), 1.

of the cross, not only as a model for our mission but also in its power as a historical event that gained the victory of God over sin and evil.

Mission in Christ's way, third, is in relationship and submission to the living and exalted Lord. The church is "connected with Christ in two distinguishable ways." It is connected to the historical Jesus as the founder of the church who gathers the church and entrusts his mission to them. But the church is also "connected with him as the living and ascended Lord" who is our Eternal Contemporary.[11] This means that the church is not simply a historically continuous institution founded two thousand years ago to continue the historical mission of Jesus. It has also been incorporated into the kingdom of God, and Christ continues to rule his church as he lives among them. The character of the church is not just historical but also eschatological. He continues to nourish the life of the kingdom with his own life in the Word and sacraments of the gospel, and he works in and through them to carry out his mission in the world. Mission means ongoing and intimate communion with the living Lord, and submission to and proclamation of the Lord of history.

Mission in Christ's way, finally, is in the power of the Spirit. The Spirit whose proper nature is eschatological is poured out on Jesus at the beginning of his ministry. Jesus carries out his mission in total and complete dependence on the work of the Spirit. That same Spirit is then poured out on the church to equip it for its mission in the world.

Mission in the Kingdom of the Father

In the 1960s Newbigin believed that reflection on mission had "perhaps been too exclusively founded upon the person and work of Christ" and therefore needed to "make a large place for the work of the Holy Spirit." At the same time, he observed that "it is equally true that a true doctrine of missions will have much to say about God the Father. The opinion may be ventured that recent ecumenical thinking about the mission and unity of the Church has been defective at both these points."[12] He himself sought to make the necessary corrections. But it may be said fairly of Newbigin's thought that

11. Lesslie Newbigin, *The Reunion of the Church: A Defence of the South India Scheme* (London: SCM, 1948), 71. Newbigin makes much of this twofold way of relating to Christ in this chapter of *Reunion of the Church*. He rejects Yves Congar's notion of the church as an extension of the incarnation because this makes the church only a historical institution related to the historical Jesus and misses the eschatological nature of the church that is related also to the living and ascended Lord. See Lesslie Newbigin, *Christ Our Eternal Contemporary* (Madras: Christian Literature Society, 1968).

12. Newbigin, *Trinitarian Doctrine*, 33.

while his development of the work of the Spirit is full and rich, his reflection on the Father is less so. Yet what he does say is significant.

Newbigin's own starting point is to note that according to the New Testament witness, Jesus carries out his mission in a relationship of the Son to the Father. Jesus's mission unfolds in relation to the Father as the sovereign ruler of history who is directing all things to accomplish his purpose. Jesus steps into the story of the Old Testament, which is the long narrative of God's mighty deeds directed toward the goal of reestablishing his sovereign rule over creation. While the focus of his redemptive work recorded in the Old Testament has been Israel, his sovereign rule extends over all nations, even world powers, as well as over all creation and history. Thus Jesus rests in God's sovereign rule to work out his purposes for the world in Jesus's own work.

Moreover, Jesus carries out his mission in relation to God as a caring Father. The rule of God narrated in the Old Testament is one not of an arbitrary despot but of a gracious and loving Father. "God's fatherly rule of all things is at the very heart of [Jesus's] teaching."[13] He is the beloved Son who carries out his mission in intimate communion with the Father. He can trust the Father's wisdom in his sovereign rule. And so mission in Christ's way is in the way of trust, love, and the obedience of a son to a father.

> God who created all things also sustains them and directs them according to his will. Even the great pagan political powers are in his hands to be used for his fatherly purposes. . . . God rules and uses them all. . . . [Jesus] submits himself wholly to the Father's ordering of events. He does not seek to take control himself of world history. He rejects every temptation to become himself a ruler and director of events. . . . He appears as the Son who lovingly submits himself to the will of him who rules all things.[14]

Newbigin's strong sense of God working out his purpose in history as narrated in the Old Testament forms the backdrop. But this portrayal of God as sovereign ruler is tied to an intimate portrait of God as Father. This leads Jesus, and us, to a joyful and unanxious witness and participation in God's mission, trusting him to work out his sovereign purpose in fatherly wisdom. This is a terribly needed reminder for a church that plans, strategizes, and manages, while trusting its own efforts to fulfill God's mission. And it is also a necessary perspective for the church in the midst of anxiety over the future. If we understand our mission in light of God's sovereign rule, "we shall be

13. Newbigin, *Trinitarian Doctrine*, 39.
14. Newbigin, *Trinitarian Doctrine*, 39.

delivered from much of the anxiety which we find around us. . . . We do not need to waste our time being anxious about whether God's Kingdom will come; what we have to be concerned about is whether or not we are being faithful witnesses to it now, whether when the Lord comes we will be found awake and alert."[15]

But I would register one plea to move beyond Newbigin: the Father's work in creation needs to be developed much more fully as a context for the mission of the church today. While this is far from absent in Newbigin's work, today it needs to be much more explicit and developed.

Mission as Bearing the Witness of the Spirit

When we turn to the work of the Spirit, we find rich reflection. Mission is "bearing the witness of the Spirit."[16] The Spirit belongs first to the age to come: in the last days the Spirit will be poured out. With the coming of the Spirit, the End has arrived. The Spirit is an advance installment of the kingdom in the world (2 Cor. 1:22; Eph. 1:14). The Spirit's work begins in Jesus, in whose life, words, and deeds the Spirit acts in power to make the kingdom present in the midst of the world. It continues as Jesus pours out the Spirit on his gathered community at Pentecost. As Luke's Gospel begins with the anointing of the Spirit on Jesus for his mission, the sequel, the book of Acts, begins with the outpouring of the Spirit on his community for their mission. Now the Spirit works in this community through their life, words, and deeds as a witness to the kingdom to the ends of the earth. And so by an outpouring of the Spirit, the church is launched on its mission[17] and throughout Acts is the "active agent of mission." The Spirit "is a power that rules, guides, and goes before the church: the free, sovereign, living power of the Spirit of God. Mission is not something the church does; it is something that is done by the Spirit, who is himself the witness."[18] It is the Spirit who witnesses to Jesus creating signs of the new age. "The Church is not so much the agent of mission as the locus of mission. It is God who acts in the power of the Spirit."[19]

This needs to be kept clearly front and center if the church is to avoid turning its mission into a military operation or a sales campaign carried out simply as a human project. "It is impossible to stress too strongly that the

15. Lesslie Newbigin, "The Mission of the Church to All the Nations" (address, National Council of Churches General Assembly, San Francisco, December 1960), 2.
16. Newbigin, *Open Secret*, 56. This is the title of the whole chapter on the work of the Spirit and mission.
17. Newbigin, *Open Secret*, 58.
18. Newbigin, *Open Secret*, 56.
19. Newbigin, *Gospel in a Pluralist Society*, 119.

beginning of mission is not an action of ours, but the presence of a new reality, the presence of the Spirit of God in power."[20] Forgetting this important reality, the church is tempted to view its own strategies and plans and efforts as the way the kingdom comes.

Newbigin tells a couple of stories to illustrate this truth. On one occasion, in an industrial area of Madras there were forty adult baptisms in a short period of time. He invited all the new converts to tell their stories. Each of their stories was different, and in each case their coming to Christ was a series of events over a period of time. It might have been a talk on the factory floor with a friend, a visit from a Christian during an illness, the reading of a tract or Scripture, an act of kindness, a sermon, a prayer, a dream, or a vision. Newbigin concludes that it must be the work of the Spirit: "No one could have programmed all this. The strategy (if that is the right word) was not in any human hands."[21]

On another occasion, as the bishop of Madurai he received a letter from a village requesting baptism for twenty-five families. There had been no evangelistic initiatives organized by the church in that area, and so he tried to piece together how these families had come to Christ. He says it was a story in four acts. Act 1: A Christian engineer from a mainline church comes to town to help install an electric pump for clean water. He tells them he is a Christian but says no more. They saw he was a good man who worked hard. Act 2: A villager purchases a copy of the Gospel of Mark in a nearby village from a colporteur (a religious bookseller) and a few folks begin to read it together. Act 3: An evangelist visits the village, preaches a fiery sermon, and leaves behind a tract asking, "If you die tonight, where will you go?" These villagers decide this is a more serious matter than they had realized, and so they ask a Christian congregation five miles away to send them someone to tell them more. Act 4: The congregation sends an injured and unemployed laborer, or "coolie," to spend a month with them answering their questions. The result: twenty-five families ready and eager for baptism. Newbigin concludes: "The point of the story is obvious. If you had assembled the engineer, the colporteur, the evangelist, and the coolie for a seminar on missionary methods, they would probably have disagreed with each other—perhaps violently. Unknown to each other, each had done faithfully the work for which the Holy Spirit had given equipment. The strategy was not in any human hands. . . . It is the Holy Spirit who is the primary missionary; our role is secondary."[22]

20. Newbigin, *Gospel in a Pluralist Society*, 119.
21. Newbigin, *Mission in Christ's Way*, 20.
22. Newbigin, *Mission in Christ's Way*, 39–40.

Missionary Dimension and Missionary Intention

A second distinction important for Newbigin's missionary ecclesiology is between missionary dimension and missionary intention. During the middle of the twentieth century, the scope of mission broadened to include everything the church was doing. Newbigin was concerned that the more specific evangelistic and cross-cultural missionary tasks of the church might be lost in this widening mission. On the one hand, Newbigin affirmed the comprehensive scope of mission that was emerging. This was undoubtedly biblical. On the other hand, the expansion of mission had the potential to marginalize if not eclipse intentional activities that had as their deliberate aim a witness to Christ to those who did not yet know him.

To preserve both concerns, Newbigin makes the helpful distinction between missional dimension and missional intention. This distinguishes "between mission as a *dimension* of the Church's whole life, and mission as the primary *intention* of certain activities. Because the Church *is* the mission there is a missionary dimension of everything that the Church does. But not everything the Church does has a missionary intention." Certain activities can be considered to have a missional intention when they are "an action of the Church in going out beyond the frontiers of its own life to bear witness to Christ as Lord among those who do not know Him, and when the overall *intention* of that action is that they should be brought from unbelief to faith."[23]

Since the whole life of the church—both as a gathered community and when it is scattered throughout the world—is the place where the Holy Spirit witnesses to God's renewing work, the whole life of the church partakes of the character of witness. If Christ is Lord of all human life, then the whole of our lives will be part of God's mission as it directs others to his sovereign rule and renewing power. All Christian life has a missional dimension.

There are certain activities, however, that are undertaken specifically with the deliberate intention of bearing witness to Jesus Christ. Flowing out of a church that is aware of the missionary dimension of its whole existence will be words and deeds whose conscious goal is to point to Jesus Christ and invite others to follow him. For example, evangelism and cross-cultural missions will be deliberate and intentional activities that aim to witness to the gospel and invite the response of faith.

Newbigin believes that both of these aspects of mission are essential. One without the other will cripple the mission of the church. "Unless there is in the life of the Church a point of concentration for the missionary intention,

23. Lesslie Newbigin, *One Body, One Gospel, One World: The Christian Mission Today* (New York: International Missionary Council, 1958), 43–44.

the missionary dimension which is proper to the whole life of the Church will be lost."[24] A church that reduces mission to only intentional activities narrows the scope of the gospel and removes the full context in which witnessing words should take their place. Each needs the other.

Mission and Missions

A third crucial distinction is helpful for understanding Newbigin's missionary ecclesiology. The broadening view of mission was threatening all intentional efforts at witnessing to Christ. However, cross-cultural missions was perhaps most threatened. This was because, throughout the nineteenth and early twentieth centuries, mission had been reduced to cross-cultural missions. But cross-cultural missions came to be viewed as oppressive in the postcolonialist period, even as "theological racism"[25] by some. Moreover, with the growth of the church in the non-Western world, it seemed to no longer be needed. To the degree that Western churches participated in the cross-cultural enterprise, it would be more through social and economic development than through evangelism and church planting. A broader vision of mission threatened the cross-cultural missionary task of the church. Again, while Newbigin sees the importance of broadening mission in light of the church's role in the biblical story, he also sees that it is essential "to identify and distinguish the specific foreign missionary task within the total Mission of the Church."[26]

Newbigin distinguishes between mission and missions (with an *s*). While mission is the total calling of the church to make known the gospel as it participates in God's mission, missions consists of particular enterprises within the total mission of the church that "have the primary intention of bringing into existence a Christian presence in a milieu where previously there was no such presence or where such presence was ineffective."[27] Thus, missions remains an essential part of the ongoing mission of the church.

Indeed, missions is important for maintaining the missional dimension in all of life. While "the church is mission, we still need 'missions' in order that it may be truly so. . . . This is not in order to relieve the rest of the church

24. Newbigin, *One Body, One Gospel, One World*, 43.
25. Lesslie Newbigin, *Unfinished Agenda: An Updated Autobiography* (Edinburgh: Saint Andrew Press, 1993), 231. He turns the table and says that if the gospel is for whites only, that is "a peculiar form of racism"; see Lesslie Newbigin, "The Pastor's Opportunities: VI. Evangelism in the City," *Expository Times* 98, no. 12 (1987): 358.
26. Lesslie Newbigin, "Mission and Missions," *Christianity Today*, August 1, 1960, 911.
27. Lesslie Newbigin, "Crosscurrents in Ecumenical and Evangelical Understandings of Mission," *International Bulletin of Missionary Research* 6, no. 4 (1982): 149.

of missionary responsibility but to ensure that its whole life is missionary."[28] Missions must be to the ends of the earth and is a test of whether one really believes the gospel. It is still important to identify need throughout the world and to commission gifted and called individuals to take the gospel to those places in evangelism and church planting. We will return to the subject of missions toward the end of the chapter.

Forms of Witness

God's end-time renewing power has broken into history. And now "God's saving power known and experienced in the life of the redeemed community has to issue in all kinds of witness and service to the world."[29] What kinds of witness and service did Newbigin focus his attention on? There are five points of special emphasis: the distinctive life of the community, the calling of the laity, deeds of mercy and justice, evangelism, and missions to places where the gospel was not known.

New Being and Communal Life

For Newbigin, mission is first of all about being—being the new humanity, being a distinctive community. The doing and the going flow from this. But to be a sign of the kingdom is first of all a matter of being a people that embody the new life of the kingdom, a picture of true humanity.

Newbigin makes this point repeatedly throughout his writings. We can note three places where this is made clear. First, his little book *Truth to Tell* records three lectures on the mission of the church in modernity. In the first he argues for the public truth of the gospel, and in the second he shows how this has been undermined as the evangelical and liberal wings of the church have each in their own way compromised the gospel. In the final lecture he is concerned with the mission of the church in the public square. He points to the calling of God's people in their vocations in the not-so-naked public square in a way that would have a shaping impact on society.[30] He concludes with these words: "The most important contribution which the Church can make to a new social order is to be itself a new social order."[31] If the local

28. Newbigin, "Crosscurrents," 179.

29. Lesslie Newbigin, "Our Task Today" (address, fourth meeting of the diocesan council, Tirumangalam, 1951), 5.

30. Lesslie Newbigin, *Truth to Tell: The Gospel as Public Truth* (Grand Rapids: Eerdmans, 1991), 81–84.

31. Newbigin, *Truth to Tell*, 85.

congregation "understands its true character as a holy priesthood for the sake of the world . . . then there is a point of growth for a new social order."[32] It is in local congregations that the first shoots of new creation life can be nourished so as to subvert the principalities and powers of culture, especially the growing economic, financial, and technical forces of globalization. The church must be visible and recognizable as a community that lives out the Father's love in every city. And so, "the chief contribution of the Church to the renewing of social order is to be itself a new social order."[33]

A second place where Newbigin makes new being the primary form of witness is in his discussion of mission as word, deed, and new being.[34] He notes the long tradition that has isolated evangelism as the first priority in mission. And today in the missionary movement, he says, there is an ongoing battle between those who affirm the priority of words and those who believe that deeds of justice and peace must take precedence.

When we turn to the Gospels, we see the inextricable connection between deeds and words. The powerful deeds call forth explanatory words. But beneath both is a powerful new reality. And what is this new reality? The answer of the gospel is the arrival of the kingdom of God in the presence of Jesus himself. In him the kingdom of God has come in power. And so in the mission of Jesus, the mighty works and the preaching point to the new reality of the kingdom in the life of Jesus.

But that presence does not come to an end with the close of Jesus's earthly ministry; it continues in the new life of the community. "What he did was to prepare a community chosen to be the bearer of the secret of the kingdom. . . . The intention of Jesus was not to leave behind a disembodied teaching. It was that . . . there should be created a community which would continue that which he came from the Father to be and do—namely to embody and announce the presence of the reign of God."[35]

The new reality is, first, the coming of the kingdom in the person of Jesus by the power of the Spirit, but second, it is in the power of the Spirit creating new life in the church. The church is incorporated into the mission of Jesus in the power of the Spirit. Like him, their deeds and words testify to a new reality: the coming of the kingdom in Jesus. To pit one against the other "is profoundly weakening the Church's witness." But "both parties have hold of an important truth." Both words and deeds are an important part of the witness to the kingdom. However, "both parties to this dispute need to recover

32. Newbigin, *Truth to Tell*, 87.
33. Newbigin, *Truth to Tell*, 90.
34. Newbigin, *Gospel in a Pluralist Society*, 128–40.
35. Newbigin, *Gospel in a Pluralist Society*, 133–34.

a fuller sense of the prior reality, the givenness, the ontological priority of the new reality which the work of Christ has brought into being."[36] That new reality is a community whose whole life is rooted in Christ as Lord and Savior, who is indwelt by the Spirit, and who challenges the idolatrous cultural powers. And so, Newbigin concludes, "It is clear that to set word and deed, preaching and action, against each other is absurd. The central reality is neither word nor act, but *the total life of a community* enabled by the Spirit to live in Christ, sharing his passion and the power of the resurrection."[37] The "new being" created by the work of Christ and the Spirit has primacy in the mission of the church. The total life of the people of God as the new humankind restored to their true humanity is the foundational witness of the church. Words and deeds flow from this restored community. "The mission of the church, following that of Jesus, has to be both word and deed and the life of a community which already embodies a foretaste of God's kingdom."[38] Note the word "embodies." It is a common word in Newbigin's vocabulary for mission and captures the point of this section: the new being of the church's life is central to mission.

There is an important point to be made here in both arguments we have sketched thus far. Neither the church as new being nor the church as a new social order is limited to the church *as a gathered community*. This is the mistake made by some interpreters of Newbigin. In both places I have referenced, this new being or new social order is expressed not only in the life of the church gathered as a community but in the life of the church scattered in their various callings. In his discussion of the church as "the first shoots of a new creation," Newbigin explicitly says that the "true character as a holy priesthood for the sake of the world" involves "its members . . . equipped for the exercise of that priesthood in their secular employments."[39] And, even more clearly, when he speaks of the "total life of a community" enabled by the Spirit to live out the new reality of Christ's life, he notes that "members have different gifts and are involved in the secular life of the society in which they share."[40] This new being is the new humankind, whether gathered together in community or scattered in their various callings.

The final place that illustrates how Newbigin makes new being the primary form of witness is his discussion of the church as a hermeneutic of the gospel. Newbigin has established that "the gospel cannot be accommodated

---

36. Newbigin, *Gospel in a Pluralist Society*, 136.
37. Newbigin, *Gospel in a Pluralist Society*, 137 (my emphasis).
38. Lesslie Newbigin, "A Missionary's Dream," *Ecumenical Review* 43, no. 1 (January 1991): 6.
39. Newbigin, *Truth to Tell*, 86–87.
40. Newbigin, *Gospel in a Pluralist Society*, 137.

as one element in a society which has pluralism as its reigning ideology. . . . To be faithful to a message which concerns the kingdom of God, his rule over all things and all peoples, the Church has to claim the high ground of public truth."[41] What would it mean for the church to live out this public and comprehensive vision of the gospel? It will not be by a return to the coercive power of earlier Christendom. Rather, it will be by local congregations who believe the gospel and shape their lives by it. "The primary reality of which we have to take account in seeking for a Christian impact on public life is the Christian congregation. How is it possible that the gospel should be credible that people should come to believe that the power which has the last word in human affairs is represented by a man hanging on a cross? . . . The only answer, the only hermeneutic of the gospel, is a congregation of men and women who believe it and live by it."[42]

There are many activities that witness to the public truth of the gospel and challenge the public doctrine shaping culture. However, "these are all secondary, and they have power to accomplish their purpose only as they are rooted in and lead back to the believing congregation."[43] Newbigin goes on to offer six characteristics of such a community that is a hermeneutic of the gospel. It will be a community of praise in a world of doubt and skepticism. It will be a community of truth in a pluralistic society that overwhelms and produces relativism. It will be a selfless community that does not live for itself but is deeply involved in the concerns of its neighborhood in a selfish world. It will be a community prepared to live out the gospel in public life in a world that privatizes all religious claims. It will be a community of mutual responsibility in a world of individualism. It will be a community of hope in a world of pessimism and despair about the future.

A community that lives like this will be a "foretaste of a different social order." They will be congregations that renounce an introverted concern for their own lives and recognize that they exist for the sake of those who are not members. This self-giving and outward-oriented life will be a "sign, instrument, and foretaste of God's redeeming grace for the whole life of society."[44]

It is quite instructive to note the origin of these various aspects of a distinctive community. At the time, Newbigin was in "retirement" but pastoring a church in Winson Green, a poor area in the inner city of Birmingham, United Kingdom. He delivered an address in a conference called to discuss the church's social calling in a cultural context divided by the "selfish society"

41. Newbigin, *Gospel in a Pluralist Society*, 222.
42. Newbigin, *Gospel in a Pluralist Society*, 227.
43. Newbigin, *Gospel in a Pluralist Society*, 227.
44. Newbigin, *Gospel in a Pluralist Society*, 233.

created by Margaret Thatcher. The situation was urgent: market forces were gaining final sovereignty over Britain's life. This was an era of ideology and idolatry. "We were coming into a confessional situation."[45] He critiques both the right-wing economics of Thatcher that were creating this idolatrous situation and the response of the left, calling both "a product of the Enlightenment's exaltation of the autonomous individual with his autonomous reason and conscience as the centrepiece of our thinking." Both have consequently separated rights from duties, freedom from responsibilities, and have drawn different conclusions. In this context he says that it is "not the primary business of the Church to advocate a new social order; it is our primary business to *be* a new social order."[46] He offers four characteristics of such a community: praise and self-giving love amid selfishness, mutual acceptance amid autonomous individualism, mutual responsibility amid a demand for rights, and hope amid despair and consumer satiation. "When that hermeneutic is available, people find it possible to have a new vision for society and to know that the vision is more than a dream."[47]

Note in these examples four important observations about Newbigin's vision for the church as a new social order. First, the church is called to live its life in a way that is distinctive from the lives of its contemporaries as they are captive to cultural idolatry. There is an alternative or contrasting way of living. Second, the scope of this new being is comprehensive: it is all of life under the lordship of Christ. Third, one must understand well the idols of culture. If one reads Newbigin's contextual address, "Vision for the City," and his analysis of the powerful idols at work in Thatcherite Britain—both on the right and on the left—one can see why he discusses the characteristics he does. He is calling the church to be distinctive in a very particular kind of cultural setting in contrast to specific idols. And finally, this new life involves both a communal embodiment and a life lived out in the context of culture. The new being is the church both gathered as a community and scattered as the new humankind to live out their lives in a different story.

Vocations of Believers in Culture

The business of the church in the biblical story is to bear witness to the comprehensive salvation that is coming at the end of cosmic history. The

45. Newbigin, *Unfinished Agenda*, 250.
46. Lesslie Newbigin, "Vision for the City," in *Renewal of Social Vision*, ed. A. Elliot and I. Swanson, Occasional Paper 17 (Edinburgh: Centre for Theology and Public Issues, University of Edinburgh, 1989), 40.
47. Newbigin, "Vision for the City," 41.

new life that is given to the church is as wide as human life: all of life is being restored—cultural, social, economic, political, artistic, academic, familial, and more. The church's first witness is by way of new being—a renewal that covers all of life.

One of the areas of the church's witness that is of primary importance to Newbigin and occupies a good deal of space is his concern to see believers live out this new being in the context of their particular vocations.[48] It is in the various callings of each member that "the primary witness to the sovereignty of Christ must be given,"[49] because the "enormous preponderance of the Church's witness is the witness of the thousands of its members who work in field, home, office, mill, or law court."[50]

He is not referring to the obligation to evangelize one's coworkers or even to manifest the gospel in microethical categories within one's vocational setting, although these are not excluded.[51] It is much deeper than that: it is the obedience in their vocations that is faithful to God's creational intent. Christ is Lord by virtue of being Creator and Redeemer. The believer who lives under Christ's lordship in the various spheres of public life witnesses "to the true purpose for which God created [those structures]."[52] When Christians believe that their work from Monday to Friday is not the "Lord's work" and thus leave those areas to the powers of cultural idolatry without challenge, they "deny Christ's cosmic Lordship."[53] Thus, "the entire membership of the Church in their secular occupations are called to be signs of his lordship in every area of life."[54] For example, Newbigin writes, "A farmer who farms his land well but neglects to say his prayers will be certainly condemned by Christians as failing in his duty. But a farmer who says his prayers, and allows weeds, bad drainage, or soil erosion to spoil his land is failing in his primary duty as

---

48. Michael W. Goheen, "The Missional Calling of Believers in the World: The Contribution of Lesslie Newbigin," in *A Scandalous Prophet: The Way of Mission after Newbigin*, ed. Thomas F. Foust, George R. Hunsberger, J. Andrew Kirk, and Werner Ustorf (Grand Rapids: Eerdmans, 2001), 37–54.

49. Lesslie Newbigin, "The Work of the Holy Spirit in the Life of the Asian Churches," in *A Decisive Hour for the Christian World Mission*, by Norman Goodall, Lesslie Newbigin, W. A. Visser 't Hooft, and D. T. Niles (London: SCM, 1960), 28; see Lesslie Newbigin, *A Word in Season: Perspectives on Christian World Missions* (Grand Rapids: Eerdmans, 1994), 154; Lesslie Newbigin, "Baptism, the Church and Koinonia: Three Letters and a Comment," in *Some Theological Dialogues*, ed. M. M. Thomas (Madras: Christian Literature Society, 1977), 127.

50. Newbigin, "Our Task Today," 6.

51. Lesslie Newbigin, "The Christian Layman in the World and in the Church," *National Christian Council Review* 72 (1952): 186.

52. Newbigin, *Trinitarian Doctrine*, 62.

53. Newbigin, *Trinitarian Doctrine*, 62.

54. Newbigin, *Unfinished Agenda*, 203.

a churchman. His primary ministry in the total life of the Body of Christ is to care rightly for the land entrusted to him. If he fails there, he fails in his primary Christian task."[55]

Sadly, many Christians working in secular areas of culture don't understand this. When it comes to the various cultural spheres, they "behave as though they were completely outside the area of Christ's rule."[56] The reductionist vision that limits ministry to the church and defines witness as evangelism leads to the "deep-seated and persistent failure of the churches to recognize that the primary witness to the sovereignty of Christ must be given, and can only be given, in the ordinary secular work of lay men and women in business, in politics, in professional work, as farmers, factory workers, and so on."[57]

On occasion Newbigin speaks of the goal of Christian vocational engagement in the public square as shaping society with the gospel or of creating a Christian society.[58] But that is not his primary emphasis. Rather, he stresses that suffering will normally be the result of our engagement in the public square because we are put on the front lines of a battle. "The 'secular' society is not a neutral area into which we can project the Christian message. It is an area already occupied by other gods. We have a battle on our hands. We are dealing with principalities and powers."[59] Thus, suffering is integral to the vocational witness of the church. "The closeness of our missionary thinking to the New Testament may perhaps be in part judged by the place which we accord to suffering in our understanding of the calling of the Church."[60]

This encounter with the religious beliefs of culture is especially acute in the public square. In a series of Bible studies on 1 Peter, Newbigin uses as one example a contrast between the gospel and the world of business, driven by the profit motive. He poses a series of questions to illustrate this antithesis: Does a Christian employee in a store persuade his customers to buy worthless products on orders from his employer or challenge the firm and risk his livelihood? Does a businessman challenge the whole standard of business ethics if it is wrong and risk status and livelihood? And so on. He then comments that "if we take seriously our duty as servants of God within the institutions of human society, we shall find plenty of opportunity

---

55. Newbigin, "Christian Layman in the World and in the Church," 186.
56. Newbigin, *Trinitarian Doctrine*, 62.
57. Newbigin, "Work of the Holy Spirit," 28.
58. Newbigin, *Truth to Tell*, 84–85; see Lesslie Newbigin, "What Kind of Society?" (lecture, Hickman Lecture Series, Duke Divinity School, Durham, NC, 1994); Lesslie Newbigin, "Can a Modern Society Become Christian?" (lecture, Kings College, London, 1995).
59. Newbigin, *Word in Season*, 150.
60. Newbigin, *Trinitarian Doctrine*, 45.

to learn what it means to suffer for righteousness' sake, and we shall learn that to suffer for righteousness' sake is really a blessed thing."[61]

Newbigin's emphasis on the work of the church as it is dispersed does not diminish the importance of the church gathered as a community. One can feel the passion of his concern in the following questions, which he poses to pastors early in his first bishopric: "Are we taking seriously our duty to support them [believers in their callings] in their warfare? Do we seriously regard them as the front-line troops? . . . What about the scores of Christians working in offices and shops in that part of the city? Have we ever done anything seriously to strengthen their Christian witness, to help them in facing the very difficult ethical problems which they have to meet every day, to give them the assurance that the whole fellowship is behind them in their daily spiritual warfare?"[62]

In his writings on the calling of individual believers, we find at least four different ways that the local congregation can support and strengthen believers for their task in the world. The first is through a *fellowship that nourishes* the life of Christ through the means of grace. In one address to church leaders he speaks of "the only source of the church's life—the gospel." If the church is to fulfill its missionary calling, they must first experience the saving presence and power of God himself through the Word, sacraments, and prayer. He asks, "Are we placing these in the very centre of our church life? . . . Do we understand, do our congregations understand, that when the Word is truly preached and the sacraments duly administered, Christ Himself is present in the midst with all His saving power?"[63] When God's saving power is known and experienced in the life of the congregation, it will issue in the faithful witness of the thousands of its members who work in field, home, office, mill, or law court.[64] But the good news proclaimed and signified in the sacrament must be an all-embracing gospel of the kingdom that calls men and women to submit their whole lives to the lordship of Christ.

The second way a congregation can strengthen believers is through a *fellowship that supports*. How does the congregation support those who face difficulty as they oppose cultural idolatry?

There are existential decisions which must be taken from time to time in the midst of the battle by those who are actually engaged in the battle and

61. Lesslie Newbigin, "Bible Studies: Four Talks on 1 Peter," in *We Were Brought Together,* ed. David M. Taylor (Sydney: Australian Council for the World Council of Churches, 1960), 112.

62. Newbigin, "Our Task Today," 6.

63. Newbigin, "Our Task Today," 4.

64. Newbigin, "Our Task Today," 5.

who will pay the price of the decision. But they are not decisions which ought to be taken in solitude. We ought not to ask each Christian in solitude to bear the burden of the real front line warfare. . . . The Church must find ways of expressing its solidarity with those who stand in these frontier situations, who have to make decisions that may cost not only their own livelihood but also that of their families.[65]

The congregation might express solidarity through encouragement, prayer, financial support, and insight.

The third form of support is *structures that equip*. Throughout his life New-bigin suggests many bold experiments in ecclesial structures to form God's people for their vocations. Perhaps one of the more important and enduring of his suggestions is "frontier groups."[66] "I am thinking of groups of men and women in—say—a particular profession, or a particular sector of commerce or industry or in one of the sectors of education or politics, who can wrestle on the basis of direct personal involvement with the claims of Christian obedience in particular situations, who can share experiences."[67]

The fourth way of strengthening and supporting is through a *leadership that enables*.[68] A leadership that equips believers in their tasks in the world is a frequent theme in Newbigin's writings, one to which we will return. The following comes from a sermon he preached as a bishop to pastors in his diocese: "At the most sophisticated level we have to think of our task in a city like Madras to train our lay members who are playing key roles in life of government, business, and the professions to become ministers of Christ in these secular situations. All of this is involved in our calling and ordination."[69] Newbigin believes that church leadership must take on the responsibility to equip and nourish believers for callings in the public life of culture.

Deeds of Justice, Peace, and Mercy

Newbigin regularly points to a threefold witness to the kingdom: "By its witness—in word and deed and common life—to the centrality of the work of Jesus in his ministry, death, and resurrection it offers to all peoples the

65. Newbigin, "Bible Studies: Four Talks on 1 Peter," 111.

66. Newbigin, *Gospel in a Pluralist Society*, 230–31.

67. Lesslie Newbigin, *Priorities for a New Decade* (Birmingham, UK: National Student Christian Press and Resource Centre, 1980), 6.

68. Newbigin, *Gospel in a Pluralist Society*, 231.

69. Lesslie Newbigin, *Good Shepherd: Meditations on Christian Ministry in Today's World* (Grand Rapids: Eerdmans, 1977), 76.

possibility of understanding . . . the meaning and goal of history."[70] There is a consistency in the way he relates the three: the presence of the new reality of the Spirit is present in the total life of the community and is attested by mighty deeds, which in turn call for an explanation—that is, the preaching of the gospel of the kingdom.[71] This gives us the logic of Newbigin's view of mission. Out of the presence of the Spirit in the total life of the community—gathered and scattered—comes deeds, which in turn call for words of the gospel, which explain the new reality. And so in the first place we turn to the witness of the church in its deeds.

Jesus challenged the powers that ruled the world by deeds of justice and mercy. These were not marginal but central to his ministry. Therefore, since the church's mission is in Christ's way, "it is clear that action for justice and peace in the world is not something which is secondary, marginal to the central task of evangelism. It belongs to the heart of the matter."[72]

This seems clear enough. But Newbigin spent so much time defending deeds of mercy and justice because he carried out his own ministry in a context in which there was a dispute between the evangelical and ecumenical traditions. It led, on the evangelical side, to a position that emphasized evangelism and neglected—and even sometimes rejected—issues of mercy and justice. On the ecumenical side, there was a diminished commitment to evangelism—to be addressed in the next section—but also a mistaken understanding of the nature of deeds of mercy, justice, and peace.

Newbigin sets the discussion in the context of the nature of salvation. First, salvation is restorative and comprehensive. It is not the escape of individuals into another world but the restoration of all of human life as part of the nonhuman creation. When those in the evangelical tradition misunderstand this, they "shall be little interested in programs for its improvement, and much interested in what happens to the individual human person as he prepares or does not prepare for his eternal destiny."[73] Second, salvation is concerned with both communion with God and commitment to justice and peace. On the one hand, "in the Bible salvation concerns the whole man and the totality of his relationships. It includes . . . the political, and social and economic." On the other hand, this vision of salvation "is never merely a secular vision. It is never just a vision of political liberation or economic progress or social peace and justice." The "true kernel of salvation" is "fellowship with the Living

---

70. Newbigin, *Gospel in a Pluralist Society*, 129.

71. See Newbigin, *Gospel in a Pluralist Society*, 133, 137.

72. Newbigin, *Gospel in a Pluralist Society*, 137.

73. Lesslie Newbigin, "The Bible Study Lectures," in *Digest of the Proceedings of the Ninth Meeting of the Consultation on Church Union (COCU)*, ed. Paul A. Crow (Princeton: COCU, 1970), 216.

Lord."[74] When churches pursue social action apart from a relationship with God, they depart from Scripture. But so do those who emphasize knowing God yet neglect political and social issues. Finally, salvation is an eschatological reality; the future has entered history. The kingdom is present but future, already but not yet, hidden but someday yet to be unveiled. Rightly determining the relationship of the kingdom to history is essential if we are to correctly understand the true nature of our social action.

The kingdom does not come as a smooth, incremental process in history. Thus, our actions of justice and peace do not build the kingdom. The kingdom will only come fully by an act of judgment and the coming of Jesus. Until that time, there will be conflict and suffering. If this perspective is lost, then an uncritical triumphalism wherein the church is an auxiliary to the social and political programs of the day will characterize the church's mission. But the kingdom is present in history and not just in the future. There will be evidence of God's renewing power at work by the Spirit. If this is lost, then a selfish withdrawal that separates salvation from culture and avoids costly engagement in society will epitomize the church's mission. So, on the one hand, there is discontinuity between the kingdom and history; this is what the ecumenical tradition needed to recover. On the other hand, there is continuity between the kingdom and history; this is what the evangelical tradition needed to recover.

The Bible offers no hope that the kingdom will be realized within history this side of the return of Christ. And further, the Bible gives us a picture of deepening conflict between the kingdom of God and the powers that produce crisis and suffering. If we cannot build God's kingdom with our political, social, and economic action, then why do we do it? What is the nature of our deeds of mercy, peace, and justice? Newbigin offers a fivefold answer.

First, our deeds are not optional, secondary, or marginal to the mission of the church; rather, they are *essential to the very nature of salvation and the church*. They belong to the nature of salvation and of the church as an instrument of the kingdom. "It is a disastrous misunderstanding to think that we can enjoy salvation through Jesus Christ and at the same time regard action for justice in the world as a sort of optional extra—or even an inferior substitute for the work of passing on the good news of salvation. Action for social justice *is* salvation in action."[75] Anyone who thinks of salvation apart from seeking "deliverance from sickness or hunger or oppression or alienation" is "very remote from the biblical use of the word."[76]

74. Newbigin, *Good Shepherd*, 105–6.
75. Newbigin, *Good Shepherd*, 109.
76. Lesslie Newbigin, "Address on the Main Theme, 'Jesus, Saviour of the World,' at the Synod Assembly of January 1972," *South India Churchman*, February 1972, 5.

Our deeds also belong to the nature of the church. "If we are faithful to the New Testament we shall recognise that care of the poor belongs . . . to the fundamental bases of the Church's life."[77] We are not dealing with one aspect of the church's life that can be left aside; it belongs to the "integrity of the church itself, its fundamental character as Church."[78] There is a terrible distortion in our understanding of the church when it becomes "no more than a self-centred community only faintly interested in justice and mercy for this earth's exploited masses but passionately devoted to our own protection and advancement as a community and, if we are piously inclined, to assuring that after a comfortable passage through this life we can look forward to a guaranteed place in the foam-rubber-padded seats of heaven."[79] In short, the "piety which can comfortably co-exist with flagrant social injustice is an abomination to God."[80]

Second, our deeds have the *character of witness* to the coming of the kingdom in Jesus. We must not believe that somehow through our deeds we are going to usher in God's kingdom. Deeds of justice and mercy are "signs of the new reality."[81] They are a "necessary part of the Church's witness to the presence and power of God's Kingdom." Yet we do not establish the kingdom through our deeds. We are to "reject the idea that Christian action is to be conceived of as 'building the Kingdom of God.'"[82] Our activities on behalf of justice and peace "are not the means by which God establishes his Kingdom. They are witnesses to its present reality." They are "signs rather than instruments."[83] They are hope in action, an acted prayer for the coming of the kingdom.[84]

Our deeds, third, are an *expression of the love and compassion* of the kingdom in Jesus. "The first outward mark of the presence of the new reality in the world will certainly be a multitude of loving service to men in their need." This is "not a conscious missionary strategy, though it is part of the Church's total mission." Rather, these are "Christian works of love" and "should be as Christ's were, a spontaneous outflowing of the love of God for men, not a means to something else."[85] The church's solidarity with those who are

77. Lesslie Newbigin, *Set Free to Be a Servant: Studies in Paul's Letter to the Galatians* (Madras: Christian Literature Society, 1969), 20.

78. Lesslie Newbigin, "The Church as a Servant Community," *National Christian Council Review* 91 (1971): 260.

79. Lesslie Newbigin, *Journey into Joy* (Grand Rapids: Eerdmans, 1972), 102.

80. Newbigin, *Good Shepherd*, 108.

81. Newbigin, *Good Shepherd*, 93.

82. Lesslie Newbigin, *Signs amid the Rubble: The Purposes of God in Human History*, ed. Geoffrey Wainwright (Grand Rapids: Eerdmans, 2003), 51; cf. 46.

83. Newbigin, *Trinitarian Doctrine*, 47.

84. Newbigin, *Signs amid the Rubble*, 51–52.

85. Lesslie Newbigin, *A Faith for This One World?* (London: SCM, 1961), 89–91.

suffering and all attempts to relieve that suffering in acts of justice and mercy are not done "with an eye on possible conversions, but because these are the things that love must do."[86] For Jesus, his deeds "were the overflowing of the love which filled his whole being. Just so, the Church's deeds of love ought to be—not contrived signs but natural and spontaneous signs of the new reality in which we have been made sharers through Christ. Those who have received so much cannot keep it to themselves. It must overflow in love to others."[87]

Fourth, our deeds are *aimed at conversion* to Jesus. This might seem surprising in light of what was just said. Yet Newbigin does speak of a concern for conversion, though he carefully qualifies it. It is not "to create a situation in which people will listen to the Gospel." There may be some truth in this, but it is "utterly repellant" to use our social work primarily as "bait to make people swallow our preaching." This is a subtle form of selfishness that earns contempt. However, if we are asked, "Have you come here to convert us?" then quite rightly the answer would be yes, because "if our social work does not change *people* . . . it has failed. . . . We are out to convert people not just to feed them." When he asks "what kind of conversion," he answers with words and deeds that point to Jesus and the kingdom and that invite people into it.[88]

Finally, our deeds may have a *transforming effect on culture*. This is certainly not a primary point for Newbigin. He speaks of our actions as a drop in the bucket or as producing only a little more justice in the world. He does affirm that we seek change, but this is not the primary goal of social concern; it is witness. We see less and less emphasis on transformation as he grows older. Yet if we love people, we will try to influence society and transform the unjust structures of society. The service of the church involves "political actions which may be necessary to break structures of injustice, which dehumanise him [my neighbor], and to create new structures wherein a genuinely human social existence is possible."[89] Yet one may become involved in proximate goals of justice but may never offer full commitment to any social or political program. This leads to cynical despair and disillusionment when the transformation does not take place. Transformation is not our primary goal but

86. Lesslie Newbigin, "The Duty and Authority of the Church to Preach the Gospel," in *The Church's Witness to God's Design*, ed. Lesslie Newbigin and Hendrik Kraemer, Amsterdam Assembly Series 2 (New York: Harper Brothers, 1948), 19.

87. Newbigin, *Good Shepherd*, 93.

88. Newbigin, *Good Shepherd*, 92–93.

89. Lesslie Newbigin, "Servants of the Servant Lord," *Vivekananda Kendra Patrika*, February 1972, 155.

may be the spillover effect, the salting of society, when a community points to the kingdom in deeds of justice and love.[90]

We see here that for Newbigin both justice and mercy are important to the social deeds of the church. Mercy does not get to the root of the problem; to attack a disease one must not simply treat the symptom but the root cause. "It is not enough to deploy Good Samaritans around the place; we must also guard the road."[91] Yet at the same time one cannot leave a person dying at the side of the road and go organize a police force. Both justice and mercy are important, but mercy will always maintain first priority. "To work for the reformation of structures, to expose and attack unjust structures . . . is as much a part of the mission of the church as to care for the sick and to feed the hungry. . . . If the legitimate call to political action is allowed to replace the call to compassionate service, then the church has betrayed the gospel."[92]

If deeds of mercy, justice, and peace are to maintain the character of witness, it must be clear that those deeds are connected to the local congregation. One way this has been obscured is when parachurch organizations or denominational arms take over the task of mercy and justice. When the church hands over this task to bodies outside the local congregation, at least two problems develop. First, the church loses its missionary consciousness and allows the expert bodies to be responsible for mission. Second, deeds of justice and mercy are not seen to flow from the body of Christ, and they lose their proper character as signs and witnesses to the kingdom. They appear to be part of a moral crusade or agency for political action. Yet these denominational and parachurch agencies can play an important role if they enable and coordinate the witness of the churches.

As Newbigin struggles with the nature of social action, he introduces a new image of the church to which he returns often: the church as a servant community. The "fundamental form"[93] and "authentic nature"[94] of the church will be as a servant community. With this image he characterizes the church as a community who follows in the way of Jesus by serving the needs of others out of a heart of sacrificial love. He points to the well-known story of Jesus stripping, taking a towel, and stooping to wash his disciples' feet. "The church will prove its faithfulness to the Lord when it is

90. Newbigin, *Signs amid the Rubble*, 54–55.
91. Lesslie Newbigin, "The Churches and CASA," *National Christian Council Review* 93 (1973): 546. For Newbigin's view on parachurch structures, this is the best article on the subject.
92. Newbigin, *Open Secret*, 109.
93. Lesslie Newbigin, "Bible Studies Given at the National Christian Council Triennial Assembly, Shillong," *National Council Review* 88 (1968): 131.
94. Newbigin, "Church as a Servant Community," 261.

seen in the same posture."[95] Being a servant church means loving solidarity with the poor and deeds of justice and mercy that flow on their behalf.[96] A servant church must be "recognisably a body which is on the side of the oppressed" and that reaches out its hand "to victims of [the unjust established] order."[97]

Newbigin does not forget the eschatological nature of the church when he speaks of the servant nature of the church. The church "is intended by God to be a first-fruit and sign and instrument of his new creation." How does the church fulfill this role? "The congregation is to be a humble servant of Jesus for the sake of its neighbours."[98] Precisely as a sign and foretaste of the self-giving love of the kingdom, the servant church must take the stooping and kneeling posture of its Lord. As an instrument, it must be ready to help meet the needs of its neighbors.

If the church is to become a faithful servant church that follows Jesus in the pursuit of justice and mercy, there must be structures that enable this kind of service to take place,[99] worship that nourishes a comprehensive mission and social vision,[100] members of the congregation equipped for their callings in the public life of culture,[101] and leadership that equips and leads the church in justice and mercy.[102] On the last, Newbigin points by way of example to the way the office of the diaconate functioned in the early church.[103] The deacon was responsible throughout the week to show compassion to the poor, to widows, to the sick, and to the marginalized. This brought care for the poor to the heart of leadership. Moreover, care for the poor penetrated the liturgy when, at the Lord's Supper, these deacons collected gifts for the poor, and at the time of intercession they stood up and shared urgent concerns for prayer for the poor. Diaconal leadership moved the early church to solidarity of the whole church with the poor.

Evangelism

The witness of the church to the cosmic salvation at the end of universal history happens in three characteristic ways: "in the existence of a new

95. Newbigin, *Journey into Joy*, 107; Newbigin, *Good Shepherd*, 95.
96. Newbigin, "Church as a Servant Community," 260.
97. Newbigin, "Church as a Servant Community," 263–64.
98. Newbigin, *Good Shepherd*, 87, 89.
99. Newbigin, "Church as a Servant Community"; Newbigin, *Good Shepherd*, 81.
100. Newbigin, *Journey into Joy*, 112.
101. Newbigin, *Gospel in a Pluralist Society*, 139.
102. Newbigin, *Good Shepherd*, 74–78, 80; Newbigin, "Church as a Servant Community," 261.
103. Newbigin, "Church as a Servant Community," 259–60.

community based upon a common sharing in the life of the Holy Spirit; in activities which reveal in action the presence of the new reality; in words which bear witness to the new reality."[104] We turn now to the last of these. God has entrusted this story to the church, and "there is no other body that will tell it."[105] And so there is a duty and obligation to announce the good news.[106]

For Newbigin, evangelism is "communication—by written or spoken word—of the good news about Jesus. In this definition there will be no evangelism unless the name of Jesus is named."[107] He is concerned for definition not simply to be systematic in his thinking but because "it confuses certain issues to extend this word beyond its proper meaning." This is precisely what has happened when evangelism or evangelization is redefined in the ecumenical tradition primarily in terms of programs of service. Then there is no confidence in the power of the gospel to bring forth fruit, and the church is guilty of depending on human endeavor rather than the Spirit. "That has often happened, and a loose use of the word 'evangelism' has been used to cover real betrayal. There is not and there cannot be any substitute for telling the story of Jesus."[108]

In this verbal communication of the message of the gospel, one must preach Jesus *and* the kingdom. To preach Jesus without the kingdom or to preach the kingdom without Jesus "distorts salvation." One turns the gospel into a political program apart from an invitation to know Christ, and the other is the pedaling of "cheap grace" that invites one only to personal salvation.[109] The danger of the first is what the ecumenical tradition succumbed to, which led to an eclipse of evangelism. The danger of the second—preaching Jesus without the kingdom—is what the evangelical tradition had fallen prey to. And so Newbigin stressed the importance of the kingdom with the evangelical tradition in view. "If I am not mistaken, our current evangelism hardly ever uses the category of the Kingdom of God. And yet the original preaching of the Gospel on the lips of Jesus was—precisely—the announcement of the coming of that Kingdom. I believe that we may recover a true evangelism for our day if we return to that original language (translated into the idiom of our own time and place) as the basic category for our proclamation of the Gospel."[110]

104. Newbigin, *Faith for This One World?*, 87.
105. Lesslie Newbigin, *Proper Confidence: Faith, Doubt, and Certainty in Christian Discipleship* (Grand Rapids: Eerdmans, 1995), 78.
106. For an articulation of Newbigin's understanding of evangelism, see Krish Rohan Kandiah, "Toward a Theology of Evangelism for Late-Modern Cultures: A Critical Dialogue with Lesslie Newbigin's Doctrine of Revelation" (PhD diss., University of London, 2005).
107. Newbigin, "Crosscurrents," 146.
108. Newbigin, *One Body, One Gospel, One World*, 22.
109. Newbigin, *Mission in Christ's Way*, 9.
110. Newbigin, *Good Shepherd*, 67.

To those in the ecumenical camp, Newbigin used strong language to remind them that the church has an obligation to make known the good news in words. He believed we need to "denounce sharply"[111] the tendency to support social concern but marginalize evangelism. "There is a gospel to be proclaimed and we are not allowed to be silent about it. However much we may wish we could, we are not allowed to deceive ourselves into imagining that anything we are, or anything we do, can take the place of the name of Jesus. We are not allowed to be silent."[112] Silence is nothing other than a betrayal of the gospel! If our presence or deeds become "a substitute for the explicit proclamation of the name of Jesus and his saving work, then we have to reject it as a betrayal of the gospel. There can be no substitute for the name of Jesus. Men must have opportunity to know him."[113]

Much of Newbigin's discussion of evangelism is in the context of affirming an indissoluble nexus between word and deed: the presence of the reign of God by the Spirit is attested by both words and deeds together. Deeds demonstrate that the new eschatological reality of the Spirit is present, and words point to Jesus as the origin. But "if nothing is happening no explanation is called for and the words are empty words. . . . They can be brushed aside as mere talk. They are only meaningful in the context of the mighty works. They presuppose that something is happening which calls for explanation."[114] The deed without the word is dumb; the word without the deed is empty. To set these over against each other is absurd. And the conflict between evangelical and ecumenical traditions, which separates the two, is profoundly weakening the church's witness. Both are essential because both are the means by which the Spirit witnesses to the presence of the kingdom. "The all-inclusive word, corresponding to the new reality of the Spirit's presence, is *witness*. Within that total reality, both evangelism and service, both word and action have their place. Both of them can be used by the Holy Spirit for the total work of witness to Christ when they belong to and spring out of the life of the new community which the Spirit creates."[115]

111. Lesslie Newbigin, "From the Editor," *International Review of Mission* 54 (1965): 418.

112. Lesslie Newbigin, "The World Mission of the Church," *South India Churchman*, September 1968, 4.

113. Newbigin, "Bible Study Lectures," 212. See Lesslie Newbigin, "Bible Studies on John 17: The Hinge of History," *Lutheran Standard (USA)*, April 4, 1967, 10; Newbigin, "Bible Studies Given at the National Christian Council Triennial Assembly," 130.

114. Newbigin, *Gospel in a Pluralist Society*, 132.

115. Newbigin, *Faith for This One World?*, 92. Newbigin offers a biblical study of the word "witness" (or rather the *martyreo* word group) in Lesslie Newbigin, "Witness in Biblical Perspective,"

In light of this, Newbigin expands further.[116] Not every word needs a deed attached to it, and not every deed needs a word. It is the combination of the two that arises out of the total witnessing life of the church in the midst of the world. And further, there are different gifts—some in evangelism, others in showing mercy, and still others in pursuing justice. All the gifts are needed. But the Spirit, who is the primary witness, uses both words and deeds to witness to Jesus and the coming kingdom. Therefore, the church may not be silent nor absolve itself from deeds of mercy and justice.

But, again, Newbigin stresses that both word and deed arise out of a congregation where the Spirit is at work creating new life. Evangelism would lose its power apart from "the life of a new kind of community [where] the saving power of the Gospel is known and tasted." He explains further: "The purely verbal preaching of the story of Jesus crucified and risen would lose its power if those who heard it could not trace it back to some kind of community in which the message was being validated in a common way of life which is recognizable as embodying at least a hint and a foretaste of the blessedness for which all men long and which the Gospel promises."[117]

So it is evident how closely Newbigin ties evangelistic words to the embodiment of the gospel in the total life of the community and the demonstration of the gospel in deeds. Evangelistic words answer questions as to the new reality created by the Spirit in life and deed. Words that have nothing to explain lose their power: "If the Church which preaches [the gospel] is not living corporately a life which corresponds with it, is living in comfortable cohabitation with the powers of the age, is failing to challenge the powers of darkness and to manifest in its life the power of the living Lord to help and heal, then by its life it closes the doors which its preaching would open." Thankfully, he adds, "That does not mean that the preaching is void, because there is no limit to the power of the word of God."[118]

Our evangelistic words aim at conversion. The gospel is not simply announced as historical facts that can be received for information. The announcement is about the arrival of the new creation, and such is the enormity and momentous significance of this "world news" that it "requires an immediate response in action."[119] There is no room for neutrality or indecision. "A

Mission Studies 3, no. 2 (1986): 80–84. This is an oft-used, comprehensive, and important term in his mission thinking.

116. Lesslie Newbigin, "Context and Conversion," *International Review of Mission* 68, no. 271 (1979): 304–9; Newbigin, *Good Shepherd*, 93–94; Newbigin, "Crosscurrents," 146–49; Newbigin, *One Body, One Gospel, One World*, 22–23; Newbigin, *Faith for This One World?*, 89–92.

117. Newbigin, "Context and Conversion," 304.

118. Newbigin, *Gospel in a Pluralist Society*, 140.

119. Newbigin, *Word in Season*, 151.

note of crisis, with the implied demand for immediate decision, runs through this as through all proclamations of the Gospel. . . . *There* is God's salvation! Stand there, and accept or reject it!"[120] Thus, in our evangelism we "have the clear duty to bring to every man this call for radical decision."[121] This call for a response follows Jesus's example of calling for radical repentance, conversion, and the forsaking of all to follow him. And so we call for a response of faith and repentance that leads to conversion.

What is conversion? This is a critical question if our evangelism is to produce a healthy church. We noted earlier that for Newbigin conversion involves three things: personal relationship to Jesus, entry into a visible community taking up its mission, and commitment to a pattern of behavior.[122] True evangelism is "concerned with the radical conversion that leads men to explicit allegiance to Jesus Christ."[123] The call to a personal relationship is with Jesus, who has ushered in his kingdom. Thus, it demands radical loyalty and commitment. But it also calls for entry into a community chosen to participate in God's mission to the world. And finally, it summons men and women to a lifestyle of obedience that is costly and comprehensive.

When evangelism makes this kind of invitation, it makes clear what is at stake in following Jesus. But if evangelism weakens the call, it produces from the outset a compromised and domesticated church. A weak form of evangelism may produce "baptized, communicant, Bible-reading, and zealous Christians who are committed to church growth but uncommitted to radical obedience to the plain teaching of the Bible on the issues of human dignity and social justice." There may be the appearance of successful evangelism with growing numbers, but alas the church remains "marked by flagrant evils such as racism, militant sectarianism, and blind support of oppressive economic and political systems." There may be mass conversions, but following Christ is reduced to "personal and domestic behavior" and sadly "has nothing to say about the big issues of public righteousness."[124] Numbers accompanied by shallow conversions do not constitute successful evangelism.

Moreover, if evangelism is selfish—that is, inviting people to enjoy the benefits of salvation—it also creates a church that is not ready to take up its mission in the world. The mission of the church is to invite people into the

120. Lesslie Newbigin, *What Is the Gospel?*, SCM Study Series 6 (Madras: Christian Literature Society, 1942), 10–11.
121. Newbigin, "From the Editor," 148.
122. Lesslie Newbigin, "Conversion," in *Concise Dictionary of the Christian World Mission*, ed. Stephen Neill, Gerald H. Anderson, and John Goodwin (Nashville: Abingdon, 1971), 147; Lesslie Newbigin, "Conversion," *National Christian Council Review* 86 (1966): 309–23.
123. Newbigin, "From the Editor," 140.
124. Newbigin, *Open Secret*, 134–35.

kingdom. That means participation in the mission of Jesus: "The ministry of the Church as a whole should be manifestly and explicitly . . . a ministry of proclamation and enlistment—the proclamation of the coming of the reign of God in Jesus, and the enlistment of men for the service of that reign."[125] Proclamation calls listeners to enlist in Jesus's kingdom mission. This kind of evangelism makes clear from the outset that there is no participation in Christ without participation in his mission.

Missions

We have been primarily concerned up to this point with Newbigin's understanding of the missionary vocation of each local congregation in their particular context. God makes known the good news of the kingdom to the world through the total life of the community gathered and scattered, through deeds and through words. But what about places where there is no missionary community like that? That is the task of missions: intentional activities undertaken by the church to create a Christian presence in places where there is no such presence or no effective presence. As noted earlier in this chapter, Newbigin distinguishes this task of the church from the more comprehensive mission of the church by using the word "missions" (with an s).

Newbigin struggled with a new paradigm of mission throughout the 1950s and 1960s, when it was clear that the colonialist paradigm of missions was breaking down. The church in the West was in trouble, and the churches throughout the Southern Hemisphere were growing. If one could no longer call the West the "home base" and the non-West the "mission field," then what was mission? Was there still a place for cross-cultural missions? The problem was that the ecumenical tradition was fleeing the whole business; development and social action replaced making the gospel known. The evangelical tradition was reacting and simply affirming much in the old paradigm. Newbigin's desire was to move beyond this stalemate to a new vision for what mission could be in the time of a global church.

His starting point is that the church is missionary by its very nature. Mission isn't simply one more task but defines the church's very nature: "Mission is not a detachable part of the Church's being, but is the central meaning of the Church's being."[126] This means, first and foremost, that each local congregation has a responsibility to make the good news known in its particular location. They are put there in that place to witness to God's ultimate purpose in history revealed in Christ in life, deed, and word. But that congregation also

125. Newbigin, *Good Shepherd*, 67.
126. Newbigin, *Word in Season*, 12.

has a responsibility to lift up its head and look to see where there are places and peoples without a witnessing community. Each church is responsible for the establishment of a witness in those places. Missions "is not the whole of the Church's mission, but it is an essential part of it."[127]

The specific task of missions is concerned with intentional activities to take the gospel to places where the gospel is not known, erecting a witness and ultimately a witnessing community in places where there is none. Missions is concerned with initial evangelism and church planting. "Missions must concentrate on the specifically missionary intention of bringing the Gospel to those who have not heard it and this must be directed to all six continents."[128] "Missions are particular enterprises within the total mission of the church that have the primary intention of bringing into existence a Christian presence in a milieu where previously there was no such presence or where such presence was ineffective."[129] Thus, when a witnessing community has been established, missions is finished and mission begins.[130]

Newbigin finds support for this understanding of missions in the church in Antioch (Acts 11, 13). He calls this "the central New Testament paradigm for missions."[131] The church in Antioch is a witnessing community that is growing as it faithfully points to Christ in word and deed (Acts 11:19–30). However, the Spirit moves the church to set aside some men for the specific purpose of taking the gospel to places where it is not known. The purpose of those sent is to establish a witnessing community where there is none. When such a body is established there then they take up the mission in that place. Paul is one of those men sent from Antioch to do just this. When he establishes a witnessing community in the various cities, he would move on and say, as it were, "You are now the mission in this place." This is something Newbigin himself did as he followed Paul's model. After establishing a church in a village, he would say, "Now you are the Body of Christ in this village. You are God's apostles here. Through you they are to be saved. I will be in touch with you. I will pray for you. I will visit you. If you want my help I will try to help you. But you are now the Mission."[132]

Missions is necessary not simply because there are many places where there is no faithful witnessing community. It is also bound closely to the

127. Lesslie Newbigin, "Mission and Missions," *Christianity Today*, August 1, 1960, 911.
128. Newbigin, *Unfinished Agenda*, 185.
129. Newbigin, "Crosscurrents," 149.
130. Newbigin, *Open Secret*, 129. Newbigin credits much of his insight into missions to Roland Allen, *Missionary Methods: St Paul's or Ours?* (Grand Rapids: Eerdmans, 1962).
131. Newbigin, "Crosscurrents," 150.
132. Newbigin, *One Body, One Gospel, One World*, 32.

very theological nature of the gospel itself and thus the extent of mission. The gospel is about the sovereignty of God in Christ over all nations and all of life. It is public truth for all, and therefore missions must be to the ends of the earth. The ends of the earth is the ultimate horizon of God's mission and the church's mission. Since Christ is Lord of all, his authority must be acknowledged by all, to the ends of the earth. Mission begins in the neighborhood of the local congregation, but by the very nature of the gospel the missionary task must move to the ends of the earth. Mission without missions to all nations is an emaciated and distorted concept. "The Church's mission is concerned with the ends of the earth. When that dimension is forgotten, the heart goes out of the whole business."[133] Missions is mission carried out faithfully toward its ultimate horizon—the ends of the earth.

Foreign missions is the true test of whether one really believes the scope of the gospel. If one believes that what Jesus has accomplished has universal validity, one will be committed to seeing that message reach all peoples.

> [The] Gospel is the truth, and therefore it is true for all men. It is the unveiling of the face of Him who makes all things, from whom every man comes, and to whom every man goes. It is the revealing of the meaning of human history, of the origin and destiny of mankind. Jesus is not only my Saviour, He is the Lord of all things, the cause and cornerstone of the universe. If I believe that, then to bear witness to that is the very stuff of existence. If I think I can keep it to myself, then I do not in any real sense believe it. Foreign missions are not an extra; they are the acid test of whether or not the Church believes the Gospel.[134]

If missions is creating a witness in places where there is none so as to reach all peoples, then it excludes much of what is done by mission boards and called "missions."[135] The leftover mental habits of colonialist missions label everything that happens overseas "missions." Specifically, various enterprises of interchurch aid in which Western missionaries were engaged overseas are all called "missions"—teaching, pastoral work, administration, and many other activities. Newbigin affirms the importance of these "fraternal workers." But they are not missionaries, and they are not doing missions. While both may "be working in a common field . . . each would have a distinct focus of concern."[136] And it is that distinct focus of concern of missions that is Newbigin's concern.

---

133. Newbigin, *One Body, One Gospel, One World*, 27.
134. Newbigin, "Mission of the Church to All the Nations," 3.
135. Newbigin, "Future of Missions and Missionaries," 216.
136. Newbigin, "Bible Study Lectures," 190.

Mission and missions—the difference might appear to be simply seman-tics. But to assume that would be a mistake. Newbigin saw the notion of missions—that is, establishing a witness in order to found a witnessing community—being lost amid all the other tasks. This particular aspect of the church's mission was not being clearly distinguished. The majority of monetary and personnel resources were being used for interchurch aid, and the most needy places were not being reached with the gospel. Newbigin believed it was important to distinguish between other cross-cultural tasks and the work of intentional missions to establish a witnessing community. That dimension of the church's mission must never be surrendered.

Missions is the task of the church and specifically the responsibility of every local congregation. Every congregation anywhere in the world is at the same time a mission to that place and part of God's mission to the ends of the earth. Newbigin writes,

> Every church, however small and weak, ought to have some share in the task of taking the gospel to the ends of the earth. Every church ought to be engaged in foreign missions. This is part of the integrity of the gospel. We do not adequately confess Christ as Lord of all men if we seek to be his witnesses only among our neighbours. We must seek at the same time to confess him to the ends of the earth. The foreign missionary enterprise belongs to the integrity of our confession.[137]

Not only does each church everywhere have the "duty and privilege" to be involved in the worldwide task, but also every Christian has the same duty and privilege to take up their role in mission to the ends of the earth.

If it is the duty of the church to be involved in missions to the ends of the earth, this raises large questions about the validity of mission boards and organizations. These are the bodies that have been the primary agents of missions for several centuries. What are we to make of these missionary bodies? Newbigin called the creation of these mission agencies, which had separated mission from the church, "one of the great calamities of mission-ary history."[138] And indeed there were fatal consequences for both bodies. For the congregation, the consequence was a loss of its missionary identity, which led to its becoming an introverted body that caters to its own members and is not concerned with mission to the world. For the mission board, its witness is not seen to arise out of a community centered in the gospel. That did not mean, however, that Newbigin believed these bodies could play no

137. Newbigin, *Word in Season*, 13.
138. Newbigin, *One Body, One Gospel, One World*, 26.

positive role. On the contrary, he believed that, if those agencies coordinated the efforts of local bodies to carry out their mission at home and abroad, they would play an important role in God's mission. They must not replace that mission but enable and facilitate local cooperation.

But missions is not only the responsibility of the local congregation; it is also the obligation of the global church together. There is a need for ecumenical partnership and sharing the task together that acknowledges the vocation of the church in each given area. The problem is that the financial and organizational structures of missions remain caught in a colonialist framework and need to be totally revamped so there could be equal partnership among churches. Newbigin has much to say about this, but we need not traverse this territory. He wrote a half century ago, and there is much detail that is not relevant for our purposes. The need that does remain today is to struggle with how to make missions the task of local congregations and the global church working together in partnership. For Newbigin missions is part and parcel of the task of the missionary congregation. The question for us is whether that same passionate conviction is part of those who claim him as an ecclesial mentor.

The Ultimate Goal of Mission Is the Glory of God

The goal of the biblical story is the cosmic renewal of the creation, and the church's mission is to participate in God's purpose by a faithful witness in life, word, and deed to what he is doing to the ends of the earth in order to invite others into it. Newbigin asks, "What, then, is the point of missions?" Is our ultimate concern the need of all people for salvation? Is it the renewal of society? These are valid concerns, but they are not our primary goal. So what is? "The answer I believe quite simply is the glory of God." If God has done what the Bible says he has done, then our response should be to witness to his love and ask, "How can I glorify God?" so that there "may be throughout the world those who turn their faces to God and give Him thanks and glorify him. The glory of God is the purpose, the goal of mission, and our one aim is that we should praise and glorify Him."[139]

Newbigin was consistently averse to any kind of anthropocentric view of mission. He believes mission in both the evangelical and the ecumenical traditions has been "terribly Pelagian." He explains: "Whether the emphasis was upon the saving of individual souls from perdition, or on the righting

139. Newbigin, *Signs amid the Rubble*, 120–21.

of social wrongs, the overwhelming emphasis has been upon missions as our program."[140] In the evangelical tradition, the whole discussion has been derailed by asking the wrong question concerning "the individual and his or her need to be assured of ultimate happiness, and not with God and his glory." When we privatize God's mighty work of grace and talk "as if the whole cosmic drama of salvation culminated in the words 'For me; for me' . . . this is a perversion of the gospel."[141] In the ecumenical tradition the discussion has centered on our task to renew society, and this too has led to a misunderstanding of mission. "The center of the picture is not the human need of salvation (from sin, from oppression, from alienation) but God and God's immeasurable grace. So the central concern is not 'How shall the world be saved?' but 'How shall this glorious and gracious God be glorified?' The goal is the glory of God."[142]

The New Testament provides us not with a Pelagian picture of human effort saving people and the world but with a picture of an overflow of gratitude and joy that arises from God's grace for us in Jesus. "For anyone who has understood what God did for us all in Jesus Christ, the one question is: 'How shall God be glorified?' How shall his amazing grace be known and celebrated and adored?" In this context he turns to a text he often quoted throughout his life: "He shall see the travail of his soul, and shall be satisfied" (Isa. 53:11 KJV). Our goal in mission is that Jesus might be satisfied when he sees the fruit of his atonement. Our whole discussion of the Christian faith is skewed if we make the main questions, "Who is going to be saved at the end?" or "How shall the world be saved?" Rather, we "have to begin with the mighty work of grace in Jesus Christ and ask, How is he to be honored and glorified? The goal of missions is the glory of God."[143]

Perhaps the most important indicators of Newbigin's focus on the glory of God are not these explicit statements. The whole of his theological work on mission has a defining theocentric cast, and it is evident in many places that he abhors the anthropocentrism and narcissism that so often corrupt Christian faith and mission. I have a vivid memory in this regard. I was present at a talk he gave on mission. He was protesting the human-centeredness that so often shapes Christian mission. He searched for language in an attempt to express what should be our focus—the glory and transcendence of the living God. He sputtered, "We are talking about . . ." and paused, looking

140. Lesslie Newbigin, "Mission in the 1990s: Two Views," *International Bulletin of Missionary Research* 13, no. 3 (1989): 102.

141. Newbigin, *Gospel in a Pluralist Society*, 179.

142. Newbigin, "Mission in the 1990s," 102.

143. Newbigin, *Gospel in a Pluralist Society*, 179–80.

skyward as he searched for the strongest word possible. Not finding a word big enough, he threw his hands straight down to his sides in frustration and finally simply blurted out, ". . . God!" And, indeed, there is no bigger word to define the goal of our mission.

Conclusion

The church's missionary existence is rooted in God's mission. The mission of the Triune God is to move history toward cosmic renewal. This has culminated in the kingdom mission of Jesus. The church participates in that mission as a firstfruit and instrument of this restoration. The church continues the mission of Jesus to make known the kingdom in Christ's own way, in the confidence that the Father is working out his purpose and the Spirit is witnessing in power to the coming kingdom. This will mean an ecclesial witness that is as broad as life; all of the church's life, both gathered and scattered, has a missional dimension. But it will also mean intentional efforts to erect signs to the coming kingdom—the witness of deed and word. This is the vocation of every congregation in the place they have been set. Their calling, however, also invites them to participation in the witness of the kingdom to the ends of the earth. And our goal is not first and foremost the salvation of individuals or the renewal of society, although we pray for that. Rather, it is that God might be glorified. The business of the missionary congregation is to embody and tell the true story of the world, narrated in Scripture and centered in Jesus, in its own place and to the ends of the earth, all to the glory of God.

4

The Missionary Church
and Its Life Together

The story of the Bible shows God leading all of human history to its appointed End, the restoration from sin of the whole life of humankind in the context of the entire creation. The church is invited to participate in this renewing work of the Triune God. Their role and vocation is to be a people that embody and announce the cosmic renewal of the kingdom. Yet, for Newbigin, if the church is to be a faithful sign of the kingdom there must be careful attention to the institutional expression or gathered form of the church. Issues such as worship, leadership, and ecclesial structures must be brought into line with the missionary identity of the church.

In the past too much attention has been given to these issues in ecclesiology; in fact, the church as institution and community has dominated ecclesiological discussion for much of church history. This has often led to an inward-facing church primarily concerned with its own institutional life. As a result it is not uncommon today to see those who have grasped the missionary nature of the church become impatient with these issues and ignore them or even react against them.[1] Many others in both the ecumenical and evangelical traditions have followed this path. Not so for Newbigin.

There were at least three reasons Newbigin did not take this path. First, the way the church organizes and lives out its life together will either hamper or

---

1. Johannes Hoekendijk is a great example of this in his book *The Church Inside Out*, ed. L. A. Hoedemaker and Pieter Tijmes, trans. Isaac C. Rottenberg (Philadelphia: Westminster, 1966).

enable the church for mission; it will inevitably do one or the other. Second, it is only as the church continuously receives the life of Christ in fellowship and worship that the church can embody it in the midst of the world. Third, witness to God's purpose flows both out of the congregation and back to the congregation. For this reason Newbigin was concerned throughout his life with ecclesial structures, forms of leadership, and the practice of worship. What we need to keep firmly in view as we continue through this chapter is that when Newbigin deals with various issues of the internal life of the church, it is always in the context of his understanding of the missionary identity and nature of the church.

In this chapter we will, first of all, attend to two important distinctions in Newbigin's understanding of the church: first, local and universal, and second, gathered and scattered. Then we will look at worship, ecclesial structures, and leadership, and their importance for the missionary congregation.[2]

Ecclesiological Distinctions

When we use the word "church," we often have certain unexamined assumptions deeply embedded in our understanding. These hidden presuppositions can sometimes be a hindrance to our being faithful to the church's missionary calling. Two distinctions are important for Newbigin and help us understand his assumptions about the church: the church is both local and universal, and the church is expressed in both gathered and scattered form.

Local and Universal

Newbigin believes that the word "church," or *ekklesia*, is used in the New Testament always to describe visible communities of humans in two senses: (1) local congregations and (2) the entire people that belong to Jesus Christ.[3] This double usage comes because the word *ekklesia* is always qualified by "of God" and "in Corinth" (or another place). This indicates that God is at work calling and drawing a community to himself as the new humankind. He is at work locally—in Corinth, Rome, Surrey, and Phoenix—and he is at work throughout the world. It is a single action of God that assembles his one new humankind in many places. And so since "it is the one Lord who assembles his people in every place, these many local assemblies form one

---

2. See further Michael W. Goheen, *"As the Father Has Sent Me, I Am Sending You": J. E. Lesslie Newbigin's Missionary Ecclesiology* (Zoetermeer: Boekencentrum, 2000), 228–73 (chap. 6).

3. Lesslie Newbigin, "The Basis and the Forms of Unity," *Mid-Stream* 23 (January 1984): 7.

assembly universally. For the same reason the assembly in each place *is* the catholic Church in that place, for it is the one Lord who is assembling them."[4] Thus, the church has both local and universal expressions. And both are to be visible expressions.

The distinction between local congregation and universal church is driven by a missionary concern. The local congregation is the new humankind in this particular place and is called to offer to all people in that place the invitation of Christ to be reconciled to God through him. At the same time, the church is a global community that is to offer the same invitation to humankind as a whole.[5] It is precisely this discussion that led Newbigin to struggle throughout his life with ecclesial structures, forms of leadership, and ecumenical expressions. How can people see the church as the expression of the one new humankind across time and place as it becomes incarnated in many places?

Newbigin did not give equal weight to each of these expressions in his writings. Repeatedly he makes clear that the local church is "the fundamental unit of the Christian church"[6] or "the primary unit of the church"[7] or "the basic unit of Christian existence."[8] He learned this from his missionary experience in India, where various forms of witness that arose from missions—such as schools, hospitals, street preachers, and literature—moved people to want to come to the place where all of this was centered.[9] Thus these village congregations were the foundation and center for every other form of witness.[10] Moreover, he believed that the "whole thrust of the 20th century rediscovery of the missionary nature of the Church is lost if it does not lead to a radical re-conception of what it means to be a local congregation of God's people."[11] And so he frequently expressed his conviction that the local congregation is

4. Lesslie Newbigin, "A Fellowship of Churches," *Ecumenical Review* 37 (1985): 176.

5. Lesslie Newbigin, "Which Way for 'Faith and Order'?," in *What Unity Implies: Six Essays after Uppsala*, ed. Reinhard Groscurth (Geneva: World Council of Churches, 1970), 118.

6. Lesslie Newbigin, "Our Task Today" (address, fourth meeting of the diocesan council, Tirumangalam, 1951), 4.

7. Lesslie Newbigin, "The Work of the Holy Spirit in the Life of the Asian Churches," in *A Decisive Hour for the Christian World Mission*, by Norman Goodall, Lesslie Newbigin, W. A. Visser 't Hooft, and D. T. Niles (London: SCM, 1960), 26.

8. Lesslie Newbigin, "The Church—Local and Universal," in *The Church—Local and Universal: Things We Face Together*, ed. Lesslie Newbigin and Leslie T. Lyall (London: World Dominion Press, 1962), 20.

9. Lesslie Newbigin, *Unfinished Agenda: An Updated Autobiography* (Edinburgh: Saint Andrew Press, 1993), 53–54.

10. Newbigin, *Unfinished Agenda*, 118.

11. Lesslie Newbigin, review of *New Ways for Christ*, by Michael Wright, *International Review of Mission* 65 (1976): 228.

the primary reality of the church and therefore the only possible hermeneutic of the gospel.[12]

Nevertheless, this did not lead him to neglect the visible expression of the universal church. He was concerned for unity "all in one place," as this gives expression to the one church in each place. He was concerned for ecumenical structures and rejected criticisms that this pursuit of unity is merely the complicated and costly machinery of committees and councils that encumbers the church. And this also led him to concern for connections through both space and time of leadership. Episcopal, Presbyterian, and papal forms of leadership all sought to visibly express that the church was a universal body.

Newbigin's concern for the ecumenical or universal expression of the church is precisely so that the local congregation will be recognized as the one true people of God who will inherit the new creation. Disunity makes it appear that the church is just one more local religious body along with others. The local congregation is misunderstood if it is not seen to be a local presence of the universal church or the new humankind. It is not a branch of the ecumenical body but is where that new humanity is made visible. "When the local congregation speaks and acts, its words and acts must claim to be the words and acts of the universal Church if they are to be authentic. But this is hard to achieve, or even to acknowledge, in our divided state."[13] In a global world where the powers are increasingly transnational, this aspect of ecclesiology is becoming more important.

As we proceed in this chapter, the distinction between local and universal should be kept in mind, though Newbigin typically spoke of local congregations when he discussed the church, and—with a few exceptions—that will be the case in this chapter as well.

Gathered and Scattered

Often when one uses the word "church" what comes to mind is a visible body gathered in a particular place that is organized as an institution to carry out certain cultic tasks. And, indeed, this is one of the ways that Newbigin believes the New Testament uses the word "church." It is a visible and communal expression of God's people gathered around Christ, where he is present in their midst especially through Word and sacrament. However, to reduce

---

12. Lesslie Newbigin, *Sign of the Kingdom* (Grand Rapids: Eerdmans, 1980), 62; Lesslie Newbigin, *Gospel in a Pluralist Society* (Grand Rapids: Eerdmans, 1989), 227.

13. Lesslie Newbigin, *Truth to Tell: The Gospel as Public Truth* (Grand Rapids: Eerdmans, 1991), 88.

the word "church" to this institutional expression would be to misunderstand the nature of the church in the New Testament.

Newbigin's understanding of the church is fundamentally eschatological. It is nothing less than the new humankind incorporated into Christ, a sign and foretaste of the coming kingdom. As the one new humankind, the church cannot be reduced to a religious body that carries out religious rituals. That was the mistake of the enemies of the early church that classified the people of God as *thiasos* and *heranos*, private religious communities concerned with individual and otherworldly salvation. It was precisely the concern to maintain the public nature of the church as the new humankind that led them to adopt the word *ekklesia*.

Thus when the church is scattered about during the week, it is not any less the church. The laity are not fragments scattered about in culture that then become the church when they gather again for worship and fellowship. They are the new humankind, or the body of Christ,[14] in both their scattered and their gathered form.

Newbigin asks, "Is it not an illusion that constantly fogs our thinking about the Church that we think of it as something which exists manifestly on Sunday, is in a kind of state of suspended animation from Monday to Saturday?" He goes on to express his ecclesiological conviction: "The truth of course is that the Church exists in its prime reality from Monday to Saturday, in all its members, dispersed throughout the fields and homes and offices and factories, bearing the royal priesthood of Christ into every corner of His world. On the Lord's day it is withdrawn into itself to renew its being in the Lord Himself."[15]

This is evident also, as we saw in chapter 3, when Newbigin speaks of the new being of the total life of the church and of the church as a new social order as being expressed both when the church gathers and when it is scattered throughout the world during the week.[16] Moreover, the distinction between missionary intention and dimension makes the same point. Newbigin says, "The basic reality is the creation of new being through the presence of the Holy Spirit. This new being is the common life (*koinonia*) in the Church. It is out of this new creation that both service and evangelism

14. Lesslie Newbigin, "The Christian Layman in the World and in the Church," *National Christian Council Review* 72 (1952): 185–89. Throughout this article he continues to refer to the church scattered in their various vocations as "the Body of Christ" and says we have forgotten this when we limit the church to the gathered congregation.

15. Lesslie Newbigin, "Bible Studies: Four Talks on 1 Peter," in *We Were Brought Together*, ed. David M. Taylor (Sydney: Australian Council for the World Council of Churches, 1960), 96–97.

16. Newbigin, *Gospel in a Pluralist Society*, 136–37; Newbigin, *Truth to Tell*, 85–87.

spring."[17] This new reality of the Spirit is the primary witness in the church. It is in the *"whole life of the Church . . .* through which the Holy Spirit carries on His mission to the world, and the whole of it thus partakes of the character of witness. The whole life of the Church thus has a missionary *dimension*, though not all of it has mission as its primary *intention*."[18] The church exists when gathered and when scattered, and the whole of its life has the character of witness, whether in intentional words and deeds or in the rest of its life in creation.

In the preceding chapter, we unfolded what it means to be church in the midst of the world. In the following sections of this chapter, we look at what it means to be the church gathered. And we are concerned especially to show that the church must be understood in terms of its missionary nature in both its gathered and its scattered expressions. Newbigin writes, "Mission belongs to the essence of the Church. . . . And you cannot have fellowship with Him without being committed to partnership in His mission to the world."[19] This raises the question: How does the communal and institutional life of the church partake in its essentially missionary nature?

Worship

Two Simultaneous Duties

In the mid-1980s a reviewer of *Foolishness to the Greeks* challenged Newbigin to apply the heady discussion of his book to the local urban congregation. As it happened, he was pastoring a poor urban congregation in Winson Green at the time, so based on that experience, he responded with reflections on what his "heady discussion" would look like in a missionary congregation. He begins with the affirmation that we have been chosen to be bearers of the good news for the whole world. The only way anyone will believe that God's final word for the world is a crucified man is if there is a congregation that believes the gospel. He says the key is the work of God himself in the Holy Spirit both when the congregation is gathered for worship and when it is scattered throughout the world: "The Holy Spirit is present in the believing congregation *both gathered* for praise and the offering up of spiritual sacrifice, *and scattered* throughout the community to bear the

17. Lesslie Newbigin, *One Body, One Gospel, One World: The Christian Mission Today* (New York: International Missionary Council, 1958), 20.

18. Newbigin, *One Body, One Gospel, One World*, 21. Emphasis added on the opening phrase.

19. Newbigin, *One Body, One Gospel, One World*, 26–27.

love of God into every secular happening and meeting."[20] He then goes on to say that the "first priority, therefore, is the cherishing and nourishing of such a congregation in a life of worship, of teaching, and of mutual pastoral care so that the new life in Christ becomes more and more for them the great and controlling reality."[21]

It is typical of Newbigin to place worship either at the beginning of a list of characteristics of a faithful church, as he does here, or at the end. Putting it first enables him to speak of it as the first priority. Putting it at the end enables him to show its crucial need for nourishing the life of Christ for mission. For example, in another list he says, this "brings me to the fifth [and last] point, which is that the church will be a worshipping community." He then comments that it "may be thought that this should have stood first in the list. But I think we understand its meaning better if we take it after we have considered the church as a serving, suffering, witnessing, open community."[22] His ensuing discussion shows why this is so important: only in worship can we recommit ourselves to the true story centered in Christ that gives meaning to human life and be nourished by his life week by week so that we can faithfully bear witness. We see here with clarity the importance Newbigin placed on the institutional and communal life of the church—and especially on worship.

The church is like an ellipse with two foci: gathered life and scattered life. The church, he says, "always has two simultaneous duties."[23] The first is to strengthen and make more real the citizenship of God's people in the kingdom of God in word and sacrament, in prayer and communion, and in an ever-deeper rooting in Christ. And if the church fails to do this, "it is liable to become salt without savour." The second duty is to involve itself more and more deeply in the affairs of the world in suffering as it bears witness to the life of Christ. And so he lists the first thing the church needs as the "strengthening of our churches in worship." The "very first essential" is a "strong liturgical life" so that their eschatological existence might be made "more real and vivid."[24]

It is important to emphasize how significant this is for Newbigin. This kind of connection between mission—that is, evangelism, deeds of mercy and

20. Lesslie Newbigin, "Evangelism in the City," *Reformed Review* 41 (Autumn 1987): 4 (my emphasis).

21. Newbigin, "Evangelism in the City," 5.

22. Lesslie Newbigin, *Journey into Joy* (Grand Rapids: Eerdmans, 1972), 112.

23. Lesslie Newbigin, "The Evangelization of Eastern Asia," *International Review of Mission* 39, no. 154 (April 1950): 142.

24. Newbigin, "Evangelization of Eastern Asia," 143.

justice, and cultural vocations—and the worship life of the church permeates his writings. He often uses the word "withdraw" to speak of the time the church meets together to be prepared and nourished. On Monday through Saturday, people carry out their task of faithful witness, and then Sunday is "the day on which the Church makes a necessary withdrawal from its engagement with the world in order to renew the inner springs of the divine life within her through word and sacrament."[25]

The church, then, has two foci: the inner life of worship and fellowship in gathered congregations, and the outer life of mission scattered in the world. The danger is that "it is always relatively easy for the Church to do one of these things and neglect the other."[26] Far too often we "allow two things which belong together to fall apart—with consequences which are fatal for the witness of the church."[27] On the one hand, the church that isolates its worship from the task of caring for its neighbors or that focuses only on its inner life without an equal concern for its community ends up distorting its witness to the gospel. The result is an inward-focused, self-serving maintenance. On the other hand, when mission is separated from the worship life of the church, it becomes another human program that loses its power and character as witness to the kingdom. "It is precisely for the sake of the mission to the world that these two things must not be allowed to fall apart."[28] A faithful missionary church will "live in the tension of loyalty to both tasks, and in that place, in that tension, . . . bear witness to the gospel."[29]

The Gospel as the Source of the Church's Life

One of the common ways Newbigin speaks of the mission of the Church is "to reproduce the life of Jesus in the life of the world."[30] The source of that life is the gospel, in which Christ communicates his life to his people. If the church is to be faithful to embody the life of Christ in the midst of the world as a sign of the End, then its whole life must be deeply rooted in and nourished by the gospel. This is the context in which Newbigin stresses our twofold relationship with Christ: (1) we are related to Jesus historically as a body rooted in certain events and sent to continue his mission, and (2) we are related to Jesus

25. Newbigin, *One Body, One Gospel, One World*, 16–17.
26. Newbigin, "Evangelization of Eastern Asia," 143.
27. Lesslie Newbigin, "Reflections on an Indian Ministry," *Frontier* 18 (1975): 26.
28. Newbigin, "Reflections on an Indian Ministry," 26.
29. Newbigin, "Evangelization of Eastern Asia," 143.
30. Lesslie Newbigin, "The Bible Study Lectures," in *Digest of the Proceedings of the Ninth Meeting of the Consultation on Church Union (COCU)*, ed. Paul A. Crow (Princeton: COCU, 1970), 211.

eschatologically as a people who constantly encounter the living and ascended Lord in the Word and sacraments of the gospel. It is where two or three are gathered together in his name that the living Lord meets and nourishes his people with his own life in the gospel.[31] "The Church lives by faith in Christ, and the Word and Sacraments are the means whereby Christ offers Himself to men."[32] When "the Word is truly preached and the sacraments duly administered, Christ Himself is present in the midst with all His saving power. . . . [Then] God's saving power known and experienced in the life of the redeemed community has to issue in all kinds of witness and service to the world."[33]

Christ's saving power is known in the fellowship of congregations by the presence of the Holy Spirit. As Newbigin reviews the stories of a number of people who came to Christ in a particular setting, he reflects on one factor that was common to all their stories: a worshiping and celebrating congregation that was deeply involved in the daily life of their neighborhood. Mission isn't a humanly devised program but "the work of the Spirit, present in the life of the congregation, flowing out into the community, through faithful words and deeds of its members."[34]

A favorite text for Newbigin was John 15:1–11.[35] If we are to follow Jesus resolutely along the road of loving obedience that he trod, we must give priority to the cultivation of the life of Christ in worship, prayer, Word, and sacraments. The image of abiding in the vine is a beautiful picture of the way we as branches receive the life-giving sap of Christ's life "through a million tiny channels hidden behind the hard bark of the trunk and branches."[36] These channels are the means of grace whereby God gives the very life of Christ to us so that we can participate in Christ. "Participation in Christ means participation in His Mission to the world, and . . . therefore . . . true means of grace will precisely be in and for the discharge of this missionary task."[37] Although Newbigin never used this particular phrase, to emphasize this crucial point we might call them the "means of *missional* grace."

31. Lesslie Newbigin, *The Reunion of the Church: A Defence of the South India Scheme* (London: SCM, 1948), 60–72.

32. Newbigin, *Reunion of the Church*, 102.

33. Newbigin, "Our Task Today," 4–5.

34. Lesslie Newbigin, *Mission in Christ's Way: Bible Studies* (Geneva: WCC Publications, 1987), 19–20.

35. Lesslie Newbigin, "Abiding in Him," in *Uniting in Hope: Reports and Documents from the Meeting of the Faith and Order Commission, Accra, Ghana (University of Ghana, Legon), 1974* (Geneva: World Council of Churches, 1975), 141–44; Lesslie Newbigin, *Good Shepherd: Meditations on Christian Ministry in Today's World* (Grand Rapids: Eerdmans, 1977), 140–44.

36. Newbigin, "Abiding in Him," 141; see Newbigin, *Good Shepherd*, 141.

37. Lesslie Newbigin, *The Household of God: Lectures on the Nature of the Church* (New York: Friendship Press, 1954), 167.

Means of Missional Grace

Newbigin speaks most often of four means of missional grace: worship, Word, sacraments, and prayer.[38]

Worship

Worship is "by far the most important thing we do"[39] and "the central work of the Church."[40] Newbigin even speaks of the church's "most distinctive character" being a community of praise.[41] For Newbigin, "worship" is an all-inclusive word that includes praise, proclamation, prayer, sacraments, and more. The missionary dynamic is one of being gathered together in worship to deepen one's life in Christ and then being sent into the world.[42] If there is to be a "committed people as the sign and agent and foretaste of what God intends, it can only be insofar as their life is continually renewed through contact with God himself" in worship.[43]

Newbigin recognizes that the danger of a strong emphasis on worship may well lead to an inward-looking church concerned with its own liturgical life. This kind of worship is false religion. True worship enables us to be "conformed more and more inwardly to the Cross of Jesus." The cross of Jesus means a total and costly identification with the world, on the one hand, and yet a radical separation from its idolatry, on the other. Worship renews us in this life of Jesus.[44]

Precisely because worship is so important to the whole life of the church, Newbigin often addresses various distortions of worship in the life of the church, including worship that is slovenly or a matter of mechanical routine;[45] worship in which the members are spectators—a "gazing-stock"—rather than participants;[46] uncontextualized and cheap music;[47] a consumerist approach that asks, What do I get out of it?; a trivial and chatty worship devoid of

38. Using Acts 2:42, Newbigin adds fellowship to the Word, the Lord's Supper, and prayer. See, e.g., Lesslie Newbigin, *Sin and Salvation* (Philadelphia: Westminster, 1956), 94–96.

39. Newbigin, *Good Shepherd*, 37.

40. Lesslie Newbigin, "Bishops in a United Church," in *Bishops, but What Kind?*, ed. Peter Moore (London: SPCK, 1982), 156.

41. Newbigin, *Gospel in a Pluralist Society*, 227.

42. Lesslie Newbigin, "The Life and Mission of the Church," in *We Were Brought Together*, ed. David M. Taylor (Sydney: Australian Council for the World Council of Churches, 1960), 59.

43. Newbigin, *Journey into Joy*, 112–13.

44. Newbigin, *Good Shepherd*, 98.

45. Newbigin, *Good Shepherd*, 28.

46. Newbigin, *Good Shepherd*, 32–34.

47. Newbigin, *Good Shepherd*, 35–36.

reverence; and the scandal of a "dry mass" that eliminates the weekly celebration of the Lord's Supper.[48]

Word

A second means of missional grace that nourishes the church's life for mission is the Word of God. For Newbigin this meant both the Scriptures and the sacraments. When the Word of God is read and faithfully preached, and when the sacraments are rightly administered, "Christ Himself is present in the midst with all His saving power."[49] And the church lives its life in the midst of the world by the power of word and sacrament. Newbigin writes,

> This life-giving word of God is the power by which the Church lives. The Church is constantly renewed by the word of God. The word is given to us in two forms—the word spoken in the reading and exposition of Scripture, and the word acted in the sacraments. The same word is active in these two different modes. In both it is active through the Spirit. . . . The Church . . . lives by the word of God given to it as the word spoken and the word acted.[50]

Anything that threatens the true preaching of the gospel or the faithful administration of the sacraments must be expelled from the life of the church.[51] And so, because of their strategic importance, Newbigin asks, "Are we placing these in the very center of the Church's life? Are we jealous that nothing shall displace them?"[52]

The importance of Scripture as the means by which Christ meets and nourishes his people led Newbigin to stress the importance of both reading and preaching the Word. Preaching is not first of all the transference of theological ideas to the mind; rather, it is "the proclamation of the event of God in Christ" since the Scriptures are "the testimony of the witnesses to God's saving act."[53] As the Christ-event is proclaimed, it is the very "means whereby Christ the Word is Himself present to speak to those who hear."[54] And so "we go to the Bible to meet Christ, our present and Living Lord."[55]

---

48. Lesslie Newbigin, "Worship—Cleaning the Mirror," *Reform*, September 1990, 7.
49. Newbigin, "Our Task Today," 4.
50. Newbigin, *Good Shepherd*, 23.
51. Newbigin, *Reunion of the Church*, 106.
52. Newbigin, "Our Task Today," 4.
53. Newbigin, *Reunion of the Church*, 132, 134.
54. Lesslie Newbigin, "The Heritage of the Church in South India: Our Presbyterian Heritage," *South India Churchman*, January 1948, 54.
55. Newbigin, *Reunion of the Church*, 131.

As bishop, Newbigin spoke to preachers under his care, reminding them that "the business of the sermon is to bring hearers face to face with Jesus Christ as he really is."[56] This means that Jesus must be preached as Savior and Lord; gospel and law must be rightly related. One must hear both the comforting promises and the costly obligations of the gospel. One may not leave without understanding God's grace but also God's demands; neglecting either distorts the gospel. When both are proclaimed, we are comforted by the assurance that we are saved and also "re-enlisted in Christ's army as fighters for the rule of God in this world."[57] Newbigin humorously captures one side of this in a limerick:

> There's a preacher I know in Turin
> Who can preach for three hours about sin;
> But he never has space
> For a word about grace
> So he doesn't get under my skin.[58]

When Newbigin spoke of the Word in the life of the church, he primarily dealt with preaching and teaching. He did not speak much about what may be called "formation" or "discipleship"—that is, other ministries of the church to equip and form the church through the Bible. However, he did speak often, usually quite generally, of the importance of deeply indwelling the biblical story, especially if the church is to be able to resist the power of the cultural story. He speaks, for example, of "remembering and rehearsing" the biblical story, which will only come by the "continual reading of and reflection on the Bible."[59] There is a burning need "to soak ourselves in this story so that we more and more understand that it is the real story and that the story we are listening to on the radio and in our newspapers is to a very large extent phoney."[60] The only way the gospel will ever be credible is if there are local congregations who believe, live, and act on the Bible, including pastors who allow the Bible to shape the way they see the world and Christians who also learn to dwell in the Scriptures and see the world through biblical spectacles. Newbigin then says he would like to refer to his own experience as an example: "I more and more find the precious part of each day to be the thirty or forty minutes I spend each morning before breakfast with the Bible. All the rest of

56. Newbigin, *Good Shepherd*, 24.
57. Newbigin, *Good Shepherd*, 25.
58. Lesslie Newbigin, *St. Paul in Limerick* (Carlisle, UK: Paternoster, 1998), 58.
59. Newbigin, *Gospel in a Pluralist Society*, 147.
60. Lesslie Newbigin, "Biblical Authority," unpublished article, Newbigin Archives, University of Birmingham (1997), 6.

the day I am bombarded with the stories that the world is telling about itself. I am more and more skeptical about these stories. As I take time to immerse myself in the story that the Bible tells, my vision is cleared and I see things in another way. I see the day that lies ahead in its place in God's story."[61]

Newbigin did not give much direction on how the church should accomplish this immersion in the true story of the world, except some discussion of small groups. However, if we are to live faithfully in the biblical story in a world that has a different story—a powerful and seductive story—to tell about the world, we need to immerse ourselves in Scripture, both in our personal reading and in our local congregations, so that it might be the real story shaping our lives. Newbigin's writing certainly motivates us to think of ways in which the Bible might more and more be our story.

Sacraments

The gospel sacraments of baptism and the Lord's Supper are the third means of missional grace. We saw above that Newbigin speaks of these as the life-giving word of God enacted. A number of controversies over the sacraments, especially baptism, moved Newbigin to write more about the sacraments than about preaching. He fought the battle on two sides. On the one hand, he developed his understanding over against Western Christendom and its individualistic understanding of the sacraments—namely, that these were the channels by which individuals were passive recipients of God's grace. On the other hand, he engaged mounting criticism from many in India who saw baptism as a Western rite that led to the self-centeredness of the church: baptism cut off members from their community and incorporated them into a Western institution separated from the life of India. Against both of these Newbigin argued that to "recover the meaning of baptism" must be "one of the most urgent tasks" of our day. "We shall not overcome the introversion and selfishness of the Church by dispensing with baptism. It is an illusion to suppose that we can. What is needed is something much more difficult and costly."[62]

He engaged both of these fronts by arguing that the sacraments, both baptism and the Lord's Supper, have to be understood in three contexts: eschatological, communal, and missional.[63] It is no accident that these are

---

61. Lesslie Newbigin, *A Word in Season: Perspectives on Christian World Missions* (Grand Rapids: Eerdmans, 1994), 204–5.

62. Lesslie Newbigin, "The Church and the Kingdom," unpublished article, 1973, 10–11.

63. Lesslie Newbigin, "How Should We Understand Sacraments and Ministry?" (paper for the Anglican-Reformed International Commission meeting, London, 1983), Newbigin Archives, University of Birmingham; Lesslie Newbigin, "Our Baptism Renewed in Bread and Wine," *Reform*, July/August 1990, 18; Newbigin, "Church and the Kingdom."

the same words used to describe the Spirit's work. These are the means used by the Spirit to incorporate us into Christ's work. Much of Newbigin's rich theological reflection on the sacraments in terms of these three perspectives may be summarized as follows: Baptism is ultimately an *eschatological* sign, a rite of entry into the kingdom. One has passed from the old age into the age to come, dead to the old and alive to the new. Therefore, it is the sign of entry into the people of God, the *communal* context wherein the sacraments are enacted. It is in the church that the powers of the coming age are present as a sign, foretaste, and deposit of the kingdom. And our incorporation into the people of God means we enter a *missional* body committed to mission in the world: "It is our incorporation into the one baptism which is for the salvation of the world. To accept baptism, therefore, is to be committed to be with Christ in his ministry for all men."[64] The church is gathered "to be with him and to be sent out (Mark 3:14)."[65]

Again, Newbigin does not diminish the individual reception of the means of grace for salvation; rather, he puts it in biblical context. The salvation that comes to God's people is eschatological: the powers of the coming age breaking into history in Jesus and by the Spirit. The salvation that comes to God's people is communal: as part of the elect body of Christ. And the salvation that comes to God's people is missional: not simply enjoying salvation as a beneficiary but also participating in the mission of Christ.

Baptism is an initiatory rite that marks off those who belong to a community that shares in the life of the kingdom and is committed to following Jesus in mission. And the Lord's Supper is the way we continue to renew and reaffirm the commitment of our baptism. "Baptism is the act through which we are committed to follow Jesus on the way of the cross. The supper is the act in which that same commitment is continually renewed. Each time we share in the Lord's Supper we reaffirm our baptism."[66] As God's eschatological people we join the mission of Jesus in the way of the cross in baptism and recommit ourselves to it in the Lord's Supper.

Prayer

The last means of missional grace that Newbigin elaborates is prayer. For Newbigin "our life of intercession is quite central to discipleship."[67] A life of

---

64. Lesslie Newbigin, "The Future of Missions and Missionaries," *Review and Expositor* 74, no. 2 (1977): 217.

65. Newbigin, "Our Baptism Renewed," 18.

66. Newbigin, "Our Baptism Renewed," 18.

67. Lesslie Newbigin, "Renewal in Mind," *GEAR (Group for Evangelism and Renewal in the URC)* 29 (1983): 6.

prayer is rooted in Christ's mission, where we see him both deeply involved in laboring so that people might see the kingdom of God in their midst and, engaged in a life of prayer so that this might be so. All our talk "about being Christ's witnesses and servants to the ends of the earth remains mere clap-trap" unless there is at the heart of it all "a life which has its roots deep down in a discipline of prayer."[68]

> All true vitality in the work of missions depends in the last analysis upon the secret springs of supernatural life which they know who give time to communion with God. All true witness to Christ is the overflowing of a reality too great to be contained. It has its source in a life of adoration and intercession. . . . Any real power that God may give them will come through those secret channels which are in this age, as in every age, the true means of blessing for the world.[69]

Newbigin regularly connects mission to prayer—both corporate prayer and individual prayer. If we are to be a holy priesthood in the midst of the world, "we need a secret altar," a place where our inmost life, every part of it, is offered up day by day to God through Jesus Christ. There we receive God's ever-new gift of grace and mercy. But we also need times of prayer "together on the Lord's Day when he can take us as a whole community and renew us for his priestly service in the world." It is precisely our daily individual prayer that enables our communal worship to be vital and to renew us for our missionary task. Our "corporate and public worship can become lifeless if it is not constantly fructified by the time we spend each day alone to keep fresh and clean the channels of love and obedience to God and of his grace and mercy to us."[70]

Newbigin's theological reflection on many of these issues in worship is more profound and detailed than we can examine here. But the main point to be made is that he tied these means of grace—worship, Word, baptism and the Lord's Supper, and prayer—very closely to the missionary task of the church. These were the means of missional grace, as it were, that nourished God's people for their task in the world. The gospel can "become public truth

68. Lesslie Newbigin, "Forgetting What Lies *Behind* . . ." (sermon, fiftieth-anniversary observance of the Edinburgh 1910 World Missionary Conference, Riverside Church, New York City, May 25, 1960), 5.

69. Lesslie Newbigin, "Developments during 1962: An Editorial Survey," *International Review of Mission* 52, no. 205 (January 1963): 14.

70. Lesslie Newbigin, "An X-Ray to Make God Visible in the World," *Reform*, December 1990, 7.

only insofar as it is embodied in a society (the church) which is *both* 'abiding in' Christ *and* engaged in the life of the world."[71]

An important point needs to be made in conclusion. We could misinterpret Newbigin's understanding of worship if we viewed it solely in an instrumental way—that is, as only a means to mission. Mission has been our primary stress because of the theme of this book, but to view worship simply as an instrumental means would be mistaken. Worship is an end in itself. The church's worship "is directed wholly to God for His glory."[72] But that important fact does not mean it cannot have a missionary dimension. In fact, worship may well be a "powerful possible form of witness," as it was in the churches of the Soviet Union for years.

Ecclesial Structures

For Newbigin it is important to pay close attention to ecclesial structures. A couple of his statements express the importance of the issue. The "structure of the church is itself an expression of the Gospel,"[73] and therefore "the highest priority must be given to bringing about those changes in the structure of the Church."[74] The reason this was urgent for him was that even though there had been a recovery of a radically missionary theology of the church, the present structures did not reflect that theology but rather hindered the missionary witness of the church. The kinds of structures Newbigin referred to were manifold: ecumenical, congregational, leadership, diocesan, institutional, budgetary, and missionary. In this section we will be concerned primarily with congregational and ecumenical structures. In the next we will focus on structures of ministerial leadership.

We have noted before that Newbigin was a highly contextual thinker. His writings are of an ad hoc and occasional nature, written to address specific situations. This is quite clear in his discussions of ecclesial structures. On the one hand, this means the issues he is addressing often are very different from ours and initially may seem irrelevant. This is no more true than in this particular subject. Many of his suggestions do not fit our situation. On the other hand, the way Newbigin returns to theological convictions

---

71. Lesslie Newbigin, *Proper Confidence: Faith, Doubt, and Certainty in Christian Discipleship* (Grand Rapids: Eerdmans, 1995), 39 (my emphasis).

72. Newbigin, *One Body, One Gospel, One World*, 21.

73. Lesslie Newbigin, review of *Canterbury Pilgrim*, by A. M. Ramsey, and *Great Christian Centuries to Come*, ed. Christian Martin, *Ecumenical Review* 27 (1975): 172.

74. Lesslie Newbigin, "The Call to Mission—A Call to Unity," in *The Church Crossing Frontiers*, ed. Peter Beyerhaus and Carl Hallencreutz (Lund: Gleerup, 1969), 263.

to think toward solutions remains extremely valuable to us today—both in his method of thinking foundationally in a theological way and in the content of the theology that he offers as his starting point. This is important to observe in our setting. There has been much continuing reflection on congregational structures in the wake of Newbigin. The quality of that reflection ranges from quite helpful to superficial. What Newbigin can provide is not so much relevant structures for our day—that would go against his own convictions—as a way of proceeding in a theologically informed way. Yet many of his suggestions are still valuable. To the extent that space allows, we will engage the historical context that provides a background and impetus for his writings.

Urgency of Structural Renewal

In the period between 1938 and 1952, a missionary ecclesiology developed in the ecumenical tradition. But the primary barrier facing the implementation of this newly developed missionary ecclesiology after 1952 was structures from an earlier time. The missionary self-understanding that was developing needed missionary structures in order to become a reality. Newbigin was very much a part of this discussion. On a number of occasions he asks, "Does the very structure of our congregations contradict the missionary calling of the church?"[75] He charges that we "are saying that we have recovered a radically missionary theology of the Church. But the actual structure of our Churches . . . does not reflect that theology." The problem was that the "actual structures continue to placidly reflect the static 'Christendom' theology of the eighteenth century."[76] These Christendom structures, for Newbigin, meant a wealthy and established church centered primarily in a building standing in a central geographical location. There was institutional inertia that hindered any structural or institutional change. These structures existed primarily to channel grace to the church's members. Thus they were directed more toward maintenance of an institution than mobilizing for mission in the world.[77] At the very worst these structures led churches to become "clubs for self-centred enjoyment of the benefits of the Christian religion."[78] But the church could no longer maintain such a Christendom existence; the West was now a mission field.

75. Newbigin, "Developments during 1962," 9.
76. Newbigin, *Unfinished Agenda*, 148.
77. Lesslie Newbigin, *Honest Religion for Secular Man* (Philadelphia: Westminster, 1966), 102–11.
78. Newbigin, "Developments during 1962," 8.

Not only was the church's place in society changing, but so was Western society itself. The secular society of the West in the twentieth century,
when Newbigin wrote, was fast becoming a highly differentiated society, in
contrast to the undifferentiated society of medieval Europe and even many
Indian villages that Newbigin encountered. Christendom structures assumed
a social organization in which the family, political, economic, and social life
were intertwined in an indivisible whole. The church located geographically
in the center of that religio-political unity could perhaps stand as a sign of
good news for the whole community. But by Newbigin's day, society was
much more differentiated, complex, and mobile. A person lived in many
"places" at the same time. The church needed new structures to be, do, and
speak good news in this new social setting.

Twofold Criteria for Structural Renewal

The inherited Christendom structures were irrelevant and did not correspond to the missionary nature of the church; they had to be overhauled.
Newbigin offers two closely related criteria for structural renewal: they have
to be faithful to the nature and calling of the church, and they have to be
relevant to the particular community in which the church is set. As Newbigin
sees it, these criteria are really two sides of the same coin.

Structural renewal has to be faithful to the nature of the church. Every
time Newbigin enters an extended discussion of structures, he begins with
one or another of his definitions or descriptions of the church. From there
he moves to discuss structures.[79] Ecclesiology is important to establish since
"every discussion of the structures of the Church presupposes a doctrine of
the Church—hidden or acknowledged."[80]

A true church is missionary by its very nature, and so it is the new humankind that exists for the sake of the world. The way Newbigin formulates this is
that the church exists *for the place* in which it is set. When the church "tries to
order its life simply in relation to its own concerns and for the purposes of its
own continued existence, it is untrue to its proper nature."[81] The church "does
not exist for itself or for what it can offer its members."[82] The church exists to

---

79. We see the same argument in these two major discussions on ecclesial structures: Lesslie
Newbigin, "The Form and Structure of the Visible Unity of the Church," *One in Christ* 13 (1977):
107–17; Lesslie Newbigin, "What Is 'a Local Church Truly United'?," *Ecumenical Review* 29 (1977):
115–28. He begins with the contemporary context of the question, moves to a discussion of
ecclesiology, and then moves to structural renewal.

80. Newbigin, "Form and Structure," 110.

81. Newbigin, "What Is 'a Local Church Truly United'?," 119.

82. Newbigin, *Sign of the Kingdom*, 45.

carry out God's mission in the particular place in which it is set. This is the way Paul speaks of the church—for example, "the church of God in Corinth" (1 Cor. 1:2). The church is related to God. It exists for God's mission, but it is also related to its place. It exists for Corinth, for Ephesus, for Surrey, for Tempe, and so on. It is of the very essence of the church that it is *for* that place, for that section of the world for which it has been made responsible.

The terminology "for the place" is ecclesiologically loaded for Newbigin, and so he takes time to unfold what he means by *for a particular place*. The word "for," he says, "has to be defined christologically. In other words, the Church is *for* that place in a sense that is determined by the sense in which Christ is *for* the world."[83] Christ, and therefore the church, is for the world in a threefold sense: First, Christ is Creator and Sustainer; this means the church must love and cherish all of its created goodness. Second, Christ is the one who will bring all things to their appointed End; this means the church is to be a sign and preview of the true end for which that place exists. Third, Christ is the one who has died and who rose again for that place. In his death Christ not only identified with the created world he loved but also separated himself from its idolatry. And so the church must in every situation be wrestling with both sides of this reality: for and against the world. "The Church is for the world against the world. The Church is against the world for the world. The Church is for the human community in that place, that village, that city, that nation, in the sense that Christ is for the world."[84]

In light of this criterion, there are four ways the church fails to be the church *for* its particular place. The first is when it is irrelevant: if it adopts ecclesial structures and practices from another place or another time, it is seen as a foreign body. It also fails when it is conformed to the world and uncritically adopts the idolatrous structures and practices of that place. It fails, third, when it lives in polemical confrontation with the place and does not see the created goodness that is already there. And finally, it fails when it takes a conservative stance and becomes a static and outdated body that does not recognize the constantly changing context. A missionary church "must be where men are, speak the language they speak, inhabit the worlds they inhabit."[85]

The church will be *for* the particular place when it adopts the given structures of society, structures that are familiar and recognizable.[86] This is precisely what the church has always done, but sometimes it is not recognized.

83. Newbigin, *Word in Season*, 53–54.
84. Newbigin, *Word in Season*, 54.
85. Newbigin, *Honest Religion*, 112.
86. Newbigin, "Form and Structure," 113.

Historically, in different times and places the church took on, for example, the structures and practices of the Jewish synagogue, the episcopal structures of cities that organized social power in this way, and the structures of the diocese in metropolitan centers. The problem is often that these inherited structures were supposedly read off the pages of Scripture as if they were simply biblical principles. However, it is not simply a matter of embracing these structures uncritically. Their idolatry must be cleansed with a gospel disinfectant. This certainly rings true today when, for example, the church is adopting corporate structures and business models as well as worship practices from popular culture and entertainment.

The church must be for the particular *place*. In the undifferentiated societies of medieval Europe and in the Indian villages of Newbigin's experience, place was understood in exclusively geographical terms. People inhabited one place, where they lived, worked, played, and so on. Newbigin notes that this is changing today as most people now tend to inhabit many places: where they live, socialize, work, and play may be four different "places." Accordingly, to define place only in terms of the geographical location of a person's residence is inadequate. The church must be good news in every place where people are.

Here as elsewhere Newbigin approaches the subject both theologically and sociologically. Theology leads, but sociology contributes insight. He couples them, for example, when he says, "The sociologist and the theologian will be one in insisting that the idea of a structure-less Christianity is a pure illusion."[87] Here he makes use of the sociological insight that if an idea is to have an impact in history, it must take on an institutionally embodied form. In other places as well, he employs the insights of sociology. But time and again it is his theology—the gospel and the doctrine of the church—that leads his discussion.

Congregational Structures

In light of the criteria discussed above, Newbigin offers two critiques of existing structures: first, the fundamental ecclesial unit is too large; second, the structure of the church emerged from an undifferentiated society. Unfortunately, Newbigin's discussion of the kinds of structures that can meet these criticisms and enable the church to be a faithful missionary body remains rather general, but again, the way he struggles with the issue is helpful. He suggests four different forms of small groups that answer the criticisms he makes.

87. Newbigin, "Form and Structure," 109.

The first is a neighborhood group. This is a small group that meets in a particular neighborhood for Bible study, prayer, fellowship, and involvement with unbelieving neighbors.

The second is a work group that provides opportunity for those working together in a particular factory or office to gather and live as a sign of the kingdom in that place. What characterizes this group is that they are in the same work space. For a short time in his life, Newbigin advocated rather daring experiments with ecclesial structures in work locations. As the bishop of Madras, a growing industrial city, he encouraged groups of Christians to establish a communal presence and be a sign of the kingdom in that place. For him these were not parachurch organizations or outstations of the local congregation but true congregations of Christ. They should be furnished with leadership (nonordained ministry), Word, and sacrament as the center of their common life.[88] For Newbigin it was important that all mission should be seen to arise out of the gospel made known in Word and sacrament.[89] This is a radical suggestion that needs to be further explored.

The third type of small group Newbigin discusses is a frontier group. These are small groups of Christians who work within the same sector of public life and meet together to struggle with what it looks like to live out their faith in light of the gospel.[90] The primary goal of a frontier group is to search for ways to faithfully bear witness to the lordship of Christ in that particular area of culture.

The fourth is an action group. This group is organized around a concern for a particular kind of evangelistic or sociopolitical endeavor.

Newbigin expresses three dangers that will be present with the formation of small groups. The first is the twin dangers of introversion or activism. These groups may, on the one hand, become egocentric—a place where the benefits of salvation are selfishly enjoyed with little concern for the world. There must be an outward orientation that strives to understand what God's will is for the office, factory, neighborhood, and so on. On the other hand, these groups may become activistic—not a witness to the kingdom but just another program to effect social change. To keep groups from becoming either introverted or activistic, Newbigin suggests four things to keep them on track: a nonordained leadership that is deeply involved in the relevant sector of life or neighborhood and is ready to give missional leadership; full access to the congregational and sacramental life of the community, either

88. Newbigin, *Honest Religion*, 111–14.
89. Newbigin, *Sign of the Kingdom*, 66–67; see his full discussion of structures on 57–67.
90. Newbigin, *Gospel in a Pluralist Society*, 230–31.

within the small group or within the wider fellowship life of the congregation; cross-confessional unity in a common commitment to a place and task; and commitments to prayer, Bible study, fellowship, and mission.

The second danger for small groups is that the great traditions of church history will be lost. Experimentation and novelty are vulnerable to the "real danger that we lose the great essentials which have been preserved and handed on through the ordered life and liturgy of the great churches."[91] The search for the new can blind one to the wisdom of the past.

The final danger is that these small groups will be disconnected from the universal body of Christ. The emphasis falls on local place, and so these groups have little connection with the wider fellowship of God's people.

A missional ecclesiology demands that we think carefully about our congregational structures so that they enable the church to live out its vocation. Much thinking today on ecclesiology has been concerned with structures. Newbigin provides us with the kind of model we need: it is both theological and missional.

Ecumenical Structures

As Newbigin struggled throughout his life with ecumenical structures, he always did so, again, on the basis of a well-defined ecclesiology: the doctrine of the church must guide our reflection and action ecumenically as well as locally. Above we sketched his views on the local congregation and universal church as he understood Scripture's teaching. He asks, "What is the form of the church order which will effectively offer to all *human beings* in this place the invitation of Jesus Christ to be reconciled to God through him? And: What is the form of church order which will effectively offer to *mankind as a whole* this same invitation?"[92] If the church is to be good news for all humankind, it must be recognizable as both a local and a global fellowship.

Throughout his life, Newbigin asked many questions and suggested many structures that need not detain us here. But he continually pressed the issue of what it would mean to be the church in each place. While this is certainly important at the local level, we might ask whether it is important at other levels as well—such as the nation-state or the global. And, if so, what should it look like? In all of this, Newbigin says, "What matters is that the Church should everywhere be recognizable as simply the new, the true humanity; as the place where every human being is given the freedom of his own home

91. Lesslie Newbigin, "Cooperation and Unity," *International Review of Mission* 59, no. 233 (January 1970): 73.
92. Newbigin, "Which Way for 'Faith and Order'?," 118.

where he can know and love and obey God as his Father, and Jesus as his Lord in the power of the Spirit who is himself the living presence now of the blessedness to which all are called."[93] Every congregation must ask from its place how it can express this universal reality of the church.

A Living Tradition

Two questions may arise at this point as to what we are to do with the structures of our past that have been bequeathed to us. First, what about parish churches? Most churches today are local congregations in places defined by geography. And second, what do we do with our inherited traditions—whether Catholic, Anglican, Presbyterian, or Congregational? Newbigin believes that the local congregation remains the fundamental structure for the church, but he also believes that daring experiments are needed that imagine structures beyond those that have been inherited. As for long-standing traditions, Newbigin employs an organic metaphor over against a mechanical one: when machines are no longer serviceable for the purpose they were constructed to fulfill, they can be scrapped, but a living organism maintains a continuity of life and must constantly adapt to its new environment. He calls for the reformation of existing structures rather than either revolutionary destruction (which many in the World Council of Churches were calling for) or conservative preservation (sought by others in reaction to the first).

A missionary self-consciousness or spirit is not enough; every church also needs missionary structures in order for that spirit to live. The structure of the church must be compatible with what it is—a missionary body. So what should not be lost in the detail of our discussion is that "the primacy of the missionary obligation" is "to be determinative of the forms of the Church's life."[94]

Leadership

It may be fairly said that the two issues to which Newbigin devotes more space than any others in his writing, at least before his "retirement" years, are ecclesial unity and ministerial leadership. Much of his struggle is deeply contextual and distant from our experience today. Nevertheless, his efforts yield helpful reflection on leadership that continues to offer insight for today.

93. Newbigin, "What Is 'a Local Church Truly United'?," 128.
94. Newbigin, "Developments during 1962," 8.

A clue to the importance he places on leadership can be found where he discusses this issue in his important book *The Gospel in a Pluralist Society*. He offers a well-constructed theology of mission in chapters 6 through 17. Then in chapter 18 it all comes to expression in the congregation as a hermeneutic of the gospel. He begins the following chapter: "If I am right in believing, as I do, that the only effective hermeneutic of the gospel is the life of the congregation which believes it, one has to ask how such congregations may be helped to become what they are called to be."[95] His answer is the title of the chapter: "Ministerial Leadership for a Missionary Congregation."[96] So we need to trace Newbigin's answer to the question he puts before us: "What kind of ministerial leadership will nourish the Church in its faithfulness to the gospel in a pluralist society?"[97]

Ministry and the Missionary Congregation

The proper place to begin to answer the question raised above is within the context of Jesus's intention for the church to continue its mission. "We cannot talk long about ministry without talking about mission. Ministry must be conceived always in terms of the Church's mission."[98] John 20:19–23 gives the substance of Jesus's intention for the church, and Newbigin uses this as a starting point to discuss ministerial leadership. In these verses we find the following points: The church is sent and therefore missionary by its nature ("I am sending you" [v. 21]). The church's mission is shaped by Jesus's mission ("As the Father has sent me" [v. 21]). Mission is in the way of the cross ("He showed them his hands and side" [v. 20]). Mission can only be carried out in the power of the Spirit as the church shares in the resurrection life of Christ ("He breathed on them and said, 'Receive the Holy Spirit'" [v. 22]). The church continues Jesus's ministry of deliverance from the power of sin ("If you forgive anyone's sins, their sins are forgiven" [v. 23]).

This shows Jesus's intention for the church. To engage the subject of leadership, Newbigin opens up a standing debate on the passage: Does Jesus speak to his circle of disciples as "the ministry in embryo" or "the church in embryo"? Are they the first church or the first leaders of the church? Do we move from leadership to the whole church or from the whole church to leadership? Newbigin's answer is, in essense, a plague on both your houses! The first leads to clericalism, which separates leadership as a higher class

95. Newbigin, *Gospel in a Pluralist Society*, 234.
96. Newbigin, *Gospel in a Pluralist Society*, 234–41.
97. Newbigin, *Gospel in a Pluralist Society*, 235.
98. Lesslie Newbigin, *Priorities for a New Decade* (Birmingham, UK: National Student Christian Press and Resource Centre, 1980), 8–9.

within the church, and the second leads to egalitarianism, which downplays the importance of ministerial leadership. To be forced to choose between these two is the result of "viewing the Church from a static, 'Christendom' perspective, rather than a dynamic and missionary one."[99] Newbigin fought against both distortions. His goal was to replace a Christendom pattern of ministry with a more missionary one.

Newbigin begins with basic insight that in John 20 Jesus speaks these words *both* to the first leaders *and* to the first members of the church.[100] On the one hand, the commission is given to the whole church. We need ministers, from this standpoint, to lead and enable the church to fulfill its calling. He uses the analogies of Sabbath and tithing. There is one day that is holy but not because the rest are not; one day is holy so that all days may be holy. We do not give 10 percent because that is what belongs to the Lord; we give that portion to remind us that all we have is the Lord's. So the whole church is sent, and leadership is tasked with making sure it is ready to live out its identity. On the other hand, the commission is given to the apostles as the first leaders. They are called to follow Jesus and then to lead and enable others to follow. "Ministry in the Church is so following Jesus on the way of the cross that others are enabled to follow and to become themselves leaders of others in the same way."[101] The boundary is fluid between leadership and other members. Leaders lead and equip so that all may follow and so that others are ready to lead and equip others to follow—and so on. It is multiplication of discipleship.

Discipleship and leadership, then, go together. Newbigin saw this in the villages of India as churches were formed. New converts learned the faith, shared it with their neighbors, and led them on to more faithful discipleship. "As those learning to follow Christ, they were at the same time leading others. In a missionary situation that is how it is. And that is how it was in the first centuries of the Church. There was no class of what we call clergy."[102] The distinction between clergy and laity arose when Christianity became the established religion of the empire.[103]

Lead and Equip

Two operative words keep appearing in Newbigin's discussion of ministerial leadership: "lead" and "equip." What is distinctive is the way he relates

99. Newbigin, "How Should We Understand Sacraments and Ministry?," 9.
100. Lesslie Newbigin, "Ministry," unpublished paper (1982).
101. Newbigin, "How Should We Understand Sacraments and Ministry?," 9.
102. Newbigin, "Ministry," 6.
103. Newbigin, *Good Shepherd*, 75.

the two: leaders are those who lead, first, by following hard after Jesus and, second, in the process, they equip others to follow after.

Two scriptural texts undergird his notion of leading: 1 Corinthians 11:1, "Follow my example as I follow the example of Christ"; and Mark 14:42, which Newbigin translates, "Come on: let's go." In the Markan text we see Jesus leading by way of example as he goes to the cross. Newbigin draws on a picture of Jesus portrayed by the Italian film director Pasolini in the movie *The Gospel according to Matthew*. Jesus is pictured as a commander leading his troops into battle. He goes ahead of the disciples, leading them while throwing words of encouragement, instruction, and challenge back over his shoulder as they follow him in their missionary task. A leader is not "like a queen bee who remains at the center while the worker bees go out into the world."[104] Nor is a leader "like a general who sits at headquarters and sends his troops into battle. He goes at their head and takes the brunt of the enemy attack. He enables and encourages them by leading them, not just by telling them. In this picture, the words of Jesus have a quite different force. They all find their meaning in the central keyword, 'Follow me.'"[105]

Newbigin makes a strategic choice with the word "leadership" precisely because he wants to convey this notion of participatory engagement in leading. He recognizes that in the New Testament there are many metaphors for leadership: shepherds, overseers, watchmen, stewards, ambassadors, servants, and so on. He notes that the primary metaphor today is that of a shepherd with the term "pastor." He says, however, that the shepherd today conveys a very different picture from in biblical times, when a shepherd was a king who governed his people and led them into battle. The word "leadership" best conveys the combined notion of discipleship and leadership found in the New Testament.[106]

As one who leads, a leader is also to equip others for the task. Newbigin uses many terms to describe this equipping: "serve," "nourish," "sustain," "guide," "enable," "encourage."[107] He points to four ways a leader may equip the congregation. First, a leader is responsible for the ministry of word and sacraments to the congregation. We have seen the importance of this role in the preceding section. Second, leaders are called to uphold their people in prayer, "to hold them up by name before God as they go out into the world day by day to wrestle with the principalities and powers."[108] Third, leaders

---

104. Newbigin, "Ministry," 3.
105. Newbigin, *Gospel in a Pluralist Society*, 240.
106. Newbigin, "How Should We Understand Sacraments and Ministry?," 5.
107. E.g., Newbigin, *Gospel in a Pluralist Society*, 234–41.
108. Newbigin, "Bible Studies: Four Talks on 1 Peter," 119; see Newbigin, *Good Shepherd*, 143.

can provide "space" and structures in which training for cultural callings may take place.[109] Finally, ministers must be deeply involved in the ministry of the world themselves if the first three are not to be carried out in a Christendom pattern. This will involve both engagement with the powers in a social and political setting and evangelism: a leader "should be ready himself to be engaged—as opportunity offers and calls—in direct evangelistic efforts or in pioneering movements of Christian action in the secular world."[110] This does not mean that the minister is directly involved in all areas of culture. Rather, as situations arise the leader is called to represent the whole church in challenging the idols and powers in public life.

Ministerial Order and the Missionary Church

Leadership is important for the health and welfare of a missionary congregation. But as a more permanent leadership arises out of the process of ongoing discipleship, the question arises: Is there one order that best exemplifies this view of ministerial leadership? Newbigin believes there was immense fluidity and variety in the forms of ministry in the early church. And no historical forms of leadership—whether papal, episcopal, presbyterial, or congregational—can be irrefutably demonstrated from Scripture. Scripture does not offer us a universally valid order of ministry. But there are criteria for judging different forms; an examination of Newbigin's vast writing on leadership shows us five.

First, ministerial order must be shaped by and appropriate to the missionary calling of the church. Newbigin's constant refrain is that the "question that has to be asked—and repeatedly asked—is whether the traditional forms of ministry which have been inherited from the 'Christendom' period are fully compatible with the faith that the Church is called to be a missionary community."[111]

A second criterion is that forms of ministry have to be flexible and contextual. Various cultural contexts and missionary situations will demand different forms of leadership in order to carry out the missionary calling of the church. The church is not to demolish forms and structures of culture but to renew them. They are to manifest the provisional form of the new humanity

109. Lesslie Newbigin, "Episcopacy and Authority," *Churchman* 104, no. 4 (1990): 338; Newbigin, *Good Shepherd*, 80–81.

110. Lesslie Newbigin, "The Bishop and the Ministry of Mission," in *Today's Church and Today's World*, ed. J. Howe (London: CIO Publishing, 1977), 246; see also Newbigin, *Gospel in a Pluralist Society*, 240; Newbigin, *Good Shepherd*, 60–61.

111. Newbigin, "Developments during 1962," 8.

in familiar forms. It is "entirely congruous with the proper character of the Church that, from the very beginning, it took over into its own life the forms of social organism which it found in the society of which it was a part."[112] Eldership arose from the forms of the synagogue, the episcopate took on forms of political leadership in the cities of the empire, and so on. It is appropriate to take over cultural forms, but it must not be done uncritically; the idolatry must be recognized and purged.

A third criterion for ministerial order is the right relationship between the personal and the corporate. Leadership should involve individual initiative but always as part of the involvement of the whole community. Leaders are neither dictators who impose their wills nor pollsters who register the desire of the majority.

A fourth criterion is that both settled and mobile forms of ministry must be present. The New Testament speaks of elders, bishops, pastors, and deacons in the local congregation. These leaders are permanently settled to lead in one place. But there are also mobile, nonlocalized ministries such as apostles, prophets, and evangelists.[113] However, with the coming of Christendom all ministerial leadership was concentrated in the local and settled ministry, which led to the "practical elimination of the universal, travelling ministry of apostles, prophets, and evangelists."[114] Modern-day missionary movements have attempted to reintroduce mobile ministries into the church, but these have not been integrated into official ecclesiologies or ministry orders.

A fifth criterion is that the ministerial order must express the local and universal dimensions of the church. There must be leadership at the local level but a connection with the broader church that expresses the universal nature of the church. Episcopal, Presbyterian, and papal forms of leadership are attempting to express this universality.

Theological Education and Ministerial Training

Newbigin believes that if ministerial leadership is to be appropriate to the nourishing of missionary congregations, there must be radical changes in theological education. He joined a good number of missionary leaders who struggled with the question of theological education at a time when the churches in the global South and East were rapidly growing. The ecumenical movement and later the evangelical tradition engaged these questions, but their rich reflection never really took hold.

112. Newbigin, "Form and Structure," 114.
113. Newbigin, "How Should We Understand Sacraments and Ministry?," 9.
114. Newbigin, "Ministry," 8.

The problem was that the Western university model of theological education was being transported to the non-Western world. Newbigin notes that the problem is "not just that the theological schools of the Third World needed to be brought up to the 'best' western standards. It was the question whether these standards really are the best; whether the models of ministerial formation accepted in Europe and North America are really the right ones for the Third World—or even for the areas where they have been developed."[115]

First, there are structural questions about whether an academic institutional model can train the kind of missionary leaders the church needs. In a university model of theological education, students are withdrawn from ministry into academic institutions that are little relevant to actual ministry. Students follow a path to become elitist professionals and lose touch with both ordinary church membership and the poorer classes of society. Newbigin points to twentieth-century educational philosophers Ivan Illich and Paulo Freire, both of whom believed that the classroom model of education was a poor way to learn. The bankers' model of education, so labeled by Freire, is a matter of passing along intellectual information for students to bank away to be drawn on for later use. This creates the professional class of clergy and leaves one unprepared for actual ministry. Ministerial training needs to be more like business and medical models, where teaching is done as leaders engage in the practice of ministry.

Second, there are urgent questions about the contextualization of the gospel. Most seminaries do not deal with cultural context and consider theology to be timeless truth when in reality it is Western theology. The light of the gospel does not engage the current issues of the day. Newbigin has reservations about the way contextualization was understood, since it often tended to diminish scriptural authority. He is also uneasy with a certain kind of liberationist epistemology that reduces theology to reflection on praxis. But, these concerns registered, Newbigin wants to see the Bible brought to bear on particular contexts in a relevant way. As long as universal Western theologies are seen as the norm, those not formed in that culture or in that time will find them irrelevant to ministry. Theology needs to be contextual. The responsibility of theology is

> to declare to each generation what is the faith, to expose and combat errors destructive of the faith, to expel from her body doctrines which pervert the faith, and to lead her members into a full and vivid apprehension of the faith. . . . This is always a fresh task in every generation, for thought is never

115. Lesslie Newbigin, "Theological Education in a World Perspective," *Churchman* 93, no. 2 (1979): 105–15.

still. The words in which the Church states its message in one generation have changed their meaning by the time the next has grown up. No verbal statement can be produced which relieves the Church of the responsibility continually to re-think and re-state its message. . . . The church has to state in every new generation how it interprets the historic faith, and how it relates it to the new thought and experience of its time. . . . Nothing can remove from the Church the responsibility for stating *now*, what is the faith. It belongs to the essence of the living Church that it should be able and willing to do so.[116]

Third, there are concerns about the content of the theological curriculum. In the West, in too many ways biblical studies and theology have allowed the gospel to be absorbed into the cultural story rather than challenging it. The Bible is no longer the narrative within which theology is done. Newbigin speaks often of biblical studies operating with a faith commitment to the "creed of modernity."[117] He laments that "as training for Christian ministry was assimilated to the critical methods of modernity, thousands of prospective ordinands in their earliest months of theological training had to be gently but firmly moved from the confessional position to the scientific one."[118] The move toward higher criticism, even though it has given much insight, "is misunderstood if it is seen as a move to a more objective understanding of the Bible. It is a move from one confessional stance to another, a move from one creed to another."[119] This kind of blind captivity to modernity needs to be challenged by those outside the Western world who are not so shaped by this story. But we are a long way from this ideal since even non-Western scholars have been well schooled in the Western story they received from their theological training in Western institutions. How can Western biblical studies and theology, so domesticated by the idolatry of the cultural story, be renewed?

But the problem with the theological curriculum isn't only its syncretistic Westernized theology; it is also its nonmissionary theology. The main patterns of theology and theological education were formed when "the ends of the earth [had] ceased to exist as a practical reality in the minds of Christians." Theology, then, is "not concerned so much to state the Gospel in the terms of non-Christian cultures as with the mutual struggle of rival interpretations of the Gospel." Church history is "taught not as the story of missionary advance

116. Newbigin, *Reunion of the Church*, 137–38.
117. Newbigin, *Proper Confidence*, 83.
118. Newbigin, *Proper Confidence*, 79.
119. Newbigin, *Proper Confidence*, 80.

in successive encounters of the Gospel with different forms of human culture and society, but rather as the story of the doctrinal and other conflicts within the life of the Church."[120] The theological curriculum needs to be reworked in terms of being both more contextual and more missional.

Fourth, the responsibility for theological education has been removed from the churches. Newbigin believes "the task of theological training cannot be simply handed over to the universities. It is the task of the church, and the church must take responsibility." It is only when theology and theological education are done "in the context of the confessing and worshipping church" that there will be a "real dialogue between gospel and our culture." Newbigin is not opposed to academic settings; it is just that those involved in that kind of institution must raise foundational "questions about the very presuppositions upon which the university faculty operates."[121]

If there are to be missionary leaders, there is a need for a new kind of theological education in structures, pedagogy, and theological curriculum.

The Ministerial Task of Discipline

Discussion of the subject of ecclesiastical discipline is relatively sparse in Newbigin's writings. Yet in his memoirs it is clear that discipline was a regular and important part of his own ministry as a bishop.[122] We refer to it here briefly because in the three or four places where he does discuss it, he makes clear that this is a crucial element in the missionary church. Discipline means more than excommunication, of course, but that is included. A church must take responsibility to enable converts to be renewed in their lives when conversion removes them from their old social spheres. They must continually be guided to leave behind sin and idolatry. It has to be both firm and gracious. And there will be times when excommunication must take place when people allow public sin to have a foothold in their lives. The goal is ultimately restoration to faithful living. If the church does not take discipline seriously, "the Church's witness to the non-Christian world becomes hopelessly compromised."[123]

In his own memoirs of his time as a bishop, Newbigin describes times where he had to exercise discipline. He stresses the importance of firm discipline in love. The exercise of discipline is "in many ways the severest test of a church's Christianity. It is easy—fatally easy—for a congregation simply to shut its eyes to the sins of its members and to do nothing about them. It is also easy for it,

---

120. Newbigin, *Honest Religion*, 102–3.
121. Newbigin, "Theological Education," 115.
122. Lesslie Newbigin, *A South India Diary* (London: SCM, 1951), 72–75.
123. Newbigin, *Household of God*, 7.

under certain circumstances, to adopt a hard legalistic attitude which is without redemptive power."[124] True discipline must avoid both of these approaches.

In a sermon Newbigin preached as a bishop to his ministers, he says, "The duty of discipline . . . is part of the whole discipline laid upon us in our ordination." He rejects a Pharisaical approach that is harsh and condemning as well as a Sadduceean path that is an "easy-going compromise with the world which merely shrugs its shoulders in the presence of evil and prefers to avoid trouble by saying nothing. Evil then goes unchallenged, and becomes comfortably established in the Church, like a tenant who cannot be evicted." The object of all discipline is that the person may be forgiven and restored to the church's fellowship; that must never be forgotten. It must be done with humility because we too are forgiven sinners. Significantly, Newbigin makes a special point of challenging those under his care "to be fearless in tackling the sins of the rich and powerful." It is easy to shrug off discipline of those with social and economic power. Yet if we only discipline those who do not hold this kind of power, we "expose ourselves as cowards and bullies."[125]

Discipline is necessary for the missionary congregation if it is to live its distinctive life in the midst of the world as a sign, foretaste, and firstfruit of the kingdom. The life of the missionary church must evidence the power of the gospel. A compromised and domesticated life blurs the witness of the church.

Conclusion

Traditionally, ecclesiology has been devoted to questions of the church as institution—worship, preaching, sacraments, organization, leadership, and so on. Moreover, in popular imagination the word "church" often stands for these things. But these aspects of the church's life have been disconnected from the mission of the church in the world. Some more recently have reacted against this institutional introversion and ignored more than a thousand years of ecclesiological reflection. Newbigin did neither. He often struggled with traditional questions but always reframed them in light of the mission of the church. If the church is to be a faithful sign, foretaste, and instrument of the kingdom, then worship, ecclesial structures, and leadership—indeed all the aspects of the church as institution and community—are important.

124. Newbigin, *South India Diary*, 73.
125. Newbigin, *Good Shepherd*, 50–53. In *South India Diary*, 72, Newbigin tells a story of where this very thing took place. A "very influential member of the church" was not disciplined for a serious sin. "Evidently the influence of Mr. T. weighed more with the Pastoral Committee than the fear of God."

5

A Missionary Encounter
with Culture

The gospel makes a remarkable and bold claim: the goal of universal history—and therefore the purpose and meaning of the whole creation—has been disclosed, accomplished, and made present in the life, death, and resurrection of one Jewish man in the middle of history. This is surely not an announcement to be slotted into a private category called "religion." Rather, it is a "secular announcement"[1] and "public truth"[2]: it is a message of ultimate importance for all people. But how can anyone ever believe that God's final word is a man hanging naked, tortured, and humiliated on a cross? By any cultural vision this message is simply ridiculous and downright foolish. "It is easy for us," Newbigin comments, "who are committed to the preaching of the Gospel, to forget how strange, and even repelling, the Gospel is to the ordinary common sense of the world."[3]

But the gospel is more than simply a message and a truth claim—it is a matter of power. The End of history breaking into the middle is the advent of God's power in the Holy Spirit to renew all things. So the question of how anyone can ever believe such a strange message can only be answered in this way: first, only if there is a people that believe and faithfully witness

1. Lesslie Newbigin, *The Finality of Christ* (London: SCM, 1969), 22, 46.
2. Lesslie Newbigin, *Truth to Tell: The Gospel as Public Truth* (Grand Rapids: Eerdmans, 1991).
3. Lesslie Newbigin, "Context and Conversion," *International Review of Mission* 68, no. 271 (1979): 301.

to that good news, and second, only if the Holy Spirit works through their lives, deeds, and words to bring people to conversion.

This missionary people is set in the midst of the world. They are not hermetically sealed off from the culture in which they live but are, consistent with their vocation, interwoven into the fabric of their cultural community. This raises the enormously important and difficult question: How is the church to live out a faithful witness in the midst of its cultural context? A wrong relationship will deeply compromise its witness. This is why the relationship of gospel, church, and culture is so significant for Newbigin's missionary ecclesiology. This chapter discusses Newbigin's view of how the church can embody and witness to a comprehensive gospel in the midst of a culture that is itself shaped by another equally comprehensive yet incompatible story.[4]

The Insight of a Cross-Cultural Missionary

Newbigin begins his important book *Foolishness to the Greeks* by asking what would be involved in a "genuinely missionary encounter" between gospel and culture. He says the "angle from which I am approaching the study is that of a foreign missionary."[5] We have to pause here and carefully consider what seems to be a quite unexceptional statement. He rightly notes that there is nothing new in proposing a discussion of the relationship between gospel and culture. It has been done many times, and in the twentieth century a number of cultural theologians have tackled the issue. H. Richard Niebuhr, for example, gave us a classic study of five models in his book *Christ and Culture*.[6] And the work of Paul Tillich was concerned with a "theology of culture."[7] Newbigin observes, "This work has been mainly done, as far as I know, by theologians who had not had the experience of the cultural frontier, of seeking to transmit the gospel from one culture to a radically different one."[8]

The work of Newbigin, especially his insight into a missionary encounter with Western culture, has been explosive precisely because of this very point.

4. See further Michael W. Goheen, "Gospel and Cultures: Lesslie Newbigin's Missionary Contribution," *Philosophia Reformata* 66, no. 2 (2001): 178–88; Michael W. Goheen, *"As the Father Has Sent Me, I Am Sending You": J. E. Lesslie Newbigin's Missionary Ecclesiology* (Zoetermeer: Boekencentrum, 2000), 331–70 (chap. 8).

5. Lesslie Newbigin, *Foolishness to the Greeks: The Gospel and Western Culture* (Grand Rapids: Eerdmans, 1986), 1.

6. H. Richard Niebuhr, *Christ and Culture* (New York: Harper, 1951).

7. Paul Tillich, *A Theology of Culture* (New York: Oxford University Press, 1959).

8. Newbigin, *Foolishness to the Greeks*, 1.

There are at least two aspects to his claim. First, he is saying that the stance or angle from which he approaches the subject is that of mission or witness—"seeking to transmit the gospel." Niebuhr, Tillich, and other cultural theologians step back and offer an assessment in terms of a theoretical analysis of the problem. It is not so much that Newbigin would speak against using academic tools; scientific insight can certainly be helpful. Rather, he is saying that the most fundamental stance we must take as Christians is in terms of the identity we have as God's people—his witnesses. It is not scientific neutrality or theoretical distance. How do we analyze the relationship between gospel and culture if we start with our fundamental missional identity? If we have been entrusted with the good news that God is restoring all of human life, how do we live in a culture with a very different story to tell? It is from this angle that he approaches the subject.

There is a second dimension to Newbigin's observation: cross-cultural missionaries have had the experience of trying to live and communicate the gospel in very different cultures from their own. This brings a depth of insight that simply cannot be obtained in any other way. When you cross over into another cultural setting and take the time to get to know the language, customs, and institutions of that culture, it begins to shake you out of the assumed familiarity you have with your own culture. That which seems to be normal and simply the way things are is now questioned. Your own embodiment of the Christian faith is reexamined; you realize that it is far more shaped by your cultural story than you had ever imagined.

Newbigin quotes a Chinese proverb: "If you want a definition of water, don't ask a fish."[9] People immersed within one cultural story all their lives can easily be unaware of their context. And what sets apart people who have had a deep engagement with another culture is the way they gain critical distance on the cultural waters in which they swim. This is exactly what happened to Newbigin in his missionary experience in India. In his writings he notes many occasions when he was awakened to the many unexamined assumptions of his European worldview and its impact on his faith. He writes, "[The] missionary, if he is at all awake, finds himself, as I did, in a new situation. He becomes, as a bearer of the gospel, a critic of his own culture. He finds there the Archimedean point. He sees his own culture with the Christian eyes of a foreigner, and the foreigner can see what the native cannot see."[10] Two of Newbigin's missionary experiences may serve to illustrate this "awakening."

9. Newbigin, *Foolishness to the Greeks*, 21.
10. Lesslie Newbigin, *A Word in Season: Perspectives on Christian World Missions* (Grand Rapids: Eerdmans, 1994), 68.

When he attempted to preach the gospel on the streets of India, Newbigin found he had to wrestle with the question of how one could communicate who Christ is in the language and categories shaped by Hinduism and still remain faithful to the gospel. The evangelist must use the language of his hearers. Yet that language reflects a worldview by which the hearers make sense of their world. It expresses deep commitments and beliefs that are irreconcilable with the gospel, and so to use them would be to reshape and distort the gospel message according to those beliefs. How, then, can the gospel be expressed in a way that is faithful to the gospel and yet heard as relevant to that culture?

What Tamil word could be used, for example, to communicate the identity of Jesus? *Swamy* might offer a possibility; it means "Lord." Would this not be like employing *kyrios* in Greek? The problem is that there are many lords in Hindu thought—thirty million of them, according to one tradition—and if Jesus is just one more lord, this is not important news. What about *avatar*? This refers to the descent of God in creaturely form to put down the power of evil and to establish the rule of righteousness. Does this not correspond well with the incarnation and gospel of the kingdom? The problem here is that *avatar* is conceived of in terms of a cyclical worldview. Therefore one cannot ascribe finality to any *avatar* the way the gospel does to Jesus in terms of a more linear historical understanding of the world. Perhaps one could just begin by telling the story of Jesus of Nazareth. But when Newbigin did this he saw listeners melt away, for then Jesus is identified merely with *maya*, the transient and illusory world. All other attempts—*kadavul*, the supreme transcendent God; *adipurushan*, the primal man who is the beginning of all creation; *chit*, the intelligence and will that constitute the second member of the triad of ultimate reality—founder on the same problem. "What all these answers have in common is that they necessarily describe Jesus in terms of a model which embodies an interpretation of experience significantly different from the interpretation which arises when Jesus is accepted as Lord absolutely."[11]

Here in his evangelistic endeavors Newbigin was face-to-face with the problem of gospel and culture. Serious involvement with another culture shook him out of his own comfortable assumption that his was a Christianity untouched by cultural idolatry. It awakened him to the reality that the gospel will always be expressed in and therefore encounter a cultural story that is incompatible with it.

> My confession of Jesus as Lord is conditioned by the culture of which I am a part. It is expressed in the language of the myth within which I live.

11. Lesslie Newbigin, "Christ and Cultures," *Scottish Journal of Theology* 31 (1978): 2–3.

Initially I am not aware of this as a myth. As long as I retain the innocence of a thoroughly indigenous Western man, unshaken by serious involvement in another culture, I am not aware of this myth. It is simply "how things are." . . . No myth is seen as a myth by those who inhabit it: it is simply the way things are. Western man is no exception to this rule.[12]

The second experience that illustrates Newbigin's awakening to the ways our unexamined assumptions shape our worldview occurred when he was teaching the Gospel of Mark to villagers in India. He was teaching the miracle stories and trying to make sense of them in the complex way he had been taught in Cambridge, wherein miracles had to be explained somehow psychologically in terms of a naturalistic worldview. If only he could induct the villager into his own culture through a proper Western education, Newbigin thought, then he would be able to see things as they really are. But his laboring to explain Jesus's miracles drew an impatient response from one unschooled villager: "Why are you making such heavy weather over such a perfectly simple story?" He proceeded to recount a number of healings and exorcisms that had taken place in his village congregation. Newbigin was struck by the fact that the villager was much closer to the meaning of Mark's Gospel than he was. He says that it "was only slowly that I began to see that my own Christianity had this syncretistic character, that I too had to some degree coopted Jesus into the worldview of my culture."[13]

This cross-cultural missionary experience made Newbigin acutely aware of the dynamic of a missionary encounter with culture[14]—an encounter that is always taking place but not often recognized. A missionary encounter is the clash between two comprehensive and religious visions of life that are to some degree incompatible. It is within the context of this missionary encounter that the issue of gospel and culture must be examined.

A missionary encounter is always the normal posture of the church in its cultural setting. It is unavoidable and constitutive of the nature of the gospel and the church's existence. The church may be unaware of the dynamic, but that doesn't mean it isn't operative; it likely means they have capitulated to the powers of the culture. There will always be a missionary encounter—it is essential to the Christian faith. And it will always be worked out in one

12. Newbigin, "Christ and Cultures," 3.
13. Newbigin, *Word in Season*, 99.
14. Newbigin also speaks of a "missionary confrontation" in "Die Kulturelle Gefangenschaft Abendlandischen Christentums als Herausforderung an eine missionarische Kirche," unpublished speech, Newbigin Archives, University of Birmingham (1984), 5.

way or another in a certain embodiment. This is what has been called "contextualization" in missionary circles. And contextualization will always be either "true" if it is faithful or "false" if it is not. It is not a matter of whether the church is involved in a missionary encounter; it is just a matter of whether we are aware of it. And it is not a matter of whether we will contextualize the gospel; it is only a matter of whether we are faithful. It is a matter of life and death for a faithful witness to the gospel.

A Missionary Encounter and the Painful Tension

Newbigin came to understand the nature of a missionary encounter through his cross-cultural missionary experience. A missionary encounter arises, first of all, because all cultures have a religious and comprehensive *credo* at the center or foundation of their life together that is incompatible with the gospel. When Newbigin discusses the nature of culture, he often starts with a rather simple dictionary definition: "the sum total of ways of living built up by a group of human beings and transmitted from one generation to another."[15] This would include language, arts, technology, and law, as well as a culture's social, political, and economic organization. But he immediately identifies something deeper and more ultimate that shapes and gives meaning to all these elements: "One must also include in culture, as fundamental to any culture, a set of beliefs, experiences, and practices that seek to grasp and express the ultimate nature of things, that which gives shape and meaning to life, that which claims final loyalty. I am speaking, obviously, about religion."[16]

Newbigin distinguishes between, on the one hand, a vast network of unified cultural elements that is visible in practices and institutions and, on the other hand, a deeper level of foundational religious beliefs that shape and integrate them all. He speaks in various ways about these foundational beliefs, calling them "committed beliefs,"[17] "basic assumptions and commitments,"[18] "the dogma that controls public life,"[19] "fiduciary frameworks,"[20] "plausibil-

15. Newbigin, "Christ and Cultures," 9; Newbigin, *Foolishness to the Greeks*, 3.
16. Newbigin, *Foolishness to the Greeks*, 3; see Lesslie Newbigin, *The Open Secret: An Introduction to the Theology of Mission*, rev. ed. (Grand Rapids: Eerdmans, 1995), 160–61.
17. Newbigin, *Open Secret*, 146.
18. Lesslie Newbigin, "Mission in the 1980s," *Occasional Bulletin of Missionary Research* 4 (October 1980): 155.
19. Newbigin, *Word in Season*, 150.
20. Lesslie Newbigin, *The Other Side of 1984: Questions for the Churches* (Geneva: World Council of Churches, 1983), 53.

ity structures,"[21] "ideologies, myths, worldviews,"[22] "a creed,"[23] a "credo,"[24] "idols,"[25] and even "gods."[26] He clarifies his distinction between the various components of culture and the underlying religious beliefs in a discussion of Romans 12:1–2. Newbigin often uses the phrase "conformed to culture" from this text, specifically citing it to refer to syncretism. But in one place he discusses the text in more detail. He says that when Paul commands us not to be conformed to the world, he is referring to culture, "which does not mean just art, literature, and music, but the whole way that our world is organised. It means our language, our thought-patterns, our customs, our traditions, our public systems of political, economic, judicial, and administrative order—the whole mass of things which we simply take for granted and never question." In all these areas, the word "world" can be used positively to refer to God's good creation. But it can also be used negatively to speak of a culture "organised around another centre than the creator's."[27] The various aspects of human culture will always be organized around *some* center. Human culture is created to find its center in the Creator God. But with the advent of sin, the Creator is replaced by idols, which integrate, organize, and shape the various facets of human culture in a way counter to God's design. "Human nature abhors a vacuum. The [central] shrine [of public life] does not remain empty. If the one true image, Jesus Christ, is not there, an idol will take its place. It is not difficult to name the idolatry that controls our culture."[28]

The problem in Western culture is that there is a strange assumption that we can discuss religious beliefs "as though they were a separable entity from the entire life of human communities," but this is "possible only in a society that has accepted the privatization of religion."[29] Religion is not one more cultural activity or institution alongside others. Religious commitments permeate and shape all our cultural endeavors even if they go unrecognized.

21. Lesslie Newbigin, *The Gospel in a Pluralist Society* (Grand Rapids: Eerdmans, 1989), 228.

22. Newbigin, *Gospel in a Pluralist Society*, 221.

23. Lesslie Newbigin, *Proper Confidence: Faith, Doubt, and Certainty in Christian Discipleship* (Grand Rapids: Eerdmans, 1995), 50.

24. Lesslie Newbigin, "Gospel and Culture—but Which Culture?," *Missionalia* 17, no. 3 (November 1989): 214.

25. Newbigin, *Word in Season*, 150.

26. Newbigin, *Gospel in a Pluralist Society*, 220; Newbigin, *Word in Season*, 150.

27. Lesslie Newbigin, "Renewal in Mind," *GEAR (Group for Evangelism and Renewal in the URC)* 29 (1983): 4.

28. Newbigin, *Foolishness to the Greeks*, 115.

29. Lesslie Newbigin, "Mission in the 1990s: Two Views," *International Bulletin of Missionary Research* 13, no. 3 (1989): 101.

Neither in practice nor in thought is religion separate from the rest of life. In practice all the life of society is permeated by beliefs which western Europeans would call religious, and in thought what we call religion is a whole worldview, a way of understanding the whole of human experience. The sharp line which modern Western culture has drawn between religious affairs and secular affairs is itself one of the most significant peculiarities of our culture and would be incomprehensible to the vast majority of people who have not been brought into contact with this culture.[30]

In these comments we see two characteristics of the central core that shapes culture. First, it is religious: the beliefs are of an ultimate nature. Second, it is comprehensive: these religious beliefs organize and shape all aspects of human life. Newbigin calls this a "hidden *credo*." The Latin word *credo* is the first word in the Apostles' Creed and means "I believe." *Credo* refers to a set of religious beliefs that give ultimate meaning to all of life. Newbigin gives us the metaphor of a *credo* that is hidden beneath our culture; it functions like the foundation of a house. These beliefs lie unnoticed beneath a culture but give shape and organization to the visible aspects of human culture above. Even though hidden, this *credo* shapes the public life of culture, including in economics, education, medicine, and media.[31]

Perhaps the most common way Newbigin speaks of the cultural *credo* is in terms of a story. The religious beliefs of a culture did not drop out of the sky but developed in the particular history of a cultural community. This is true for all cultures. But the West in particular has understood the meaning of human life in terms of a story as a result of the impact of the Bible on our culture, especially through Augustine. Western culture has a story to tell about itself and about the goal of human history. This is a story that clashes with the gospel.

All Christians are born into a particular culture, and their lives are inevitably narrated by these religious beliefs from their earliest years. Christians, also from their earliest years, breathe the cultural air common to all. Or, to change the metaphor, believers are born into and continue to swim in the waters of their culture. They come to share these comprehensive religious beliefs about the world. The problem is that they are idolatrous and incompatible with the gospel. The cultural water is polluted.

A missionary encounter is inevitable, second, because the gospel makes an equally comprehensive claim and demands absolute allegiance. In earlier chapters, we have seen that the gospel is the good news of the kingdom of

---

30. Newbigin, *Gospel in a Pluralist Society*, 172.
31. Newbigin, "Gospel and Culture—but Which Culture?," 214.

God—the restoration of God's rule over the entirety of human life. This gospel is a counterstory to the one told in culture and demands nothing less than complete and final loyalty. For "if it is really true that God has done what the Gospel tells us he has done . . . it must, it necessarily must become the starting point and the controlling reality of all thought, all action, and all hope."[32] Thus, we have in the gospel and the cultural story two religious and comprehensive visions of life. Both are religious: they demand ultimate commitment and submission. Both are comprehensive: they demand the entire scope of human life. And these stories are incompatible. They will shape, integrate, and unify life in very different ways.

And so, third, a missionary encounter is a clash between two incompatible stories that creates a painful tension. The Christian affirmation that in Christ we know the true story of the world comes into direct conflict with a "different dogma" that shapes the public life of culture. The church that is faithful to the gospel "must necessarily clash with contemporary culture. It must challenge the whole 'fiduciary framework' within which our culture operates."[33] This is the perennial experience of the church in the world when it is faithful. What is at stake for the church in every place and time, if it is true to its witnessing identity, is nothing less than a "clash of ultimate commitments."[34]

With the notion of a missionary encounter, Newbigin seeks to counter a deep syncretism in the Western church that has simply tried to carve out a small "religious" space for the gospel within the cultural story. The sad reality is that when this happens, the church has made peace with the idols of the cultural story by tailoring its own message to fit into it. The Western church has "in general failed to realize how radical is the contradiction between the Christian vision and the assumptions that we breathe in from every part of our shared existence."[35] Newbigin wants to somehow awaken the church, as he was himself, to see afresh this radical contradiction between the gospel and the cultural vision of life.

This clash is not simply a matter of differing worldviews or philosophies of life. There is a religious or spiritual dimension; this is idolatry. Newbigin alerts us to this by his use of the Pauline language of "powers."[36] Idolatry gives

32. Lesslie Newbigin, "The Gospel and Modern Western Culture," unpublished article, Newbigin Archives, University of Birmingham (n.d.), 13.

33. Newbigin, *Other Side of 1984*, 53.

34. Newbigin, *Open Secret*, 154.

35. Lesslie Newbigin, "Evangelism in the City," *Reformed Review* 41 (Autumn 1987): 4.

36. Newbigin's views on the powers are confusing and need clarification, which he himself recognized. See Al Wolters, "Creation and the 'Powers': A Dialogue with Lesslie Newbigin," *Trinity Journal for Theology and Ministry* 4, no. 2 (Fall 2010): 85–98 (special issue, "The Gospel in

a foothold to spiritual powers, and these powers do not take the victory of Christ lying down. The powers will always strive for the established cultural idolatry to become and remain the exclusive controlling vision of life. Thus, if the church is faithful to the gospel, the clash will bring a "painful tension."[37] This "belongs to the essence of the Church's life in the world."[38]

Newbigin illustrates this painful tension with a story from India. He describes a situation where all the members of the church in a village came from the same caste. It is difficult in this situation, he says, for the church to understand its role as God's new humankind and therefore to challenge the assumptions of the old community. It is easy to continue to live life within the caste system. "Yet eventually the Church, as a totally new kind of community, must challenge the older forms of community, and a painful tension is set up. It is part of the mission of the Church to set up such a tension. It must not evade it either by seeking to deny and repudiate all the ties of kinship, or by capitulating to them and allowing them to have control. It must demonstrate its character as something of a wholly different order."[39] The church, as a "totally new kind of community," must challenge in its life the idolatrous social structure of the caste. Quite naturally, a painful tension emerges, one that cannot be evaded by syncretism or withdrawal. And Newbigin is clear that this is an essential dimension to the church's mission. Evading it is to fail to live out our missional vocation.

We need to beware as we hear this story, especially if we are from the West, lest we simply confine this problem to non-Western cultures. It is always easier to see idolatry in others. Readers who are not from India can easily nod in agreement and miss that what Newbigin is describing here ought to be the universal experience of the church. Believers everywhere will experience a painful tension if they are faithful. We may see the idolatry of caste systems, but do we have eyes to see our own idolatry? Churches everywhere must constantly ask the question: What are the idolatrous social, economic, and political structures of our culture?

---

the Public Square: Essays by and in Honor of Lesslie Newbigin"). About Wolters's perspective Newbigin says: "Here I must say that his criticisms have a great deal of weight in them. I think he is right in pointing out the weaknesses of my treatment, both as regards the exegesis of scripture and as regards the internal coherence of my arguments. I have to confess that I ought to do some real rethinking." He goes on to say, though, that he believes "there is more to my argument than Wolters grants." See Lesslie Newbigin, "Response to the Colloquium by Bishop Lesslie Newbigin," unpublished response to Leeds Colloquium (June 1996), 6–7.

37. Lesslie Newbigin, *A South India Diary* (London: SCM, 1951), 49.

38. Lesslie Newbigin, "The Bible Study Lectures," in *Digest of the Proceedings of the Ninth Meeting of the Consultation on Church Union (COCU)*, ed. Paul A. Crow (Princeton: COCU, 1970), 202.

39. Newbigin, *South India Diary*, 49.

In another example, Newbigin describes this painful tension in terms of the "secular-apostolic dilemma."[40] In a paper on education, he grapples with the question of how Christians can be involved in the public school system when there are two different understandings of education based on two different visions of the purpose of human life. The secular state mandates that education fall in line with their purpose of national interest based on their public doctrine. Yet their "secular" involvement in the school system will bring a tension with their "apostolic" calling to be faithful to the gospel. How can Christians fall in line with the idolatrous purpose of public education?

Faithfulness in the midst of this painful tension may bring suffering. Suffering comes because we follow Jesus, whose message of the kingdom challenged all powers that stood in opposition to it. "His ministry entailed the calling of individual men and women to personal and costly discipleship, but at the same time it challenged the principalities and powers, the rulers of this world, and the cross was the price paid for that challenge. Christian discipleship today cannot mean less than that."[41] Suffering is unavoidable if the church follows Jesus in a missionary encounter with idolatrous culture.

> No human societies cohere except on the basis of some kind of common beliefs and customs. No society can permit these beliefs and practices to be threatened beyond a certain point without reacting in self-defence. The idea that we ought to be able to expect some kind of neutral secular political order, which presupposes no religious or ideological beliefs, and which holds the ring impartially for a plurality of religions to compete with one another, has no adequate foundation. The New Testament makes it plain that Christ's followers must expect suffering as the normal badge of their discipleship, and also as one of the characteristic forms of their witness.[42]

Newbigin tells a story that significantly shaped his views on the painful tension and suffering during his bishopric in Madurai.[43] After independence, the government of India required all elementary schools to switch to the Ghandian model of education in which Hindu syncretism was built into the program. A village boy who took up a teaching position in Madurai lost his teaching certificate because he refused to conform and compromise his faith.

40. Lesslie Newbigin, "The Secular-Apostolic Dilemma," in *Not without a Compass: Jesuit Education Association Seminar on Christian Education in India Today,* ed. T. Mathias (New Delhi: Jesuit Educational Association of India, 1972), 72–78.

41. Newbigin, *Gospel in a Pluralist Society,* 220.

42. Lesslie Newbigin, *Trinitarian Doctrine for Today's Mission* (1963; repr., Carlisle, UK: Paternoster, 1998), 46.

43. Newbigin, *South India Diary,* 90–93, 115.

Newbigin reports, "The costly witness of a village boy who was willing to lose his teaching certificate rather than compromise his faith so shook the whole institution that I was soon baptizing students within the college campus."[44] This event convinced Newbigin of three things: the incompatibility of the gospel with the dominant doctrine shaping culture and public institutions, the cost of suffering one must often pay for a faithful witness, and the power suffering may have to draw others to Christ.

There is a fourth point to be made about the nature of the missionary encounter: the painful tension is embodied in the very life of the church as it inhabits both stories. We have seen that the deepest beliefs of our culture, as well as the gospel, are religious and comprehensive. But they are also communally held. They are not the fruit of individual insight, nor are worldviews peculiar to particular individuals. Rather, a religious vision is the product of human life together in a community over time. Worldviews are shared, and they are expressed and transmitted from generation to generation in a common language. They are embodied in shared ways of life in customs, institutions, practices, symbols, and more.

Newbigin speaks of "plausibility structures." This points to a process whereby humans form and construct a culture that expresses and embodies their deepest beliefs about the world. Then as people inhabit those institutions and customs, they are socialized into a way of life and the beliefs embedded in the various cultural products. The church is not exempt from this socialization process. They too inhabit the cultural story and way of life. As they inhabit the cultural institutions, customs, and practices, the beliefs embedded in them become plausible. The church internalizes the fundamental beliefs woven into the cultural way of life and finds it difficult to question them.

The church is a community that inhabits this cultural story. But it is also a community that is called to live in another incompatible story told in Scripture. As they take hold of the gospel, they do not extract themselves from culture but embody and articulate it in the cultural forms they know. This establishes the painful tension at the very heart of the church's life.

This leads Newbigin to an important insight into the nature of the relationship between gospel and culture. Newbigin asks whether, in the way we pose the question of the relation of the gospel to culture, we have already implied "an unacknowledged and disastrous dualism." We treat the gospel-and-culture question "as though it were a matter of the meeting of two quite separate things: a disembodied message and a historically

---

44. Lesslie Newbigin, *Unfinished Agenda: An Updated Autobiography* (Edinburgh: Saint Andrew Press, 1993), 120.

conditioned pattern of social life." The gospel is not "an ethereal something disinfected of all human cultural ingredients."[45] It is always incarnated and expressed in the lifestyle and patterns of a particular culture. The church does not somehow transcend culture when they embrace the gospel; they share the same life and beliefs as members of the cultural community. In other words, the gospel always flows together with cultural beliefs and meets in the life of the church. Neither the gospel nor the culture exists in the abstract—"out there." The church is a community that inhabits both stories: narrated and socialized into the cultural story from birth, then renarrated and resocialized with the biblical story through the hard work of discipleship and formation. And so it is precisely within the very life of the church and in the heart of every believer that gospel and culture meet. A painful tension is the essence of the church's life in the midst of culture; it is the inevitable outcome of living in two communities that embody two incompatible stories.

A final point about the missionary encounter: the term "missionary" qualifies this encounter. Up to this point we have simply been describing an encounter, but it is always qualified by the term "missionary." What does Newbigin mean by that qualifying adjective? Islam also understands the notion of an encounter between two equally religious, comprehensive, and communally embodied visions and ways of life. Sadly, many Muslims probably understand this better than most Christians. But an encounter in the Christian faith differs from that of Islam, and the word "missionary" helps to pinpoint that difference.

The term "missionary" points, first, to the fact that the gospel can be translated into every culture of the world. The gospel is not a comprehensive vision and way of life that must completely displace every element of another vision. While there is a "radical discontinuity," even "radical contradiction" between the gospel and culture, there is not "total discontinuity."[46] This, of course, departs from Islam. One cannot translate the Qur'an from Arabic into any other language. All translations are called interpretations. Moreover, the social, political, and economic vision and way of life expressed in a comprehensive sharia law must displace all other rivals.

Moreover, the witness to the comprehensive vision of the gospel is noncoercive. Our witness must be in the power of the Spirit and not in any coercive methods that would compel people to convert under pressure. The gospel must be embraced freely, and space must be given for a response.

45. Newbigin, *Gospel in a Pluralist Society*, 188.
46. Newbigin, *The Finality of Christ*, 59; Newbigin "Evangelism in the City," 4.

Rejection of the witness and suffering is what may be expected and embraced when it comes. The witness must be the appealing life, deeds, and words of a seemingly weak community rather than the pressure tactics of the strong. Suffering love must characterize the witness of the church. Ultimately the witness to the gospel must be the work of the Spirit. In Islam, since the goal of history is an intrahistorical victory, the Muslim mission may and even must use coercive means to usher in the end. The only question is how far that coercion can go—does it include violence?

"Missionary" points to one more thing: even though the church may not use coercion, this does not imply a weakened commitment to the truth of the message. Quite the opposite, in fact. Adherents to a witness that is missionary in nature believe that its message is universally valid and therefore must be made known to all people. And so, while the church may not use any pressure tactics, it remains steadfast and firm in its commitment to the truth and to the ultimate victory of the gospel when Christ returns. There may be an unanxious and joyful witness that leaves the results in God's hand. Witness will be one of humble yet confident boldness in the truth of the gospel. It will be accompanied by a trust in God's work that follows Jesus's path of suffering love.

The Church for and against the World

If there is a missionary encounter, how can the gospel be translated into a way of life without compromising its all-embracing demands? Or, to approach the issue from the standpoint of the church's mission, how can the church faithfully witness through its life, deeds, and words to the lordship of Christ over all of cultural life in a particular place where other lords rule? Newbigin approaches these questions from the angle of the church's missionary vocation. The church struggles with the issue of a missionary encounter precisely so it can faithfully carry out its vocation to mediate the call of Christ to a people living in a certain place. He insists that the "whole existence of the congregation must be such as to mediate to the people of that place the call of Christ which speaks to them as they are but calls them from what they are in order that—in Christ—they may become God's new creation."[47] The call of Christ affirms their cultural identity—speaks to them as they are. But it also rejects their cultural identity—calls them from what they are to become God's new creation. This raises the question: How is the church to translate

47. Lesslie Newbigin, "What Is 'a Local Church Truly United'?," *Ecumenical Review* 29 (1977): 120.

the gospel into a particular culture in such a way as to faithfully mediate the call of Christ in that context?

The Cross and Resurrection as the Determining Criteria

The starting point for a faithful witness in culture is the cross and resurrection of Jesus Christ; these events form the pattern for the life of the missionary church.[48] The church must be for the world in the same way that Christ is for the world, but the church also must be against the world in the same way that Christ was against the world. Christ's relationship to the world must be the determining criterion. And this is seen most clearly in the cross and resurrection: "The Cross is in one sense an act of total identification with the world. But in another sense it is an act of radical separation. It is both of these at the same time."[49] Both solidarity and separation belong "to the essence of the Church's life in the world."[50] And so, following its Lord, the church must be against the world and for the world.

Earlier we noted Newbigin's observation that the Bible uses the word "world" in two different senses: the world is God's good creation as developed in human culture, and the world is human culture as it is distorted by idolatry. The cross says no to the idolatrous form, and the resurrection says yes to the good creation. "A society which accepts the crucifixion and resurrection of Jesus as its ultimate standards of reference will have to be a society whose whole style of life, and not only its words, conveys something of that radical dissent from the world which is manifested in the Cross, and at the same time something of that affirmation of the world which is made possible by the resurrection."[51]

So to mediate the call of Christ faithfully, the church must assume a twofold posture toward its culture. On the one hand, the church will identify with its culture, living in solidarity with and affirming it, while mediating the call in terms and forms that are familiar. On the other hand, the church will be separate from its culture, living in opposition to and rejecting its idolatry, mediating a challenging call to repentance and conversion. A loss of either side of this double stance will compromise the church's witness. We need to probe further this twofold orientation.

---

48. Lesslie Newbigin, "Bible Study Lectures," 195.

49. Lesslie Newbigin, *The Good Shepherd: Meditations on Christian Ministry in Today's World* (Grand Rapids: Eerdmans, 1977), 98.

50. Newbigin, "Bible Study Lectures," 202.

51. Lesslie Newbigin, "Stewardship, Mission, and Development" (address, Annual Stewardship Conference of the British Council of Churches, Stanwick, 1970), 6.

A Twofold Posture for Faithful Witness

Newbigin begins with affirmation: the church is for the world.[52] It is precisely because the church loves and identifies with its culture that it opposes the idolatry that distorts the fullness of life in God's good creation. The church is against the world precisely because it is for it. The starting point is God's love and faithfulness to his creation, and that must be the starting point for his followers. Because God loves his creation and human culture, he hates the sin that corrupts it and ruins the lives of its inhabitants.

The reason that the missionary church must take this stance of affirmation and solidarity is the confession that creation is very good. This includes human cultural development as a part of that good creation. Newbigin distinguishes between the good creation and the distortion of evil. "The world is itself not evil, but is under an evil power."[53] Sin is pervasive in its scope, and it pollutes all parts of human culture. But the creation and cultural development remain good. Thus, the church must be at home in its cultural setting and participate in its development for the flourishing of all. That is what it means to be human. It must affirm all of the created goodness its history has uncovered.

The affirmation of the creational good of culture will lead to a full identification and solidarity of the church with its culture. It will adopt its language, customs, symbols, institutions, and systems. The good news then may be embodied and communicated in understandable and familiar patterns.[54]

The other side of the stance the church must take is that it is against the world. Not only is the church at home in its culture; it is also at odds with it. Not only does it participate in cultural development; it also calls for repentance and conversion. There is to be not only identification with the world but also radical dissent from it. The reason for this is that sin and idolatry have twisted every aspect of it. The gospel comes as both a yes and a no—a word of salvation and a word of judgment. And both come at the same time on every part of culture.

Newbigin speaks strongly and often about this side of the church's posture. He speaks of the church in terms of a "dissenting otherworldliness" and as

---

52. Newbigin, *Word in Season*, 53–54.

53. Lesslie Newbigin, "Bible Studies on John 17: Just Who Is the Enemy?," *Lutheran Standard (USA)*, May 2, 1967, 12; Lesslie Newbigin, "What Is a 'Local Church Truly United'?," in *In Each Place: Towards a Fellowship of Local Churches Truly United*, ed. J. E. L. Newbigin (Geneva: World Council of Churches, 1977), 119.

54. Newbigin, *Gospel in a Pluralist Society*, 141.

"discriminating non-conformists."[55] We are to be "radical dissenters,"[56] "radical critics and misfits" with a relationship of conflict, contradiction, and radical discontinuity with the world.[57] "There is a stark contrast between the faith by which the Church lives and the mind of the world."[58]

Thus the Christian church lives as a minority in its culture, "questioning the things that no one ever questions." The church offers another story—the true story—which has a more rational and comprehensive way of understanding and living in the world. We live in a "different fiduciary framework" that is "an alternative to the one that is dominant in our culture." Our life and words call our neighbors to conversion—a radical shift in perspective. To question what no one questions and invite others into this alternative story requires "the boldness of a foreign missionary who dares to challenge the accepted framework, even though the words he uses must inevitably sound absurd to those who dwell in that framework."[59] So our lives and message will be familiar but will also appear absurd.

We noted that Newbigin begins with solidarity and affirmation. But it is also true that he speaks more often of separation and rejection—the church against the world. This has led some to characterize Newbigin's thought as counter- or even anticultural.[60] But Newbigin was a deeply contextual thinker; the problems he encountered needed the emphasis of a radical dissent of the church from culture. We especially see this in two places: as he engaged the World Council of Churches and as he developed his Mission and Western Culture project. He believed that the World Council of Churches often identified with culture to the point of departing from the gospel. He also believed that the Western church was an advanced case of syncretism. Both had "failed to realize how radical is the contradiction between the Christian vision and the assumptions we breathe in from every part of our shared existence."[61]

55. Lesslie Newbigin, *Behold, I Make All Things New* (Madras: Christian Literature Society, 1968), 26.

56. Newbigin, "Stewardship, Mission, and Development," 6.

57. Newbigin, *Behold, I Make All Things New*, 26.

58. Lesslie Newbigin, "Bible Studies Given at the National Christian Council Triennial Assembly, Shillong," *National Christian Council Review* 88 (1968): 13.

59. Newbigin, *Open Secret*, 112.

60. See Stephen B. Bevans, *Models of Contextual Theology*, rev. ed. (Maryknoll, NY: Orbis, 2002), 117–37; Sander Griffioen, "Newbigin's Philosophy of Culture," trans. Al Wolters, *Trinity Journal for Theology and Ministry* 4, no. 2 (Fall 2010): 99–111 (special issue, "The Gospel in the Public Square: Essays by and in Honor of Lesslie Newbigin"). I have responded to this charge in Michael W. Goheen, "Is Lesslie Newbigin's Model of Contextualization Anticultural?," *Mission Studies* 19, no. 1 (2002): 136–56.

61. Newbigin, "Evangelism in the City," 4.

Both led him to stress the negative and antithetical side of cultural engagement. If there is a very large person sitting on one side of the teeter-totter, it is necessary to jump very hard on the other side. And this is what Newbigin is doing: jumping hard on the side of opposition to the idolatry of culture.

The rejection of cultural idolatry will lead the church to a radical separation from and opposition to its culture. Precisely because the church loves and identifies with its culture, it will oppose the idolatry that destroys the flourishing of human life. Even as it adopts its culture's language, customs, symbols, institutions, and systems, the church will do so critically aware of its idolatrous shaping. The good news, although necessarily embodied and communicated in understandable and familiar patterns, will always issue a call to repentance and conversion. There will be an invitation to join the new humankind that will one day fill the new creation. This is a call not to reject culture but to embody a sign of what that place is meant to be.

The question that arises is whether Newbigin is simply speaking out of two sides of his mouth. Do we not really have an outright contradiction between identification and opposition, affirmation and rejection, yes and no, at home and at odds? Newbigin resolves the painful tension with the notions of "subversive fulfillment" and "challenging relevance." But before we discuss those terms, we note briefly two ways of avoiding the painful tension that Newbigin rejected.

Avoiding the Painful Tension

Newbigin often contrasts two ways of avoiding the painful tension: irrelevance and syncretism.[62] The experience of being a cross-cultural missionary had taught him that there are always two opposite dangers, the Scylla and Charybdis, between which one must steer. On the one side, there is the fear of the idolatrous culture. This leads to an attempt to withdraw from the culture into a ghetto. One may withdraw to another form of perceived faithfulness that comes either from another place or from another time. Thus the gospel is made irrelevant, and the witness of the church is subverted. When the church attempts to freeze the gospel in another time or transport it from another place to protect it from the idolatrous forces of culture, it becomes a petrified fossil, the dead remnant of life from another time. On the other side, there is an attempt to so identify with the culture that the church ends up uncritically taking on the idols of the culture. The church is absorbed into and domesticated by the cultural story. This is syncretism,

---

62. Newbigin, *Word in Season*, 67; Newbigin, *Foolishness to the Greeks*, 7.

and this too leads to the subversion of a faithful witness. This is the life of a chameleon that takes on the color of its surroundings or a jellyfish that is moved to and fro with the tide.[63]

Newbigin believed that the evangelical tradition, rightly concerned to protect the truth of the gospel, resembles the first danger. It ends up in a sterile and repellent sectarianism that shuns culture and often lives in polemical confrontation with it. Evangelicals attempt to be faithful by holding on to theology and forms from another time. Theirs is a separation without solidarity. The ecumenical tradition is threatened by the second danger. Christians in the ecumenical tradition are motivated by a genuine concern to sympathize and identify with the struggles of humankind, attempting to be relevant to the needs of the world and meet the world on its own terms; theirs is a solidarity without separation that ended "near or at the point of apostasy."[64]

In reality, though, it is impossible to withdraw. One cannot escape culture. And so the attempt to withdraw will only take place in certain confined areas of life. The rest will be vulnerable to syncretism. This is clear enough in Newbigin's analysis of evangelicalism. While he critiques them for their repellent sectarianism and irrelevance, he also interprets their approach to the Christian faith as syncretistic in a variety of ways. It is quite common, for example, for Newbigin to place those from the evangelical and ecumenical traditions on different sides of the fact-value dichotomy. In that case, both have capitulated to the religious vision of the Enlightenment.

So Newbigin's biggest concern throughout his life is that the painful tension would be resolved in terms of syncretism—a capitulation in life and word to the idolatry of culture. For him the "crucial question" is, What is the story that we think we are really a part of? He answers, "If the biblical story is not the one that really controls our thinking then inevitably we shall be swept into the story that the world tells about itself. We shall become increasingly indistinguishable from the pagan world of which we are a part."[65]

This syncretism is almost always unacknowledged. There usually is real sincerity in confessing Christ. Yet there may be a difference between one's professed religion and one's real religion. A person's real religion may be

63. Lesslie Newbigin, *The Reunion of the Church: A Defence of the South India Scheme* (London: SCM, 1948), 142. Newbigin speaks of a "jelly fish" and "petrified fossils." The imagery of a chameleon comes from Jürgen Moltmann, *The Experiment Hope*, trans. M. Douglas Meeks (Philadelphia: Fortress, 1975), 3.

64. Newbigin, "Bible Studies on John 17: Just Who Is the Enemy?," 12.

65. Lesslie Newbigin, "Biblical Authority," unpublished article, Newbigin Archives, University of Birmingham (1997), 2.

something quite other than what he or she professes. Someone's real religion is what is "ultimately authoritative" in all of their thinking and acting. If, for example, Christians limit the gospel to a restricted area of life and allow the modern scientific worldview to shape the rest of their public lives, then their real religion is not the gospel they profess but the cultural worldview that actually shapes their lives. "In this case the commitment to Christ will be conditioned by the person's commitment to the overriding 'myth,' and the latter will be his or her real religion."[66] This is one of the urgent reasons that Christians need to be awakened from a syncretistic slumber to the missionary encounter that should be integral to their faith.

Subversive Fulfillment and Challenging Relevance

In light of the above discussion, how do we live faithfully in the painful tension that arises from living in two incompatible stories? How can the church be both for and against the world? This is especially pressing if every cultural product and institution is both creationally good and idolatrously twisted and the two are inextricably intertwined.

Faithful contextualization, for Newbigin, can be summarized in the terms "subversive fulfillment" and "challenging relevance." He borrows the term "challenging relevance" from veteran Indian missionary Alfred Hogg[67] and the term "subversive fulfillment" from his two primary mentors, Hendrik Kraemer and Willem Visser 't Hooft.[68] The coupling of "challenging" and "relevance" shows that Newbigin is looking for a way to both employ and indwell familiar and relevant cultural forms while at the same time challenging the idolatry embedded in them. Subversive fulfillment is an attempt to express the same thing. The gospel fulfills the creational longings or design or structure but subverts the idolatry that has twisted it. Both expressions recognize that all cultural products—language, institutions, customs, and so forth—have both a creational structure and an idolatrous distortion. Both want to hold on to what is creational and reject the idolatrous.

66. Newbigin, *Open Secret*, 161.

67. Alfred G. Hogg, *The Christian Message to the Hindu: Being the Duff Missionary Lectures for Nineteen Forty Five on the Challenge of the Gospel in India* (London: SCM, 1947), 9–26.

68. Kraemer uses the term "subversive fulfilment" in Hendrik Kraemer, "Continuity and Discontinuity," in *The Authority of Faith*, Madras Series 1 (New York: International Missionary Council, 1939), 4. Following Kraemer, Visser 't Hooft uses the term "subversive accommodation" in Willem A. Visser 't Hooft, "Accommodation: True and False," *South East Asia Journal of Theology* 8, no. 3 (January 1967): 13; see also Lesslie Newbigin, "The Legacy of W. A. Visser 't Hooft," *International Bulletin of Missionary Research* 16, no. 2 (1992): 80.

Two biblical examples make this clear. The first, and the one that functions quite often as a model for Newbigin, is the way the Gospel of John communicates the gospel. John freely uses the language and thought forms of classical religion and culture that formed the world of his hearers. The classical dualisms of word-flesh, spirit-body, heaven-earth, light-darkness, and more are all the fruit of pagan idolatry. Nevertheless, John uses this language and these thought forms in such a way as to confront them with a fundamental question and indeed a contradiction. For example, John begins with the announcement, "In the beginning was the *logos*." As he continues it becomes apparent that *logos* is not the impersonal law of rationality that permeated the universe, giving it meaning and order, as his pagan hearers would have assumed, but is rather the man Jesus Christ. John identifies the classical longing for order but subverts, challenges, and contradicts the idolatrous distortion of the classical world. Newbigin writes, "I suppose that the boldest and most brilliant essay in the communication of the gospel to a particular culture in all Christian history is the gospel according to John. Here the language and thought-forms of that Hellenistic world are so employed that Gnostics in all ages have thought that the book was written especially for them. And yet nowhere in Scripture is the absolute contradiction between the word of God and human culture stated with more terrible clarity."[69]

On the one hand, John embraces the creational longing to know the origin of order and meaning in the world. This question is intrinsic to the very creational makeup of humanity. This longing is good and can be affirmed. However, the answer that is given is shaped by classical idolatry. The *logos* is an idolatrous fiction of the pagan mind. So, on the other hand, John subverts the Hellenistic religious vision and contradicts its accepted rationality. He challenges the pagan answer and offers Jesus as the true source. The language is baptized, cleansed of the idolatry while affirming the true creational intent. The language of *logos* or eternal life, for example, is burst open, emptied of its idolatry given by the framework of the classical-pagan worldview, and filled with new meaning.

It is important to see that Newbigin is not just talking here about a strategy for verbal communication. Rather, this model of communication is a way of understanding the whole way we relate to culture. Language is only one of the cultural forms that have been shaped by deeper religious beliefs. We deal with all institutions and structures within a culture—economic, political, artistic, educational, technological, family, judicial, and so forth—in this way. We discern the creational design and the idolatrous distortion. We do not destroy the cultural practice in an anarchist way because there is creational

69. Newbigin, *Foolishness to the Greeks*, 53.

good. Nor do we maintain the custom in a conservative way because it is sinfully twisted. Rather, the goal is "to subvert them from within and thereby to bring them back under the allegiance of their true Lord." This is how Paul deals with the various cultural forms and structures of Rome. "The structure is not simply to be smashed. . . . It is to be subverted from within."[70]

An example of the way Newbigin approaches various issues of mission in the public square with this kind of distinction is his discussions of power and especially political power. The first time he discusses this issue is in the 1970s when, after the Bangkok Conference, there were many attacks on so-called First-World churches that held overwhelming economic, political, cultural, and ecclesiastical power. This rejection, he believed, was a naïve sort of philosophical anarchism and gnostic rejection of power as evil. To treat all power as evil is to fall into the Manichaean heresy, which does not distinguish between the good creation and sinful corruption.[71] Yet, for Newbigin, power is a good part of the creation, and the problem is the misuse and abuse of power.[72] Power is creationally good and is God's gift for some to serve others. The abuse of power comes from idolatrous corruption. The need of the hour is "help for those entrusted with power to learn how to use it."[73] Political tyranny embodies both the creational goodness of political power and the sinful distortion of oppressive abuse.[74]

The church's task is to faithfully translate the gospel into each culture so that the witness to the good news is both challenging and relevant, fulfilling the creational intent and longing while subverting the idolatry. The trouble is that every cultural institution, custom, and practice is both creationally good and idolatrously twisted. How can one distinguish between the two? And how can one faithfully embrace and embody all the good creational gifts? This is incredibly difficult and demands discernment.[75]

The Process of True Contextualization

The process of discernment that leads to true contextualization involves three things: an ultimate commitment to the biblical story, a dialogue with culture, and an ecumenical dialogue with Christians from other cultures.

70. Newbigin, *Truth to Tell*, 82.
71. Newbigin, *Foolishness to the Greeks*, 102.
72. Lesslie Newbigin, "The Taste of Salvation at Bangkok," *Indian Journal of Theology* 22 (1973): 51; Newbigin, *Foolishness to the Greeks*, 126.
73. Newbigin, *Foolishness to the Greeks*, 126.
74. Newbigin, *Word in Season*, 143–44.
75. Newbigin, *Gospel in a Pluralist Society*, 195–96.

Allegiance to the Biblical Story

Faithful contextualization requires, in the first place, an ultimate allegiance to the biblical story. Newbigin says that true contextualization "must begin and continue by attending to what God has done in the story of Israel and supremely in the story of Jesus Christ. It must continue by indwelling that story so that it is our story, the way we understand the real story."[76] For Newbigin, to begin with Scripture and offer our ultimate allegiance to the gospel means at least three things: understanding Scripture as a narrative of universal history, the church's indwelling of this story, and discerning the gospel's yes and no to the cultural story.

Newbigin states categorically, "I do not believe that we can speak effectively of the Gospel addressed to our culture unless we recover a sense of the Scriptures as a canonical whole, as the story which provides the true context for our understanding of the meaning of our lives—both personal and public."[77] If Scripture is fragmented into bits, whether those bits are historical-critical, theological, moral, devotional, or narrative, then the Bible will be absorbed into the bigger cultural story. There will be no encounter. "If this biblical story is not the one that really controls our thinking then inevitably we shall be swept into the story that the world tells about itself. We shall become increasingly indistinguishable from the pagan world of which we are a part."[78]

The church must indwell this biblical story and interpret the culture from within it. The "gospel gives rise to a new plausibility structure, a radically different vision of things from those that shape all human cultures apart from the gospel. The Church, therefore, as the bearer of the gospel, inhabits a plausibility structure which is at variance with, and which calls into question, those that govern all human cultures without exception."[79] The continual danger is that we interpret the Bible from within the culture rather than the other way around. "Do you try to understand the gospel through the spectacles provided by your culture, or do you try to understand your culture through the spectacles provided by the gospel?"[80] The gospel must hold ultimate priority, and the cultural story must be subjected to the scrutiny of the Bible. The gospel is to become like a pair of spectacles through which we view, interpret, and live in the world. The biblical story "provides us with such a set of lenses, not something for us to look *at*, but for us to look *through*. . . .

76. Newbigin, *Gospel in a Pluralist Society*, 151.
77. Lesslie Newbigin, "Response to 'Word of God?,' John Coventry, SJ," *Gospel and Our Culture Newsletter* 10 (1991): 3.
78. Newbigin, "Biblical Authority," 2.
79. Newbigin, *Gospel in a Pluralist Society*, 9.
80. Newbigin, *Word in Season*, 99.

This calls for a more radical kind of conversion than has often been thought, a conversion not only of the will but of the mind, a transformation by the renewing of the mind so as not to be conformed to this world, not to see things as our culture sees them, but—with new lenses—to see things in a radically different way."[81]

To be able to do this, we will need to remember and rehearse the story through individual and communal reading and reflection on the biblical story so that we indwell the story and it becomes ours.[82] We need "to soak ourselves in this story so that we more and more understand that it is the real story and that the story we are listening to on the radio and in our newspapers is to a very large extent phoney."[83]

As we indwell the biblical story, we attempt to discern the word of grace and judgment that Scripture pronounces on our culture. "True contextualization accords the gospel its rightful primacy, its power to penetrate every culture and to speak within each culture, in its own speech and symbol, the word which is both No and Yes, both judgment and grace."[84]

Dialogue with Culture

By what process do we discern the yes and the no, the grace and the judgment of the gospel on our culture? Faithful contextualization demands, second, a dialogue with culture in which the cultural story is always brought under the scrutiny of the biblical story. Newbigin writes, "We must always, it seems to me, in every situation, be wrestling with both sides of this reality: that the Church is for the world against the world. The Church is against the world for the world."[85] Newbigin describes this as an internal dialogue with culture that takes place in the heart of each Christian and a communal dialogue with culture within the church. The people of God are to more and more indwell the biblical story "as the true story of which our story is a part." But we are fully socialized into our cultural story as well. "By all our cultural formation from infancy onward, we are made part of the story of our nation and our civilization." The competing understandings of the world are internalized, and "there is necessarily an internal dialogue within us."[86] The clash of two incompatible

81. Newbigin, *Gospel in a Pluralist Society*, 38.

82. Newbigin, *Gospel in a Pluralist Society*, 147.

83. Newbigin, "Biblical Authority," 6.

84. Newbigin, *Gospel in a Pluralist Society*, 152.

85. Newbigin, *Word in Season*, 54.

86. Lesslie Newbigin, "Truth and Authority in Modernity," in *Faith and Modernity*, ed. Philip Sampson, Vinay Samuel, and Chris Sugden (Oxford: Regnum Books, 1994), 76. See also Newbigin, *Gospel in a Pluralist Society*, 65.

stories makes this internal dialogue inevitable. Indeed, if it does not occur, it is likely that the biblical story has been accommodated to the cultural story.

If this dialogue is to lead to growing discernment, three things we have discussed earlier in the chapter will be important. The first is that we must immerse ourselves more and more in the biblical story. This will be both an individual and a communal task. The cultural story will naturally form us, but it takes hard work to indwell the biblical story.[87] Second, there is a need for a missionary analysis of the cultural story. This will require the church to understand the religious beliefs of the culture, the story that has formed those beliefs, and how those beliefs are embodied in the culture. To the degree the church does not understand its own cultural story, it is vulnerable to its idolatry. This is why Newbigin spends so much time rehearsing and analyzing the Western story from so many different angles. And finally, we need an understanding of subversive fulfillment. Discernment involves distinguishing between the creational structural good in every cultural institution and product and the idolatrous distortion that misdirects it. If the church is to subvert the cultural structures and practices within which it lives and bring them back under the allegiance of their true Lord, then it must distinguish between the design of the creation and its idolatrous spirit.

This is an ongoing process that will take place in the life and heart of every believer. But this internal dialogue must not only be an individual affair. Contextualization takes place in the life of the congregation that rehearses and remembers the story the Bible tells in Word and sacrament and that together brings the biblical story to bear on its culture.[88]

Ecumenical Dialogue across Cultures

There is a danger that even a vigorous dialogue with culture may result in a local contextualization being absorbed into the idolatry of that place. And so faithful contextualization requires, finally, an ecumenical dialogue with the church outside of one's own culture. There is the need for new eyes that come from believers from other cultures. Thus, writes Newbigin, the dialogue must move beyond cultural boundaries and be "open to the witness of the church in all other places." Only thus will the church be "saved from absorption into the culture of that place and enabled to represent to that place the universality, the catholicity of God's purpose of grace and judgment for all humanity."[89]

87. Newbigin, *Gospel in a Pluralist Society*, 65, 147.
88. Newbigin, *Gospel in a Pluralist Society*, 147–48.
89. Newbigin, *Gospel in a Pluralist Society*, 152.

This dialogue will involve both mutual enrichment and mutual correction. All contextualizations of the gospel are incomplete: there is a need in every church for enrichment. All contextualizations of the gospel are also to some degree shaped by the idolatry of their place: there is a need for mutual correction.[90] Our understanding of the gospel will be shaped by the cultures that have formed us. The only way we can be shaken out of these culturally conditioned interpretations of the gospel is through the correcting witness of other believers who have read the Bible within the context of other cultures.

There are real hurdles to be faced if this kind of dialogue is to become a reality. On the one hand, this dialogue at present only takes place within the language and thought forms of Western culture. Because of the dominance of this cultural pattern, Christians living in the West do not receive from Christians in other cultures the correction they need.[91] On the other hand, the forum in which this dialogue has most often taken place has been the World Council of Churches. But this body has become increasingly infected by a pluralism and loss of confidence in the truth of the gospel.[92] Moreover, many Pentecostal and evangelical churches with insight to offer remain outside this fellowship. These are not easy problems to solve.

Newbigin points to the possibility of this dialogue arising from the return of cross-cultural missionaries to their own culture. The cross-cultural missionary has the gift of new eyes to see their own culture critically. At the same time, they know their own culture and are able to translate that insight for the church. Newbigin, of course, is a sterling example of this dynamic.

Conclusion

Throughout the biblical story and church history, cultural idolatry has constantly threatened to derail the church's witness to the End of universal history. In his understanding of a missionary encounter with culture, Newbigin has offered a gift and a challenge. As a cross-cultural missionary, he offers a gift: he is acutely aware of the essential reality of a missionary encounter and has wrestled with ways to faithfully live in the painful tension it fostered. His challenge to embrace the painful tension of a missionary encounter and pursue a path of faithful contextualization is a call we must embrace if we are to be faithful to our missionary vocation.

90. Newbigin, "Christ and Cultures," 13; Newbigin, *Gospel in a Pluralist Society*, 196; Newbigin, *Open Secret*, 149–50.
91. Newbigin, *Open Secret*, 152.
92. Newbigin, *Word in Season*, 125.

6

A Missionary Encounter
with Western Culture

According to Newbigin, "The Church exists to embody and to tell the story which is the true story."[1] The church makes the "stupendous claim" that "the story it tells, embodies, and enacts is the true story . . . the true interpretation of all human and cosmic history." If this is so, there are two implications. The first is that all "others are to be evaluated by reference to it . . . and that to understand history otherwise is to misunderstand it, and therefore misunderstanding the human situation here and now."[2] The second is that the church "is bound to call into question any plausibility structure which is founded on other assumptions."[3] If the biblical story is true, then all other cultural stories misunderstand the nature of the world and the meaning of human life. The church's very existence is to live and tell the biblical story as the true story in such a way as to call its cultural story into question and invite conversion. This is what is involved in a missionary encounter.

This is exactly where Newbigin believed the Western church had lost its way. If he is correct, it is no small failure: the very reason for the existence of the church is endangered. He was at pains to communicate that this was

1. Lesslie Newbigin, "The Gospel and Modern Western Culture," unpublished article, Newbigin Archives, University of Birmingham (1993), 12.
2. Lesslie Newbigin, *Proper Confidence: Faith, Doubt, and Certainty in Christian Discipleship* (Grand Rapids: Eerdmans, 1995), 76–77.
3. Newbigin, *Proper Confidence*, 93.

a serious matter. Surely "the most urgent task facing the universal church at this time" is to recover a missionary encounter with Western culture.[4]

The Urgency of a Missionary Encounter between the Gospel and Western Culture

Newbigin believes that there is "no higher priority" than "to ask the question of what would be involved in a genuinely missionary encounter between the gospel and this modern Western culture."[5] He offers five reasons why this task is so urgent.

First, Western culture is the most *powerful* global force at work in the world today. In the process of globalization, Western culture now "has more worldwide influence than any other culture, including that of Islam."[6] "What we call the modern Western scientific worldview, the post-Enlightenment cultural world, is the most powerful and persuasive ideology in the world today."[7] The nations of the world are eager to adopt this understanding of the world, and urban areas in particular have been drawn into this story.

Second, it is the most *pervasive* cultural force in today's world. It has spread through the process of globalization to all the urban areas of the world. It has become a global culture. "Among all the cultures with power in the contemporary world, the culture which originated in Western Europe is the most powerful and pervasive. It dominates the cities of most of the world. What is called 'modernization' in Asia and Africa is usually co-option into this way of thinking and behaving."[8]

Third, Western culture is the most *dangerous* foe the church has ever faced in its long history. "The church is awakening slowly to the fact that modernity is the most powerful enemy it has faced in its two thousand years of history."[9]

4. Lesslie Newbigin, "Culture of Modernity," in *Dictionary of Mission: Theology, History, Perspectives,* ed. Karl Muller, Theo Sundermeier, Steven B. Bevans, and Richard H. Bliese (Maryknoll, NY: Orbis, 1997), 98. For an analysis of Newbigin's mission and Western culture project, see Michael W. Goheen, "Liberating the Gospel from Its Modern Cage: An Interpretation of Lesslie Newbigin's Gospel and Modern Culture Project," *Missionalia* 30, no. 3 (November 2002): 360–75; Michael W. Goheen, *"As the Father Has Sent Me, I Am Sending You": J. E. Lesslie Newbigin's Missionary Ecclesiology* (Zoetermeer: Boekencentrum, 2000), 371–416 (chap. 9).

5. Lesslie Newbigin, *Foolishness to the Greeks: The Gospel and Western Culture* (Grand Rapids: Eerdmans, 1986), 3.

6. Newbigin, "Culture of Modernity," 98–99.

7. Lesslie Newbigin, *A Word in Season: Perspectives on Christian World Missions* (Grand Rapids: Eerdmans, 1994), 67.

8. Lesslie Newbigin, *Mission and the Crisis of Western Culture*, ed. Jock Stein (Edinburgh: Handsel, 1989), 1.

9. Lesslie Newbigin, *Living Hope in a Changing World* (London: Alpha International, 2003), 83.

Newbigin often employed a metaphor used by Walter Lippman of the "acids of modernity," which have proved powerful in dissolving the Christian faith wherever this culture has penetrated. "The Christian gospel continues to find new victories among the non-Western, premodern cultures of the world, but in the face of this modern Western culture the Church is everywhere in retreat."[10] The churches of the West are in retreat at present, and there is nothing to suggest that as modernity penetrates other non-Western cultures the same thing won't happen to those churches as well.[11] "In all the great and growing urban centres of the world, 'modernisation' is in progress and is spreading its influence even into the remotest villages. Everywhere it has the effect of marginalising religion—including the Christian religion. It is, without possibility of doubt, the most powerful and pervasive of human cultures. Wherever it goes it becomes the controlling doctrine for public life and drives religion into a smaller and smaller enclave."[12]

Fourth, "it is precisely this powerful culture which is most *resistant* to the Gospel."[13] The long association of Western culture with the Christian faith appears to make it immune to the critique of the gospel. Western culture has deep Christian roots but has rejected the gospel as public doctrine, relegating it to the sphere of private opinion. It has developed many powerful defenses against the gospel that make it difficult to mount a missionary encounter.

> The peaceful co-existence of Christianity with post-Enlightenment culture . . . has endured so long that it is hard for the Church now to recover the standpoint for a genuinely missionary approach to our "modern" culture. . . . The Church has lived so long as a permitted and even privileged minority, accepting relegation to the private sphere in a culture whose public life is controlled by a totally different vision of reality, that it has almost lost the power to address a radical challenge to that vision and therefore to "modern Western civilization" as a whole.[14]

Most powerful, most pervasive, most dangerous, and most resistant to the gospel—surely this global culture constitutes an enormous challenge. Yet it is the fifth reason, perhaps more than the others, that makes the issue so urgent: the church in the West is living in a state of *syncretism* with this

10. Newbigin, *Word in Season*, 66.
11. Newbigin, *Word in Season*, 185.
12. Lesslie Newbigin, "Gospel and Culture—but Which Culture?," *Missionalia* 17, no. 3 (1989): 213.
13. Newbigin, *Mission and the Crisis of Western Culture*, 1 (my emphasis).
14. Lesslie Newbigin, *The Other Side of 1984: Questions for the Churches* (Geneva: World Council of Churches, 1983), 22–23.

culture. Instead of challenging its idolatry, it has been content to live in a "cozy domestication with the 'modern' worldview."[15] The problem is with the church: it has accepted the cultural story as the true story and allowed the gospel that it exists to tell and embody to be accommodated to the more comprehensive cultural narrative. This constitutes the biggest problem.

And so Newbigin does not primarily address the unbelieving world. Indeed, one should expect those outside the church to dismiss the Christian faith as a private option; this is precisely how grand narratives work. It is the church that must be addressed, since they have accepted a place in the private sphere and been unfaithful to the gospel entrusted to them. "The churches have so largely accepted relegation to the private sector, leaving the public sector to be controlled by the other story."[16] Even Western missionaries live in "symbiotic alliance with their culture"[17] and have analyzed every other culture in terms of contextualization but, surprisingly, have "largely ignored the culture that is most widespread, powerful, and persuasive among all the contemporary cultures—namely, what I have called modern Western culture."[18] Newbigin is not utilizing apologetics to convince people outside the church. He is directing his critique and challenge to the church so that they might again understand and gain confidence in their own gospel—"everything depends on a recovery of confidence in the gospel."[19] When he examines and exposes the idolatrous roots of Western culture, it is so that Christians may more confidently affirm their faith.[20] For Newbigin the most powerful apologetic is a church that believes the gospel and lives by it.

Loss of a Missionary Encounter: An Advanced Case of Syncretism

Upon his return to England after almost forty years of missionary service in India, Newbigin found the West to be as much of a mission field as the nation of India he had entered four decades earlier. He found a "very tough form of paganism," which he believed was "the greatest intellectual and practical task facing the church."[21] The problem was not simply the tremendous

15. Lesslie Newbigin, "Pluralism in the Church," *ReNews (Presbyterians for Renewal)* 4, no. 2 (May 1993): 1.

16. Newbigin, *Word in Season*, 156.

17. Newbigin, "Culture of Modernity," 99.

18. Newbigin, *Foolishness to the Greeks*, 2–3.

19. Newbigin, *Word in Season*, 187.

20. Lesslie Newbigin, *The Gospel in a Pluralist Society* (Grand Rapids: Eerdmans, 1989), 7 (my emphasis).

21. Lesslie Newbigin, *Unfinished Agenda: An Updated Autobiography* (Edinburgh: Saint Andrew Press, 1993), 236.

power of the global culture he found, although that was true. It was that the church was not living out its vocation in terms of a missionary encounter with this culture.

Just prior to his return he had been sitting next to an Indonesian leader at a missionary conference in Bangkok and heard him mutter under his breath, "Of course the number one question is: Can the West be converted?"[22] This question reverberated in his mind afterward. As a missionary he understood well the ever-lurking danger of syncretism. When the church's message and life is accommodated to the idols of the culture, the church is unfaithful to its very being and vocation. He believed that this was what had happened to the church in the West. He characterized it as a "timid syncretism"[23] and made the serious charge that the Western church was "an advanced case of syncretism. . . . Instead of confronting our culture with the gospel, we are perpetually trying to fit the gospel into our culture."[24] This is the "cultural captivity of Western Christianity."[25] Western Christians are often quick to point out the syncretism in the churches of Asia and Africa, but the "most obvious examples of syncretism . . . are to be found in the Western churches, which have worked so hard to tailor the gospel to fit the so-called requirements of modern thought."[26]

On a number of occasions Newbigin offers an arresting image of just how serious he is in making this charge. In the great hall of Ramakrishna Temple, there is a gallery of all the great religious teachers of humankind. Among them is a portrait of Jesus. Each year on Christmas Day, Hindus offer their worship to Jesus as one of many manifestations of deity in human history. Newbigin comments, it was "obvious to me as an English Christian that this was an example of syncretism. Jesus had simply been co-opted into the Hindu worldview; that view was in no way challenged." He continues, "It was only slowly that I began to see that my own Christianity had this syncretistic character, that I too had—in a measure—co-opted Jesus into the worldview of my culture."[27] Jesus had been absorbed into the Hindu worldview accepted as one of many in the pantheon of gods. Similarly the

22. Lesslie Newbigin, "Can the West Be Converted?," *Princeton Seminary Bulletin* 6, no. 1 (1985): 25–37.

23. Lesslie Newbigin, "The Bible and Our Contemporary Mission," *Clergy Review* 69, no. 1 (1984): 11.

24. Newbigin, *Word in Season*, 67; see Newbigin, *Other Side of 1984*, 23.

25. Newbigin, *Word in Season*, 66.

26. Newbigin, *Word in Season*, 130.

27. Lesslie Newbigin, "England as a Foreign Mission Field" (address, Assembly of the Birmingham Council of Churches, Birmingham, UK, 1986), 2. See also Newbigin, *Gospel in a Pluralist Society*, 3; Newbigin, *Word in Season*, 99.

gospel had been accommodated to the modern Western worldview along-side its many gods.

The question, then, is how the Western church, which has been co-opted into the idols of its culture, could recover the normal position, the faithful posture, of a missionary encounter with its culture. "How, then, can there be a genuine encounter of the gospel with this culture, a culture that has sprung from the roots in Western Christendom and with which the Western churches have lived in a symbiotic relationship ever since its first dawning?"[28] What is needed is an Archimedean point from which the church can challenge the culture in which it has been absorbed. Newbigin believed that the experience and insights of cross-cultural mission offered this Archimedean point. And Newbigin brought his extraordinarily broad and rich cross-cultural experience to the task of liberating the Western church for a missionary encounter.

Liberating the Western Church for a Missionary Encounter

"The gospel is like a caged lion. It does not need to be defended, just released."[29] Newbigin believed the gospel was caged by the idolatry of Western culture. His task was to bring the insights of the cross-cultural missionary experience to bear so that the gospel might be liberated for a missionary encounter. We can see at least three tasks in Newbigin's copious writing on the issue: cultural, theological, and ecclesiological.

Cultural Task: Uncovering the Hidden Credo

The first task of any missionary is a diagnosis of culture.[30] Newbigin says that a "missionary going to serve in another country is advised to make a thorough study of its culture."[31] This is precisely so the missionary will not be unwittingly seduced into a syncretistic alliance with the reigning religious vision of the culture. To do so would spell death for the missionary task. Cultural analysis, for the missionary, is a matter of life and death for faithfulness to the gospel. And so it is for the church.

28. Newbigin, *Foolishness to the Greeks*, 9.
29. This has been attributed to Martin Luther but I have never been able to verify it. Charles Spurgeon has used a similar analogy at least three times but not just these words. See https://elliot ritzema.com/2012/07/31/spurgeons-let-the-lion-out-of-the-cage-quote/. Accessed 18 April 2018.
30. Newbigin, *Word in Season*, 100.
31. Newbigin, *Foolishness to the Greeks*, 21. It is remarkable, if this is true, that we spend al-most no time in theological education teaching pastoral leaders how to understand their culture.

We might start with the following paragraph as summarizing some of the key issues that would be important in his diagnosis of Western culture:

> Incomparably the most urgent missionary task for the next few decades is the mission to "modernity." . . . It calls for the use of sharp intellectual tools, to probe behind the unquestioned assumptions of modernity and uncover the hidden credo which supports them. . . . At the most basic level there is need for critical examination from a Christian standpoint of the reigning assumptions in epistemology (How do we know what we claim to know?) and in history (How do we understand the story of which we are part?). . . . It means probing the hidden assumptions behind our practice in economics, in education, in medicine, and in communications (the media). All of this has to be seen and done as part of missionary obedience.[32]

Missionary obedience calls for a diagnosis and analysis of the post-Enlightenment West. A diagnosis aims to uncover the hidden *credo* that lies at the foundation of the public life of our culture. And the hidden *credo* may be exposed to view and unmasked in its true religious nature by analyzing both history and epistemology.

Diagnosis: Unmasking Our Unquestioned Religious Assumptions

Our first problem is that we hold unquestioned assumptions. If we have been immersed in one culture all of our lives, we have no critical distance from it. Newbigin references the Chinese proverb, noted earlier, that if you want a definition of water you do not ask a fish. Water is the only environment it has ever known. How can we gain some critical distance from our assumed environment? In other words, "what is the Archimedean point from which we can challenge the culture of which we are ourselves a part?"[33] What is needed is a kind of cultural analysis that somehow will give the church critical distance to examine the unquestioned assumptions of culture.

But for the church the problem is far more serious. The waters in which we swim are polluted by idolatry. The unquestioned assumptions that need to

---

32. Newbigin, "Gospel and Culture—but Which Culture?," 214. Newbigin's reference to these six areas of modern culture (history, epistemology, education, economics, medicine, and media) set an agenda for the gospel and culture movement in the UK, a movement spawned by Newbigin's gospel and Western culture project. A book that was prepared for a national conference in 1992 was published with a chapter on each of these six areas, with two more added—science and the arts. See Hugh Montefiore, ed., *The Gospel and Contemporary Culture* (London: Mowbray, 1992).

33. Newbigin, *Word in Season*, 68.

be examined are radically religious and to some degree stand opposed to the gospel. And one of the deepest unquestioned assumptions is that our culture is not religious. This is difficult indeed. If the church is to be freed from its captivity to Western culture, one of the first tasks is to expose the deeply religious nature of our culture's public doctrine. A peculiarity of Western culture is that we have judged religion to be one more cultural product alongside others such as politics, economics, sports, medicine, media, and education. However, religion is a directing power at the root of culture that integrates and shapes all those other areas. Newbigin gets at this with his imagery of a hidden *credo*. We observed in the last chapter that he believed that religion is not separate from the rest of life. The whole life of Western society is permeated and shaped by beliefs that are religious. He mentions here probing the hidden assumptions behind education, economics, medicine, and the media. Religion is "a whole worldview, a way of understanding the whole of human experience"[34] and a "set of beliefs, experiences, and practices that seek to grasp and express the ultimate nature of things, that which gives shape and meaning to human life, that which claims final loyalty."[35] All cultures have a *credo*, ultimate beliefs that lie at the foundation of culture and integrate, shape, and give meaning to the whole of cultural life together. And the West is no exception.

The problem in the West is that there is the dangerous belief that we live in a neutral and secular culture: "Modernity pretends to have no creed. It pretends to stand for an 'open' society in which all creeds are tolerated. It applies to itself the adjective *secular*, with the implication that it is neutral in respect to beliefs that come under the name 'religion.' In this way it conceals from its adherents the fact that it is itself based on a particular view of the human situation, a view that is open to question."[36] But Newbigin rejects the "idea that we ought to be able to expect some kind of neutral secular political order, which presupposes no religious or ideological beliefs."[37] And he calls this assumption a myth in two senses: first, as an unproven belief accepted uncritically to justify a social structure and, second, as a belief that is mistaken.[38]

Denis Munby believes a secular society is one that is uncommitted to any religious vision. It is pluralist and is tolerant of all visions of life.[39] It rejects

34. Newbigin, *Gospel in a Pluralist Society*, 172.
35. Newbigin, *Foolishness to the Greeks*, 3.
36. Newbigin, *Word in Season*, 194.
37. Lesslie Newbigin, *Trinitarian Doctrine for Today's Mission* (1963; repr., Carlisle, UK: Paternoster, 1998), 46.
38. Newbigin, *Gospel in a Pluralist Society*, 211.
39. D. L. Munby, *The Idea of a Secular Society and Its Significance for Christians* (London: Oxford University Press, 1963).

all religious claims and builds its common aims for the good of all citizens on scientific facts. Newbigin subjects Munby's argument to a withering critique. Munby's own vision, observes Newbigin, is that "his secular society *is* committed to a very particular view of society."[40] And it is not pluralist and tolerant; it excludes Islam, Judaism, and Christianity, which believe that all of human society is under the sovereign rule of God. We do not have a "secular society but a pagan society . . . a society which worships gods which are not God." And sadly, the "idea of secular society has been accepted by many Christians uncritically because it seemed to offer the Church the possibility of a peaceful coexistence with false gods, a comfortable concordat between Yahweh and Baalim."[41] The secular society "is not a neutral area into which we can project the Christian message. It is an area already occupied by other gods. We have a battle on our hands. We are dealing with principalities and powers."[42]

The belief in a neutral secular or pluralistic society is a powerful myth that blinds people to the reality of the spiritual battle in our world. It is certainly an unproven collective belief that is accepted uncritically. But even more than that, it is an assumption that requires the church in its mission to follow in the way of Jesus to unmask and challenge the principalities and powers and the ruler of this world. "It calls for a new kind of enlightenment, namely the opening up of the underlying assumptions of a secular society, the asking of unasked questions, and the probing of unrecognized presuppositions."[43] Discipleship and mission must challenge "in the name of the one Lord all the powers, ideologies, myths, assumptions, and worldviews which do not acknowledge him as Lord."[44]

These religious beliefs that enslave Western culture, and sadly often the church, *lie hidden below* the surface level of culture like tectonic plates, unseen yet shaping all that is above. They are the directing power of the ruler of this world that molds a cultural way of life. Diagnosis of Western culture, then, is an excavation task. It requires sharp tools to dig below the surface level of our lived culture so as to uncover the hidden *credo* that gives form, unity, and significance to the inhabitants of Western culture.

40. Newbigin, *Gospel in a Pluralist Society*, 217.
41. Newbigin, *Gospel in a Pluralist Society*, 220. Newbigin suggests that an important task will be the "identification, the naming of the false gods that our society worships. Ours is not a secular society, it is a society which worships false gods" (Newbigin, *Mission and the Crisis of Western Culture*, 14).
42. Newbigin, *Word in Season*, 150.
43. Newbigin, *Gospel in a Pluralist Society*, 220.
44. Newbigin, *Gospel in a Pluralist Society*, 221.

Or, to change the metaphor: these religious beliefs *lie hidden behind* the mask of the claim to a secular and neutral society. "The church has to bear witness to the truth that unmasks the illusions and falsehoods of modernity."[45] Diagnosis is, therefore, an unmasking task that requires tearing away the presumed mask that hides the religious beliefs of Western culture.

Historical Analysis: Unmasking the Religious Story We Live By

Newbigin employs two tools to unmask the public doctrine of Western culture and expose its idolatry—historical and epistemological analysis. One of the ways Newbigin believes it possible to gain some critical distance from the polluted waters of Western culture is to tell the story of just how this particular vision of the world came to be. "One way to gain a perspective on our culture is to look at it from the angle of history. European culture was not always so."[46] What we take for granted as the way things are is not incontrovertible truth but a constructed way of life that falsely claims universality. It is simply a product of one particular tribal history of the European peoples.[47] The illusion of self-evident truth can be unmasked by telling the story. With regularity, Newbigin examines the roots of our culture historically to show that the universal claims to truth are constructed and "that the axioms and assumptions of our modern culture are not simply an objective account of 'how things really are,' but are themselves questionable and vulnerable."[48]

An African proverb says: "Until the lions have their historians, the hunter will always be the hero of the story." Newbigin is aware that the "hero" of the story will shape the way the story is told—from the facts selected as significant to the way those facts are arranged and interpreted in a narrative.[49] The question is, What is the point of the story? Where is history going? What is the purpose of the human story? The telling of the Western story assumes an answer to those questions. It is the triumph of autonomous humanity over evil through the application of scientific reason to technology and social organization in order to master nature and human affairs with the goal of building a better world. This is not simply a neutral recording of the facts. Rather, it is a way of understanding the story and meaning of human life within it. It offers a way of salvation from evil and an eschatology. It is a religious narrative.

45. Lesslie Newbigin, "A Missionary's Dream," *Ecumenical Review* 43, no. 1 (January 1991): 9.
46. Lesslie Newbigin, "The Gospel and Modern Western Culture," unpublished article, Newbigin Archives, University of Birmingham (1990), 2.
47. Newbigin, *Proper Confidence*, 74.
48. Newbigin, "Bible and Our Contemporary Mission," 16.
49. Newbigin, *Gospel in a Pluralist Society*, 171–72.

Like the biblical story, the metanarrative of Western humanism offers a comprehensive vision of life and demands ultimate allegiance. There is a clash between two religiously ultimate and comprehensive, yet incompatible, stories.

> The way we understand human life depends on what conception we have of the human story. What is the real story of which my life story is part? . . . In our contemporary culture . . . two quite different stories are told. One is the story of evolution, of the development of species through the survival of the strong, and the story of the rise of civilization, and its success in giving humankind mastery of nature. The other story is the one embodied in the Bible, the story of creation and fall, of God's election of a people to be the bearers of his purpose for humankind, and the coming of the one in whom that purpose is to be fulfilled. These are two different and incompatible stories.[50]

An early experience in Newbigin's life sheds light on this view of the Western story as the true human story. The strongest impact on Newbigin's thinking during his last year of school, he says, was made by a book by F. S. Marvin titled *The Living Past*. "It gave me a belief in the human story as an upward striving towards growing mastery over all that stands in the way of man's full humanity." The book invited him to participate in this story, which he says led him to join lustily in singing the words of John Addington Symonds's hymn at the school assembly: "Spill no drop of blood, but dare all that may plant man's lordship firm on earth and fire and sea and air."[51] He comments, "I saw myself as part of that noble campaign."[52]

That book articulates the metanarrative that Newbigin sees gripping Western culture. He engages it already in his Bangalore Lectures in 1941 and uses the same language fifty-four years later to describe his analysis of gospel and culture.[53] It is "the master-narrative which 'modernity' since the Enlightenment has told. In this narrative human history is the progressive triumph of 'civilization,' understood as the mastery of nature and of human affairs by means of the universal power of 'reason' as the Enlightenment understood it."[54]

---

50. Newbigin, *Gospel in a Pluralist Society*, 15–16.

51. Newbigin observes that this hymn expresses well the Western grand story of progress and, strangely, is included in many Christian hymnbooks. See Lesslie Newbigin, *Signs amid the Rubble: The Purposes of God in Human History* (Grand Rapids: Eerdmans, 2003), 5–6.

52. Newbigin, *Unfinished Agenda*, 6.

53. Newbigin, *Signs amid the Rubble*, 3–55; Lesslie Newbigin, "Gospel and Culture" (unpublished speech, Denmark, November 1995).

54. Lesslie Newbigin, "The Gospel and Our Culture: A Response to Elaine Graham and Heather Walton," *Modern Churchman* 34, no. 2 (1992): 8.

Seminal to this Western master narrative is the notion of progress. "The idea of progress raises for Christianity in a very acute form the question of God's purpose for history as a whole."[55] Progress is more than simply the development of human culture. Rather, for "our modern Western world," progress is our "eschatology." While the medieval world, taught by the Bible, saw the holy city of Revelation as the goal of history, the "eighteenth century transferred the holy city from another world to this."[56] The Western story is progress toward paradise created by humanity, a society of freedom, brotherhood, and peace.[57]

This new world is created by human effort and is "no longer a gift of God from heaven." Rather, "it is the final triumph of science and skill of the enlightened peoples of the earth."[58] It is humanistic in a deeply religious sense of confidence in humans to save themselves. This story of progress toward a better world is rooted in an understanding of humanity that we are godlike, good, and capable of liberating ourselves from the misery and evil of the world.[59] In this metanarrative of modernity, the way humanity will move history to this paradise is summarized in four words Newbigin often strings together: science, technology, economics, and politics.[60] Universal reason is disciplined by the scientific method to liberate it from dogma, tradition, and superstition. This emancipation from "dogma, tradition, and superstition, and the purposeful exercise of the newly liberated powers of human reason would lead to such a growing understanding and a growing mastery that all the evils that enslave men and women would be conquered."[61] The growing mastery to conquer evil would come as science is translated into technology to subdue nature and into economic and political social organization to control human culture.

This vision of universal history came to maturity in the eighteenth-century Enlightenment, the point where, "after a long period of gestation, modern Europe came to birth and to consciousness of its own unique character."[62] This is the period that Newbigin often focuses much of his attention on. He signals the religious nature of this story as he observes that people living at this time refer to this period as the "enlightenment." There is a "collective conversion" as Europe is converted to a new religious vision.[63] "Light had dawned.

---

55. Newbigin, *Signs amid the Rubble*, 5.
56. Newbigin, *Foolishness to the Greeks*, 28.
57. Newbigin, *Signs amid the Rubble*, 6.
58. Newbigin, *Foolishness to the Greeks*, 28.
59. Newbigin, *Signs amid the Rubble*, 6.
60. E.g., Newbigin, "Gospel and Culture," 8, 12.
61. Newbigin, *Foolishness to the Greeks*, 28.
62. Newbigin, *Unfinished Agenda*, 251.
63. Newbigin, *Foolishness to the Greeks*, 23.

Darkness had passed away. . . . 'Enlightenment' is a word with profound religious overtones. It is the word used to describe the decisive experience of Buddha. It is the word used in the Johannine writings to describe the coming of Jesus: 'The Light had come into the world' (John 3:19)."[64] Europeans were convinced that the light of "a true scientific method" had dawned. "Nature and Nature's laws lay hid in night; God said: 'Let Newton be', and all was light."[65] Those living before Newton or living elsewhere, outside his influence, were in darkness. And if you have the light in a dark world, you are obligated to share the light with others; you become a missionary religion. "They were the bearers of light in a world still strangely dark. They had therefore both the duty and the capacity to carry their civilization into every corner of the world. And they proceeded to do so."[66]

What happens in the Enlightenment is a profound conversion. It is "the substitution of one credo by another. It is a conversion . . . of one creed to another."[67] This conversion meant that no longer was the biblical story "the locus of truth. Rather, truth was to be found by the exercise of autonomous reason."[68] Newton's scientific method now functioned as the paradigm of truth. Scientific truth, rather than the biblical story, was now the "ground for human unity. The long period of the Christianization of Europe was now seen as the dark ages, or—at best—the middle ages between two periods when reason reigned, the ancient classical world and the present."[69]

As the new ground for human unity, it begins to reshape every aspect of public life. Newbigin's analysis of Western culture shows how this vision sets out to reform all of human life, from politics to scholarship to economics to gender. What we call "modern Western culture . . . is a whole way of organizing human life that rests on and in turn validates" the Enlightenment vision.[70] His discussion of public education serves as a good example of this.

> With the rise of the doctrine of progress in the eighteenth century, as a direct result of the Enlightenment and Age of Reason, a conscious movement arose throughout Europe to take the education of the young out of

64. Newbigin, *Other Side of 1984*, 7.
65. Newbigin, *Other Side of 1984*, 10.
66. Newbigin, *Other Side of 1984*, 8.
67. Lesslie Newbigin, "The Bible: Good News for Secularised People" (keynote address, Europe and Middle East Regional Conference, Eisenach, Germany, April 1991), Newbigin Archives, University of Birmingham, 2.
68. Lesslie Newbigin, "Mission Agenda" (lecture, Trinity College, Dublin, November 2, 1992), 3.
69. Newbigin, "Mission Agenda," 3–4.
70. Newbigin, *Foolishness to the Greeks*, 29; see the full chapter, "Profile of a Culture," 21–41.

the hands of parents and churches. A system of government-controlled
state education was developed that inculcated into successive generations
a different view of the world. The whole idea that education should be
the responsibility of the government is a very recent concept and is one of
the implications of that new doctrine of progress.[71]

While the Enlightenment is the focal point of Newbigin's analysis, his
writings abound in clues for the way he would construct the whole Western
metanarrative, from the ancient Greeks to the present. This is important since
Newbigin often relies on a background grand story to buttress his arguments.
He refers to the source of Western culture in terms of two incompatible
streams: classical rationalistic humanism and the biblical story.[72] The difference between these streams is the location of reliable truth. In the humanist
vision, truth is timeless ideas that stand above history, while in the Bible truth
is found in a story of historical events centered in Jesus. These two streams
are brought together in Augustine in the fourth and fifth centuries, and for
the better part of a thousand years it is the biblical story, in which faith leads
reason, that is ascendant, and it is the biblical story that is the source of truth,
not humanism's timeless truths. These two traditions are pried apart in the
thirteenth-century work of Aquinas and the scholastics who followed him
through their introduction of Aristotle into Western European culture.[73] The
humanist vision began to gain growing cultural power with the flood of
classical ideas that flowed into Europe in the Renaissance,[74] in the religious
wars following the Reformation that discredited the Christian faith,[75] and
especially in the triumph of the new physics of the scientific revolution.[76] All
of this led to the conversion of the West in the Enlightenment.

Newbigin also offers much on the way the Enlightenment vision developed, especially in the twentieth century.[77] The events in twentieth-century
Europe have led to a growing loss of confidence in promises of Enlightenment

71. Lesslie Newbigin, *Discovering Truth in a Changing World* (London: Alpha International,
2003), 103.

72. Newbigin, *Gospel in a Pluralist Society*, 1–3; *Proper Confidence*, 3.

73. Newbigin, "Gospel and Culture," 6; Lesslie Newbigin, "The Gospel and the University,"
unpublished sermon, Chapel of Royal Holloway, University of London, June 27, 1993, 2.

74. Newbigin, *Other Side of 1984*, 6–7.

75. Newbigin, *Proper Confidence*, 30.

76. Newbigin, *Other Side of 1984*, 10.

77. Reflection on Newbigin's analysis of the post-Enlightenment West has usually centered
on how his sustained focus on the modern scientific worldview relates to scattered comments
he makes about the postmodern West, especially in the area of epistemology. Not enough attention has been paid to his growing concern in the last decade of his life for the way the modern
idolatry of the Enlightenment has taken an economic and global form.

progress, since it has "failed disastrously to deliver what was promised." The rational planning of society has been abandoned in favor of leaving all to the irrational forces of the market.[78] In one part of our culture—the private sphere—there is a collapse of modernity into postmodernity: a growing relativism and pluralism and the reduction of truth claims to power.[79] However, the bigger threat is that the public life of Western culture still embodies the modern vision of life, albeit in a new global and economic form. And therefore modernism is still the major challenge the world faces.[80] This economic form of modernity had its roots in the eighteenth century: it is in economics that "the Enlightenment was to have perhaps its most far-reaching consequences."[81] The "new economics" of the Enlightenment vision would "create unlimited material growth" and "higher levels of fulfilment and happiness" through the operation of the free market. It is true that the "free market is a good way of balancing supply and demand," but "if it is absolutized and allowed to rule economic life, it becomes an evil power."[82] This is what has happened at the end of the twentieth century. And this economic idolatry is reshaping all of cultural life and becoming a global culture. Modernity in an economic form—the "modern, scientific, liberal, free-market culture"[83]—is spreading across the globe in the process of globalization. After the collapse of the command economies in the Soviet Union and Eastern Europe, the whole world "has become locked together in a single economic-financial-technical unit." With the development of information technology, all the peoples of the inhabited earth are being sucked into this global "financial-economic system."[84] This is modernity or modernization on a global scale, and to understand it we must dig down to a "deeper level" than political and economic systems, down to "the level of fundamental beliefs, of ultimate commitments, in fact of idolatries."[85]

78. Lesslie Newbigin, *Truth and Authority in Modernity* (Valley Forge, PA: Trinity Press International, 1996), 73–74.

79. Newbigin, *Proper Confidence*, 27; Lesslie Newbigin, "Religious Pluralism: A Missiological Approach," *Studia Missionalia* 42 (1993): 231–34; Newbigin, *Truth and Authority in Modernity*, 7–9, 82.

80. Lesslie Newbigin, "Modernity in Context," in *Modern, Postmodern and Christian*, ed. John Reid, Lesslie Newbigin, and David Pullinger, Lausanne Occasional Paper 27 (Carberry, Scotland: Handsel, 1996), 8.

81. Newbigin, *Other Side of 1984*, 11.

82. Lesslie Newbigin, "Speaking the Truth to Caesar," *Ecumenical Review* 43, no. 3 (July 1991): 375.

83. Newbigin, *Word in Season*, 188.

84. Newbigin, "Missionary's Dream," 5.

85. Lesslie Newbigin, "The Gospel as Public Truth: Swanwick Opening Statement" (unpublished address, 1992), 6.

Economic modernity has produced in the latter part of the twentieth century the "meaningless hedonism of a society."[86] Our confession is "I shop, therefore I am," or "Tesco ergo sum."[87] We are dealing with the "depth and power of a religion whose cathedrals are the great shopping malls and supermarkets where families come week by week for the liturgy of consumerism."[88] This religious vision is creating a growing divide between rich and poor. In 1960, at the beginning of the first development decade, the world's richest billion received 30 times the income of the poorest billion. In 1990 that number had moved to 150 times. Moreover, this economic and consumer way of life is destroying the environment. If the whole world were to live at the level of the developed world, the planet could not sustain us.[89] Economic modernity and consumerism—this is the central idolatrous threat to the church today.

There may be much to quibble about in Newbigin's analysis of Western culture or the way he told the story. However, what must be firmly fixed in our minds, if we are to understand what he is doing, is that he does not see himself as a cultural analyst or a historian. Rather, he is attempting to expose the roots of our culture that are enervating the church's witness. His concern is that the church gain confidence to embody and tell the gospel as the true story, unencumbered by the powerful idols of the West. In other words, it is not an academic task, first of all, but a missionary task. The church is compromised and timid because of the power of the Western story. Newbigin wants the church to see it as a rival story to the gospel—just as comprehensive, just as religious, just as rooted in faith. Nevertheless, it is to some degree incompatible with the gospel. And, if the church's very nature is to embody and tell the biblical story, then to accommodate the gospel to this rival story is unfaithfulness.

Epistemological Analysis: Unmasking the Idol of Reason

Time and again Newbigin says that the real issue is whether the gospel is *true*. And if it is, the churches need the confidence that it is so. The brief sketch of the Western story above shows us why Newbigin spent so much time exposing the myth of neutral reason. For Newbigin, the public doctrine of Western culture was the march of autonomous reason to master the world and build a paradise on earth. But our confidence in reason to build

---

86. Lesslie Newbigin, "It Seems to Me," *Transmission* (Spring 1997): 4; see Newbigin, *Foolishness to the Greeks*, 30–31.

87. Lesslie Newbigin, "What Is Culture?" (unpublished address, 1990), 4. Tesco is an enormous multinational chain superstore in the UK.

88. Newbigin, "Gospel as Public Truth," 6.

89. Newbigin, "Gospel as Public Truth," 5–6.

paradise is based squarely on our trust that scientific reason tells us the truth: we *know* the truth by reason. The enthronement of reason challenged the truth of the gospel, and Christians had become timid and lost confidence in the gospel. That confidence had to be recovered if there was to be a missionary encounter. The messianic pretensions of scientific reason had to be unmasked. And so Newbigin spilled a lot of ink on fairly nuanced analyses of the epistemological questions of how we know. "The fundamental issue is epistemological: it is the question about how we can come to know the truth, how we can know what is real."[90] Interestingly and tellingly, he often begins with an analysis of the knowing process before turning to discuss the mission of the church.[91]

It would be easy to mischaracterize Newbigin's concern with epistemology and ask the question I often received from my students: Why are we spending time on epistemology when we are studying mission? The answer, quite simply, is that we live in a culture that "has prized above all the autonomy of reason."[92] This idol must be exposed because our culture, and the church with it—which, again, was his primary concern—is captive to this vision. The church has become timid about proclaiming and living the gospel as public truth. It has meekly acquiesced to the confinement of the gospel to the wholly unsuitable place of private values and personal preferences. In other words, a misunderstanding of the nature of knowledge has constructed a cage that imprisons the gospel and confines the church's mission.

Epistemological analysis may help to remove those bars. We have become captive to a scientific approach to knowledge as the only way to valid truth, and this has emasculated a missionary encounter. To liberate the church from its captivity to the idol of autonomous reason, Newbigin engages frequently in a "resolute attack on the fundamental problem which is epistemology, the way we formulate an answer to the question: 'How do you know?'"[93]

Newbigin's attack is twofold. First, he challenges the unquestioned epistemology that lies at the heart of Western culture. He does so through historical analysis and the exposure of the false dualisms that have emerged from that history. The hero of the story is Augustine, for whom reason worked in the context of faith. And the primary villains are René Descartes, John Locke, and Francis Bacon, who turned that around. His analysis also draws on the insights of postempiricist philosophy and history of science to show the

---

90. Newbigin, *Word in Season*, 104.
91. E.g., Newbigin, *Gospel in a Pluralist Society*, 1–65; Newbigin, *Discovering Truth in a Changing World*, 1–20.
92. Newbigin, *Other Side of 1984*, 51.
93. Newbigin, *Gospel in a Pluralist Society*, 25.

naïveté of assuming neutral reason. Second, he offers a more truthful model of the way we know the truth, drawing on such philosophers as Michael Polanyi, Alasdair MacIntyre, and Nicholas Wolterstorff.[94]

In the work of Enlightenment philosophers Descartes, Bacon, and Locke, scientific reason was extracted from its proper creational place amid faith commitments that shaped a communally embodied tradition. It was crowned as the final arbiter of all truth claims, including the truth of the gospel and the Christian faith. This set up a number of artificial dichotomies that are deeply embedded in the Western worldview: reason and revelation, knowing and believing, fact and value, doubt and dogma, public and private, truth and opinion, and objective and subjective. In each case, the first term correlates with scientific knowledge and the second with the role and place of the gospel. Yet these are false dichotomies that misunderstand the nature of knowing. The pretensions of autonomous scientific reason must be unmasked to liberate the gospel from its cage in the private realm of opinions and values.

These are not simply the theoretical dualisms of scholars. Rather they are deep-rooted assumptions that lie at the foundation of our culture. "The most distinctive feature of our modern culture is its sharp division of human affairs into a public world of 'facts' and a private world of 'values.' The former is the world of public doctrine. . . . The latter is the world of free personal choice."[95] When scientific reason is the final authority for truth, only what can be proved by reason is validated as truth and thus able to play a role in the public square. All other truth claims must be relegated to the private realm of values and opinion. They are mere tastes, like chocolate ice cream, that are subjective and have no objective grounding in the world. Thus we have a bifurcated culture in which science and technology, acknowledged as truth, provide the main dynamic for public life. But there is no shared public doctrine on the purpose of human life that may guide public life, including science and technology. All claims to the meaning of human life are mere subjective preference and have lost touch with reality, which has left much of what matters in human life to degenerate into subjectivism and relativism.

The idol of autonomous reason has been masked by a false claim to objectivity: scientific knowledge is assumed to be objectively true and tells us the way things are. Autonomous reason, disciplined by the scientific method, can rise above our subjectivity to gain objective knowledge. It judges all traditions and beliefs with an air of invincible authority. Yet this is simply not

94. Paul Weston has offered a detailed analysis of Newbigin's epistemology, especially in its dependence on Michael Polanyi, in Paul Weston, "A Critical Engagement with the Writings of Lesslie Newbigin" (PhD diss., University of London, 2001).

95. Newbigin, "Culture of Modernity," 100.

how scientific knowledge works. Rather, to pursue scientific knowledge one must embrace and indwell a fiduciary framework or a faith-based perspective. This is a framework of beliefs, assumptions, practices, and skills that the scientific community assumes and trusts when it carries out its work. This framework contains a vast array of tacit beliefs and unexamined, unquestioned knowledge. It is passed along to a student who wants to be a participant in the scientific tradition; they receive and trust the whole faith framework they have been given.

Thus, autonomous reason is an illusion; reason always works in the context of the authority of some tradition with all of its beliefs and assumptions.[96] Reason always works to make sense of the world within some socially embodied tradition. In the case of science, reason functions within a community of scientists who work together in carrying forward this tradition and bringing its foundational insights to bear on various situations and experiences. So even the tradition of science works in the light of an unquestioned faith commitment: the scientific method will guide us to truth. This light is not questioned; it is trusted in faith to provide illumination for further understanding.

Newbigin appropriates these scientific insights in a missiological way. He draws an analogy between the scientific tradition and the Christian tradition.[97] In both cases, reason only operates within the context of a continuing tradition; the tradition is socially embodied by a community; the tradition works with a faith commitment that functions as the ultimate light in which the community works and lives; and the tradition continues as that community brings the light of the original disclosure to bear on new contexts and situations. The only questions are: Which tradition? Whose light?

While there is an analogy between the scientific and Christian traditions, there are also fundamental differences. First, the scientific tradition begins with "I discovered with the scientific method," while the Christian tradition begins with "God has spoken in Jesus Christ."[98] One begins with I-It knowledge, while the other begins with the trustful listening characteristic of I-Thou knowledge. In the Christian faith, reason has become the servant of a listening and trusting openness to God's revelation rather than the servant of a masterful autonomy over creation in the humanist tradition.[99]

Second, the faith commitment that gives rise and light to the Christian tradition concerns ultimate questions of purpose and meaning, whereas the scientific tradition is limited to issues of cause and effect that probe the

96. Newbigin, *Gospel in a Pluralist Society*, 58.
97. Newbigin, *Gospel in a Pluralist Society*, 52–65.
98. Newbigin, *Gospel in a Pluralist Society*, 60.
99. Newbigin, *Word in Season*, 93.

rational structure of the cosmos. Indeed, science has eliminated purpose from the outset. If someone finds a machine that has never been seen before, they may well be able to analyze its structure. But the only way one may know the purpose of the machine is if someone explains it to them. Science may analyze the structure of the universe, but we can only know its purpose if the Creator reveals it. The gospel reveals the purpose and meaning of the creation and thus serves as a more comprehensive rationality tradition that can account for the findings of science. The ultimate purpose of the world revealed in Jesus Christ can find a place at lower levels of analysis for cause-and-effect scientific knowledge that probes the structure of the creation.[100] But it does not work the other way.

Newbigin believes that not only are these dichotomies false; they are dangerous and destructive. When we put our "trust in the findings of science," we may well gain insight into the structure of our world, but we will be "left with no answer to the question of ultimate meaning." Thus, the way is open "to develop a pantheon of idols"[101] that guide our public life. Moreover, a faith commitment to the critical principle of doubt engendered by autonomous scientific reason is ultimately proving to destroy Western culture. We are being led inexorably to a nihilistic relativism and subjectivism that threatens our society. Descartes inevitably begets Nietzsche.[102]

Newbigin calls for a return to the insights of Augustine: *credo ut intelligam* (I believe so that I may understand). The idols of pagan classical culture, like the idols today, produced dichotomies that threatened its very existence.[103] There was a need for a new starting point or *arche*, and the church offered the gospel. It was this good news offered as public truth that ultimately saved all the insights and gains of classical culture. So today the church must take up its missionary task to embody and proclaim the gospel as public truth. Only in its light can the true nature of the world be understood and Western culture be saved from descent into the meaningless hedonism of a consumer society. And only in its light can all the marvelous treasures of Western culture be saved from destruction.[104] Religion has been wrongly imprisoned within the bounds of reason for two centuries. This must be reversed: reason must be liberated to rightly function within the bounds of true religion.

---

100. Newbigin, *Gospel in a Pluralist Society*, 49.

101. Newbigin, *Word in Season*, 150.

102. Newbigin, "Gospel and the University," 3.

103. Newbigin develops this thesis in dependence on Charles Cochrane, *Christianity and Classical Culture: A Study in Thought and Action* (New York: Oxford University Press, 1939). He refers to this book as one of the three or four most important books crucial to his thinking (Newbigin, *Truth to Tell*, 15).

104. Newbigin, *Truth to Tell*, 15–39.

Theological Task: Gospel as Public Truth

If there is to be a missionary encounter with Western culture, observes Newbigin, there is an "urgent need for the development of a coherent and intellectually tenable doctrine of Scriptural authority."[105] Elsewhere he writes that "one of the central issues involved in a missionary encounter with our culture is the question: How do we appeal to scripture as the source of authority for our mission?"[106] The problem that confronts the Western church is that the Bible has been part of the culture for so long that it has accommodated itself to the fundamental assumptions of the culture and appears unable to challenge them. Newbigin asks, "Have we got into a situation where the biblical message has been so thoroughly adapted to fit into our modern western culture that we are unable to hear the radical challenge, the call for radical conversion which it presents in our culture?"[107]

Newbigin tells the story of biblical authority in the West to give us a perspective on the problem. For a one-thousand-year period, the Bible was read and interpreted "from within the Christian tradition."[108] What that means for Newbigin is a twofold affirmation:

(a) It is Jesus Christ, the total fact of Christ as witnessed in the apostolic testimony, which is the touchstone for the interpretation of all Scripture; and

(b) We are to understand Jesus as he understood himself, namely as the one who brings the story of Israel to its crisis and fulfillment. In other words, Jesus is totally misunderstood if we detach Him from his place in the history of Israel.

Newbigin explains that "to bring (a) and (b) together, we require the whole canon of scripture—the Old and New Testaments together."[109] For a millennium, Scripture was interpreted within this faith commitment: it is the true story of the whole world that finds its climactic point in Jesus Christ. This is the confession and creed that shaped the reading of Scripture within the church.

105. Lesslie Newbigin, "New Birth into a Living Hope" (keynote address, European Area Council of the World Alliance of Reformed Churches meeting, Edinburgh, Scotland, August 28, 1995), 7.

106. Newbigin, "Bible and Our Contemporary Mission," 13.

107. Newbigin, "Bible and Our Contemporary Mission," 11.

108. Newbigin, "The Bible: Good News for Secularised People," 1.

109. Lesslie Newbigin, "Biblical Authority," unpublished article, Newbigin Archives, University of Birmingham (1997), 2.

This all changed in the eighteenth century when a new creed took hold of Europe with a faith commitment to autonomous reason disciplined by the scientific method. The Bible was read and interpreted now from within another belief system, another worldview, another creed, another *credo*, another dogma.[110] The Bible moved from the church to the university, from the hands of ordinary Christians into the hands of scholars who could deploy this scientific method in their interpretation of Scripture. The Bible was "no longer Holy Scripture, but a corpus of ancient writings to be understood and assessed in the light of a different creed. . . . The ordinary Christian needed the scholar to interpret it . . . [as] a person certified as competent in terms of the new credo."[111]

The new world of biblical scholarship claimed the high ground of truth with an attempt "to distinguish a scientific approach to the Bible from the confessional approach." But "this move is misunderstood if it is seen as a move to a more objective understanding of the Bible. It is a move from one confessional stance to another, a move from one creed to another." And the deep-rooted faith and commitment to this new belief system made it "very hard to persuade the practitioners of the historical-critical method to recognize the creedal character of their approach."[112] This so-called objective scholarship that substitutes the Enlightenment faith for the biblical faith as the rightful context for true interpretation is not simply neutral with respect to the biblical message; it is unbelieving scholarship. The biblical texts are written from faith to faith; they testify to God's acts from a believing position with the purpose of evoking faith in the hearers (e.g., John 20:31). The "objective" standpoint is a decision not to believe the gospel on the basis of a rival *credo*.[113]

And scholars were faithful to their new *credo*. The Bible was no longer considered to be God's Word but an object of methodological analysis. An I-It scientific analysis of an ancient text replaced an I-Thou listening to the voice of God. Specifically, the methods of Isaac Newton in physics became the model by which Scripture was analyzed. Newton broke down the world to its smallest bits and then reassembled it based on his understanding of the laws of the cosmos. "Modern scholarship, following the models of modern science, has worked by analysing and dissecting the material into smaller and smaller units and then re-classifying and re-combining

110. Newbigin employs all these various terms—"belief system," "creed," "dogma," "worldview," and *"credo"*—to describe the Enlightenment approach to biblical studies.

111. Newbigin, "The Bible: Good News for Secularised People," 1.

112. Newbigin, *Proper Confidence*, 79–80.

113. Newbigin "Bible and Our Contemporary Mission," 14.

them—obviously on the basis of a modern understanding of 'how things really are.'"[114] This led to a fragmentation of the Bible into historical-critical bits. "Theological students, unfortunately, are asked to spend so much time analyzing and dissecting the various strands which make it up that they often miss the shape of the whole. It is like trying to understand a photograph in the morning paper by taking a magnifying glass to it. You see only a lot of black dots; you don't see the picture."[115] And when you break the big story into bits, those bits are incorporated into a different picture or absorbed into the modern worldview. There is no challenge to the idolatry of modernity—only capitulation. There is no authoritative Scripture and no missionary encounter.[116]

The impact of this kind of post-Enlightenment dogma on biblical scholarship permeated the churches, especially those in the more liberal and mainline camps, as it shaped generations of pastors and leaders within the church who during their theological training were "gently but firmly moved from the confessional position to the scientific one."[117] But the Enlightenment faith gained a foothold in the more conservative churches as well.

The triumph of higher criticism and the Enlightenment religious vision split the church into two camps: liberal and fundamentalist. The liberal tradition reduced the Bible to a mere "collection of records and religious experience, part of the history of religions, having therefore no unique authority which sets it apart from all other books."[118] This brought forth the rightful reaction of conservative Christians who want to preserve the authority and truth of the Bible. However, they have done so with the very Enlightenment tools that produced the liberal tradition they reject. The conservative churches defend the truth of Scripture by reducing it to an account of timeless dogmas and objective truths about God, nature, and humankind in which human subjectivity plays no part. In terms of the foundational fact-value dichotomy characteristic of the post-Enlightenment West, conservatives fall on the side of facts and liberals on the side of values. And both undermine the given narrative unity producing their own construct. The liberal tradition breaks

---

114. Newbigin, "Bible and Our Contemporary Mission," 14. See Lesslie Newbigin, "The Role of the Bible in Our Church" (unpublished speech, United Reformed Church Forward Policy Group, April 1985), 1.

115. Lesslie Newbigin, "The Other Side of 1990" (unpublished lecture, Clare College, Cambridge University, 1989), 2.

116. Lesslie Newbigin, "Canon and Mission," unpublished notes, Newbigin Archives, University of Birmingham (n.d.), 1.

117. Newbigin, Proper Confidence, 79.

118. Newbigin, "The Bible: Good News for Secularised People," 6; see Newbigin, Truth to Tell, 43–44.

down the Bible into historical-critical and ancient religious bits and then reassembles it in terms of a whole tailored to fit the dictates of the prevailing modern worldview. The conservative tradition breaks down the Bible into theological bits and reassembles it according to their own systematic theologies and apologetics schemes.

This analysis leads Newbigin to a threefold diagnosis of the problem with current views of Scripture and a threefold response that is needed if there is to be a missionary encounter. First, the Bible has been lost as the authoritative Word of God; it must be recovered *as truth*. Second, the Bible has lost its comprehensive authority and been relegated to the realm of private values; it must be recovered *as public truth*. Third, the Bible has been reduced to either a record of religious experiences or a collection of theological propositions; it must be recovered *as narrative truth*. What is given to us in Scripture is neither religious experiences nor timeless propositions but the story of universal history with its center in Jesus. A missionary encounter is only possible if we recover the Bible as comprehensive and narrative truth. In a word, if there is to be a missionary encounter between the gospel and Western culture, then the Bible must be regained as the true story of the whole world with authority over all of human life.

Newbigin does not want to cast aside all the gains in biblical scholarship that have been made in the post-Enlightenment period. The Enlightenment did bring real light—not ultimate light, but real light. Higher criticism has brought much insight into the human component of Scripture. And so, for Newbigin, there is no return to the precritical days of the West before the Enlightenment or of, for example, India, where people can still read the Bible without post-Enlightenment glasses. That route is not open to us. We have to face both the insight and idolatry of the Enlightenment. If a jellyfish syncretism is not an option, neither is a fossilized return to precritical days. The way forward is to recover the Bible as public truth in its narrative and comprehensive authority so that there might be a missionary encounter with the religious vision of Western culture.

Ecclesiological Task: A Missionary Church beyond Privatization and Christendom

It should not surprise us that in his major publications on a missionary encounter with Western culture, as well as in his smaller papers on the issue, Newbigin often concludes with the ecclesiological task. In the final chapter of *Foolishness to the Greeks*, titled "What Must We Be? The Call to the Church," Newbigin says,

The church is the bearer to all the nations of a gospel that announces the kingdom, the reign, and the sovereignty of God. It calls men and women to repent of their false loyalty to other powers, to become believers in the one true sovereignty, and so to become corporately a sign, instrument, and foretaste of that sovereignty of the one true and living God over all nature, and all nations, and all human lives. . . . What does the calling imply for a church faced with the tough, powerful, and all-penetrating culture [of the West]?[119]

There are two options that the faithful missionary church is barred from: privatization and Christendom.

Neither Privatization nor Christendom

Newbigin is constantly concerned with the foundational dichotomy in Western culture between the public world of facts that are known and the private world of values that are simply believed. The gospel and the church's mission had been consigned to the latter place. This understanding of the gospel as a private religious message stands in stark contradiction to the gospel's own claim for itself. On this misunderstanding of the gospel, the church and its mission are similarly misconstrued. The church is the new humankind called to embody the comprehensive sovereignty of God in all of life. It is no accident that in the quote above, Newbigin uses the word "sovereignty" three times and stresses the comprehensive gospel of the kingdom—*all* nature, *all* nations, and *all* of human life. In this Western setting split by public and private life, what is the church to be?

Clearly we must not accept the privatized place that the humanistic narrative of the West assigns to us. It is nothing less than unfaithfulness to the message of the gospel and to our missionary calling. Newbigin insists we cannot "accept the view that the only task of the church is to provide for individuals a place in the private sector where they can enjoy an inward religious security but are not required to challenge the ideology that rules the public life of nations."[120]

There are at least three reasons that the church has been willing to accept its role in the private realm, and each of these must be challenged. The first is that the church has often accommodated itself to a pagan Greek anthropology and eschatology. When humanity is conceived in terms of an immortal soul dwelling in a physical body that awaits a return to its true home in heaven, an

---

119. Newbigin, *Foolishness to the Greeks*, 124. See Newbigin, *Other Side of 1984*, 55–62; Newbigin, *Gospel in a Pluralist Society*, 222–32.
120. Newbigin, *Foolishness to the Greeks*, 124.

ancient pagan dichotomy has overruled biblical teaching. The goal of human life, according to Scripture, is a renewed humankind liberated from sin and its curse, living the fullness of creational life together in resurrected bodies in the context of a restored nonhuman creation. This biblical goal of history gives meaning to the church's engagement with public life. A spiritualized and individualized eschatology is not concerned with history and will weaken any resolve to engage the public life of culture. A proper eschatology will be essential for a recovery of the church's missionary calling in the West.

A second reason the church has accommodated itself to the private realm is a misconstrual of the gospel as something less than the kingdom that Jesus announced. God's reign is comprehensive, and the community that is sent to tell and embody that reign cannot neglect its obligation "to declare the sovereignty of Christ over every sphere of human life without exception."[121] To embody the good news of the kingdom will mean the church is called to challenge the idolatry of the public life of culture. To call for submission to Christ as Lord is to reject all other lords. But if the church reduces its gospel to individual salvation, it misunderstands its gospel and neglects its comprehensive vocation. "The Gospel is vastly more than an offer to men who care to accept it of a meaning for their personal lives. It is the declaration of God's cosmic purpose by which the whole public history of mankind is sustained and overruled, and by which all men without exception will be judged. . . . Only an interpretation of the Gospel which puts in the centre God's total purpose for human history is true to the Bible."[122]

Thus, the gospel calls the church to a far-reaching mission that engages all of cultural life. To refuse engagement with the public life of culture and to seek a safe place in the private realm is to misunderstand the gospel and accept a role that the early church refused to accept. The private realm offers the possibility of peaceful accommodation to culture. "As long as the Church is content to offer its beliefs modestly as simply one of the many brands available in the ideological supermarket, no offense is taken. But the affirmation that the truth revealed in the gospel ought to govern public life is offensive."[123]

Here we are reminded of the way Newbigin contrasts the contemporary Western church with the early church. The early church could have accepted the designation of a *cultus privatus* by embracing the terms of its enemies— *heranos* and *thiasos*. These terms pointed to a community that proclaimed an individual and otherworldly salvation that did not confront Roman idolatry.

---

121. Newbigin, *Truth to Tell*, 71–72.
122. Lesslie Newbigin, *Honest Religion for Secular Man* (Philadelphia: Westminster, 1966), 46.
123. Newbigin, *Gospel in a Pluralist Society*, 7.

Imperial Rome was happy to permit and protect this kind of private religion because it did not challenge the public order. Newbigin asks, "Why, then, did the church refuse this protection? Why did it have to engage in a battle to the death with the imperial powers?" He answers, "Because, true to its roots in the Old Testament, it could not accept relegation to a private sphere of purely inward and personal religion. It knew itself to be the bearer of the promise of the reign of Yahweh over all nations."[124] Since the early church understood its gospel as the rule of God over all nations and all of life, it refused to be called a private religion and instead took on itself the designation of *ekklesia tou theou*, a public assembly. "In other words, the early Church did not see itself as a private religious society competing with others to offer personal salvation to its members; it saw itself as a movement launched into the public life of the world, challenging the *cultus publicus* of the Empire, claiming the allegiance of all without exception."[125] This challenge "made a collision with the imperial power inevitable."[126] Newbigin believes the Western church has become what the early church refused to be. Our task is to recover the Old Testament roots of the gospel and understand it again as the summons to serve the sovereign Lord, who rules all of life. This will entail a challenge to the public doctrine of our culture.

The third reason Newbigin notes that the church has accommodated itself to the private realm is that it does not rightly understand the religious and idolatrous nature of Western culture. It misunderstands the Bible's teaching on the spiritual powers. The power of secularism has led the church to have to accept the presumed neutrality of the public square. But the "truth is that, in those areas of our human living which we do not submit to the rule of Christ, we do not remain free to make our own decisions: we fall under another power."[127] The shrine of the public square is not empty, nor is it neutral; it has fallen under the power of other gods. To restrict Christ's lordship to the private realm has serious consequences: the majority of life will be lived under the sovereign rule of another lord.

Privatization is not a legitimate option if the church is to be faithful. But neither is a return to Christendom. The primary problem in Christendom was that the church forgot that it existed in a missionary situation. Churches defined themselves apart from their vocation in the world.[128] The lack of a

124. Newbigin, *Foolishness to the Greeks*, 99–100.
125. Lesslie Newbigin, *Sign of the Kingdom* (Grand Rapids: Eerdmans, 1980), 46.
126. Newbigin, *Foolishness to the Greeks*, 100.
127. Newbigin, *Other Side of 1984*, 39.
128. Lesslie Newbigin, *Household of God: Lectures on the Nature of the Church* (New York: Friendship Press, 1954), 1–2; Newbigin, *Honest Religion*, 104.

missionary identity shaped all manner of churchmanship including congregational structures, patterns of ministry, sacraments, and theological education.[129] The church in Christendom, writes Newbigin, "thinks primarily of its duty to care for its own members, and its duty to those outside drops into second place. A conception of pastoral care is developed which seems to assume that the individual believer is primarily a passive recipient of the means of grace which is the business of the Church to administer."[130]

But Newbigin's primary concern with Christendom was that the church lost its critical relationship to culture. The church has two relationships to its culture: solidarity in cultural development and dissent from its idolatrous direction. While the Christendom church takes responsibility for the cultural development and social life of culture, it forgets the antithetical tension that comes with it. "We are painfully aware of the consequences of [Constantine's] conversion; for centuries the Church was allied with the established power, sanctioned and even wielded the sword, lost its critical relation to the ruling authorities."[131] When it loses its prophetic-critical stance in relation to culture, it accepts a role as the "protected and well decorated chaplaincy in the camp of the dominant power."[132]

Yet Newbigin is not entirely negative about Christendom. He believes that the church was right in taking responsibility for the cultural, social, and political life of medieval Europe.[133] Christendom was the "first great attempt to translate the universal claim of Christ into political terms."[134] The result was that "the Gospel was wrought into the very stuff of [Europe's] social and political life."[135] It shaped our science, political democracy, and traditions of ethical behavior,[136] and "we still live largely on the spiritual capital it generated."[137] Yet "we cannot go back to the *corpus Christianum*," nor for that matter can we "go back to a pre-Constantinian innocence." The challenge for us, according to Newbigin, is to "learn how to embody in the life of the church a witness to the kingship of Christ over all life—its politic and economic no less than its personal and domestic morals—yet without falling into the

129. Newbigin, *Honest Religion*, 102–5.
130. Newbigin, *Household of God*, 166–67.
131. Newbigin, *Sign of the Kingdom*, 48.
132. Lesslie Newbigin, "Christ, Kingdom, and Church: A Reflection on the Papers of George Yule and Andrew Kirk," unpublished paper, 1983, 4.
133. Newbigin, *Foolishness to the Greeks*, 100–101.
134. Newbigin, *Sign of the Kingdom*, 47.
135. Newbigin, *Household of God*, 1.
136. Newbigin, *Foolishness to the Greeks*, 124.
137. Lesslie Newbigin, *Priorities for a New Decade* (Birmingham, UK: National Student Christian Press and Resource Centre, 1980), 6.

Constantinian trap. That is the new, unprecedented, and immensely challenging task given to our generation. The resolute taking of it is fundamental to any genuinely missionary encounter of the gospel with our culture."[138]

No matter how hard Newbigin tried to distance himself from advocating a return to Christendom, that accusation continued to cling to him. No doubt the primary reason was his insistence that the gospel is public truth for all of cultural life and that the church must not allow its mission to be confined to the private sphere. If the church must press the claims of Christ in every area of cultural life, then what other possibility can there be besides Christendom? Christendom seems like the only option available if one rejects privatization, and so "there is suspicion that in talking about public truth we are motivated by nostalgia for a lost security, for the time when Christianity was either acknowledged or enforced as public truth—a nostalgia for lost Christendom."[139]

Nevertheless, for Newbigin there is no way back to Christendom: it is neither possible nor desirable. Yet the very nature of the gospel demands we confess it as public truth. So what is the way forward? How can the church embody the lordship of Christ in every area of public life without returning to Christendom? "We are now faced with a new task which may be defined as follows: how to embody in the life and teaching of the Church the claim that Christ is Lord over all life, without falling into the Constantinian impasse?"[140] This was the difficult ecclesiological challenge Newbigin tackled.

Distinctive People: Alternative Social Order and Callings in Public Life

As the people of God living in Western culture today, we ask, What must we be? There is a sense in which this whole book up to this point has been an answer to that question. The primary motivation for this book is that Newbigin offers a weighty call to the church today, and even though his writings are from the last century, the call remains profoundly relevant. Indeed, all the areas of a missionary ecclesiology that I have elaborated in the earlier chapters can be found in Newbigin's challenge to the church in Western culture today.

What must we be? We must be a people who believe the gospel of the kingdom and live in the Bible as the true story of the world. We must be a people whose lives, deeds, and words bear witness to the gospel of the kingdom both nearby and far away. We must be a people whose worship,

138. Newbigin, *Foolishness to the Greeks*, 102.
139. Newbigin, "Gospel as Public Truth," 2.
140. Newbigin, *Other Side of 1984*, 34.

leadership, and structures nourish a comprehensive obedience. We must be a people who understand the religious core and the controlling story of our culture so as to joyfully affirm God's creational gifts and resolutely reject our idolatrous ways. All of this answers the question, What must we be? But there are at least two emphases in Newbigin's writings that deserve mention in this chapter on a missionary encounter with Western culture.

The first is the repeated dual responsibility to "tell and embody" the story of God's mighty acts revealed and accomplished in Jesus Christ.[141] Newbigin constantly insisted "that God has entrusted to [the church] this story and there is no other body that will tell it."[142] And so one of the most urgent tasks is the recovery of confidence in the public truth of the gospel so that the church will tell it faithfully. "The first requirement is, quite simply, a recovery of confidence in the truth of the Gospel."[143] Much of Newbigin's work in epistemology was precisely for this purpose—to renew confidence in the public truth of the gospel. But if that telling is to be credible, there must be an embodiment. And if the telling is the announcing of a gospel of the kingdom that calls all areas of human life to submit to Christ the Lord, then the embodiment must correspond to the message. This is why Newbigin stressed two areas of this embodiment: the church as an alternative social order and its callings in the public life of culture. Both stress the importance of the church being distinctive over against the syncretism that corrupts the Western church. And both emphasize the comprehensive breadth of the gospel's authority across the spectrum of human life. For Newbigin this is the way beyond privatization and Christendom.

While these two emphases are common in Newbigin's writing, it is perhaps in *Truth to Tell: The Gospel as Public Truth* that the logic is made most clear. The book contains three lectures. The first compares the early church to the church in the West today. In the Roman Empire various dichotomies produced by cultural idolatry were destroying the empire. The church offered the gospel as the truth that Jesus Christ is Lord of public and private life. The second lecture deals with the way the church has had trouble in both its liberal and its conservative wings with affirming the public truth of the gospel. Both have been captive to Enlightenment assumptions. If the church

---

141. Newbigin, *Proper Confidence*, 76–78; Newbigin, "Gospel and Modern Western Culture," 7; Lesslie Newbigin, "Human Flourishing in Faith, Fact, and Fantasy," *Religion and Medicine* 7 (1988): 409; Lesslie Newbigin, *The Gospel in Today's Global City*, Selly Oak Occasional Paper 16 (Birmingham: Selly Oak Colleges, 1997), 6; Lesslie Newbigin, *The Gospel and Our Culture* (London: Catholic Missionary Education Centre, 1990), 4.

142. Newbigin, *Proper Confidence*, 78.

143. Newbigin, "New Birth into a Living Hope," 6.

is to embody and tell the gospel as public truth in the midst of culture, it must itself affirm the truth.

The third lecture, "Speaking the Truth to Caesar," turns to the mission of the church in the public life of culture. Newbigin begins by closing off two options: Christendom and pre-Constantinian innocence. He proceeds by challenging the church with its task to unmask the various ideologies of Western culture, especially economic idolatry, in a way analogous to the German Confessing Church during World War II. He then offers three ways the church is to embody the gospel as public truth. First, "it must be the responsibility of the Church to equip its members for active and informed participation in public life in such a way that the Christian faith shapes participation."[144] Second, "if such training were widely available, we could look for a time when many of those holding responsible positions of leadership in public life were committed Christians equipped to raise the questions and make the innovations in these areas which the gospel requires."[145] And third, "the most important contribution which the Church can make to a new social order is to be itself a new social order."[146] Here we see two things Newbigin stresses—being a distinctive community and our vocations in public life—that enable the church to embody the gospel as public truth.

It is significant that these two emphases pick up on two traditions that have been hard at work for centuries attempting to understand what it means to embody a gospel that is as wide as creation—the Anabaptist and Reformed traditions. The Anabaptist tradition has emphasized that the church is a countercultural community called to challenge the idolatry of culture in its own life together. The Reformed tradition has stressed the callings of its various members in culture.

The question that arises is whether stressing the distinctiveness of the church in its gathered and scattered life really moves us beyond Christendom. On this, three things may be said. First, Newbigin offers the notion of "committed pluralism" as a way of thinking about participation in the public life of culture. The way of committed pluralism rejects both a coercive Christendom and a privatized faith. He distinguishes between an "agnostic pluralism" and a "committed pluralism." An agnostic pluralism believes that truth is unknowable and therefore that there are no criteria to judge truth from falsehood in the public square. Supposedly all traditions may be equally tolerated. Over against this, a committed pluralism is devoted to a search

144. Newbigin, *Truth to Tell*, 81.
145. Newbigin, *Truth to Tell*, 84.
146. Newbigin, *Truth to Tell*, 85.

for truth, justice, and freedom in the public square. The truth claims of all traditions must be taken seriously. A committed pluralism is committed to dialogue between different traditions to find a way to public justice. It is modeled on what Polanyi calls the "republic of science"—the way the scientific community searches for truth. "Because it is believed that there is a reality to be known, differences of opinion are not left to coexist side by side as evidence of the glories of pluralism. They are the subject of debate, argument, testing, and fresh research until either one view prevails over the other as more true, or else some fresh way of seeing things enables the two views to be reconciled as two ways of seeing one reality."[147] The believer in his or her calling engages their area in public life, pursuing truth, justice, and freedom from the standpoint of the gospel and attempting to convince others that this comports with reality.

Second, Newbigin recalls the Dutch neo-Calvinist notion of sphere sovereignty. This tradition argues that the problem with Christendom is not that Christians exercised power in their particular cultural callings. The problem is that the institutionalized church coercively exercised power. There is a distinction between the church as an institution and the church as the new humankind, as well as the church gathered and the church scattered. God has given a measure of autonomy to the various areas of human life such as art, science, politics, and economics. The institutionalized church does not mediate God's authority in these areas. Rather, each of these spheres is ruled directly by God's Word and implemented by people who work within those spheres. This avoids both the post-Enlightenment notion of the total freedom and autonomy of the various social spheres and the medieval idea that the church rules over all of them. The church has no right to dictate how these areas are to be shaped, but Christians with insight and vocations in each of these areas must seek to shape these areas in conformity with God's Word.[148] People with cultural power in the various spheres are to use that power in a way that is directed by the gospel. This corresponds with Newbigin's long-running defense of power as creational and the problem being its misuse. Some vision of truth will shape the public square. And if the gospel is true, then the truth, justice, and freedom of God's Word should most faithfully correspond with reality and may find a response in the hearts of those who do not believe the gospel.

Finally, and perhaps most important, the story of the Bible that the church is called to embody in the public realm has as its center the cross of Jesus

147. Newbigin, *Truth to Tell*, 58.
148. Newbigin, *Foolishness to the Greeks*, 143–44.

Christ. The cross pictures for us that God does not coerce or compel but gives freedom for rejection. The metanarrative of the Bible does not look for an intrahistorical triumph. God's victory is beyond history, and until then, suffering love is the way power is exercised. Newbigin writes, "The fact that the cross stands as the central Christian symbol must forever forbid the identification of the gospel with political power. The Church's witness to the gospel must always be made in the knowledge that the manifest reign of God can only be at the end when he brings all things to final judgement, that for the present age the reign of God must be veiled in the weakness and foolishness of his Church, and that it is God alone who can reveal to people his presence within this veil."[149] The victory of the gospel comes at the return of Christ. Thus, until that day, Christians in their various offices are free to witness to and work for the justice and freedom God wills in the light of the gospel and to let God work out his purposes. Suffering and rejection may well be the response. But there should be no attempt to coerce or compel. Rather, there may be a trusting and joyful witness to the truth that leaves room for God to work and for others to respond in freedom.

Conclusion

In C. S. Lewis's *The Silver Chair* from the Chronicles of Narnia series, the Lady of the Green Kirtle, the witch-queen of the Underland, begins to seduce and hypnotize Puddleglum, Eustace, and Jill. With soothing words and music, and with magic smoke produced by the powder she throws in the fire, she begins to gradually take them under her spell. As they listen to the music and inhale the smoke, they are slowly enslaved and drawn under her power. They forget the mission given to them by Aslan to free Rilian from the witch-queen and turn themselves to serve her. The Marshwiggle Puddleglum realizes what is going on. He rouses himself from his own enchantment and attempts to foil her plan by stomping his webbed foot on the fire to put it out. The children come to their senses and are awakened from their enchantment. They rise up and slay the queen, who has now revealed herself in her true nature as a serpent.

Newbigin is like Puddleglum.[150] With the fresh eyes of someone who has lived in another culture for four decades, Newbigin has seen how the church has been seduced and enslaved by the idols of Western culture. He has

149. Newbigin, *Word in Season*, 167–68.
150. I borrow this analogy between Newbigin and Puddleglum from my wife, Marnie, who once suggested it to him, much to his great amusement.

awakened many of us to see ways in which we have come under the spell of the gods of our culture. But this is only a small beginning. Surely Newbigin was right: the most powerful, pervasive, and dangerous culture to the gospel is that of the West, which has now spread to every part of the urban world, seducing its millions. The church is called to rouse itself from its enchantment and, rooted in Christ, to show what it really means to be human.

7

Lesslie Newbigin's Legacy for Today

N. T. Wright says, "Lesslie Newbigin was quite simply a gift to the church in so many ways."[1] This has been said by many people. Certainly a big part of that gift is the theological legacy he left behind in his writings. In this chapter I elaborate eight areas where Newbigin's theology offers valuable and needed insight to the church today. To select eight areas is difficult, because each aspect of his missionary ecclesiology that we have covered in the pages above has relevance for the contemporary church. But in this final chapter I will be more selective, highlighting the aspects of Newbigin's theological legacy that I believe are most urgent for the church today.

Gospel of the Kingdom

There is a growing recognition today among evangelicals in North America that we need to get back to basics and ask the most foundational question we can ask: What is the gospel? This is evident, for example, in the formation of the Gospel Coalition and in its well-attended conferences. It is also clear in the number of books rolling off the presses that pose this question. Newbigin lived his life with this question in a missionary situation and constantly

1. Private email correspondence, July 28, 2017.

returned to the gospel as his starting point to address many topics. His insight is important for us today.

Where one starts in the Bible to answer this question is of fundamental importance. There is not just one place to start, of course, but Newbigin's consistent practice was to begin with Mark 1:14–15. This is the first announcement of the gospel by Jesus, and Newbigin believed that was crucial. Starting with the kingdom sets the gospel within the context of the Old Testament narrative and establishes its eschatological nature from the outset. Far too often the background story for the gospel is personal testimonies, evangelistic presentations, and systematic theologies. The Old Testament story and the eschatological nature of the gospel are eclipsed.

Newbigin was consistent in placing the gospel within the Old Testament context. And by making the election of Israel the central theme, he made clear that the gospel had to be the climactic moment of Israel's story. Specifically, Israel's vocation to reveal and accomplish God's redemptive purposes in the midst of the world is fulfilled in Jesus. This enables us to understand the very helpful, if not initially puzzling, formulation that the gospel is the revelation and accomplishment of the End of universal history. Israel was to reveal God's creational intentions for humanity in their lives and thus to accomplish his purpose to draw nations to himself. Jesus fulfills the calling of Israel in his life, death, and resurrection by fully revealing and accomplishing God's purpose to renew the whole life of humanity.

The starting point in the gospel of the kingdom also counters an other-worldly and individualistic understanding of the gospel and salvation. This understanding continues to ravage the church today, not just in North America but well beyond. The gospel of the kingdom preached by Jesus, if it is taken in its original context, simply cannot be twisted into this shape. It is an announcement about cosmic renewal—a salvation that is comprehensive in scope and restorative in its nature. God is restoring the whole creation and the entire life of humankind. This understanding of the gospel and the kingdom is critical for the church's life and mission today.

Newbigin's refusal to allow the person of Jesus to be separated from the kingdom continues to be a timely challenge. It is easy for those interested in the costly nature of mission in the areas of politics, economics, and society to turn mission into a social program and to forget that at the heart of the gospel is an invitation to personal communion with the person of Jesus. It is also easy for those who want to stress a personal relationship with Jesus to turn mission into evangelism and to forget that loving and knowing Jesus means following and joining him in his costly kingdom mission in the public square. Keeping Jesus and the kingdom together in the gospel is an important insight for us today.

The Bible as the True Story of the Whole World

If one gets anything from reading Newbigin, it will be his insistence on the Bible as the true story of the whole world. And there is so much in his reflection on this theme that is crucial for us today. His reflection on the status of story in the Christian faith is important. It has been my consistent experience that it is difficult to communicate this, especially, quite surprisingly, among those trained theologically. For Newbigin, story is not about a particular literary genre found in the Bible;[2] the historical books narrate that story, to be sure, but it means more. Neither is it about a redemptive-historical or narrative hermeneutic, which reduces story to its importance for biblical interpretation; nor is it about biblical or narrative or redemptive-historical theology, which confines story to a way of doing theology. Certainly each of these is shaped by the story, but it is only these because story is much more.

Newbigin's approach to the biblical narrative can be contrasted, for example, with Tim Keller's synchronic and diachronic approaches to theology. Synchronic or systematic theology deals with Scripture topically arranged and makes propositional statements about God, sin, Christ, and faith, for example. A diachronic or redemptive-historical theology "organizes what the Bible says by stages in history or by the plotline of the story."[3] The first deals with the themes of Scripture and the second with its story line. In the end, Keller advocates both approaches and warns that to lose either approach invites distortions. For Keller there is no priority: story is one of two ways to do theology.

This is very different from Newbigin. Newbigin may well be happy to speak of two theological methods. But these are both second-order activities that enable us to be faithful to the biblical story. Tracing themes through Scripture by employing a more narrative approach or articulating themes propositionally by utilizing a more topical method may well produce deepened insight into Scripture, may be mutually enriching, and may in different ways protect Scripture's teaching from distortion. Newbigin probably would

---

2. Surprisingly, John Frame seems to misunderstand N. T. Wright precisely at this point. See Frame, "N. T. Wright and the Authority of Scripture," in *Did God Really Say? Affirming the Truthfulness and Trustworthiness of Scripture*, ed. David B. Garner (Phillipsburg, NJ: P&R, 2012), 111–12.

3. Timothy Keller, *Center Church: Doing Balanced, Gospel-Centered Ministry in Your City* (Grand Rapids: Zondervan, 2012), 40.

not dispute Keller at this point. But Newbigin would say that story cannot be reduced to redemptive-historical theology; the very nature of Scripture is the true story of the world that provides the all-encompassing framework for or the overarching umbrella under which *any* kind of second-order theological reflection must be done, whether systematic or redemptive-historical theology. For Newbigin, story cannot be reduced to theology; it is much bigger and more significant than that. The Bible is an interpretation of universal or cosmic history. It is what Richard Bauckham means by "metanarrative" or what N. T. Wright means by "the basic worldview-story."[4]

Consequently, story is the overarching category for understanding the very nature of the Christian faith. The Christian faith *is* a story that begins in creation, moves through human rebellion and the election of Israel as a solution to sin, ultimately finding its climactic moment in the person and work of Jesus and then moving throughout the world in the mission of the church until Christ returns and completes his work. Story is the very *structure* of the Christian faith for Newbigin. This is the same point that N. T. Wright makes when he says that "the whole point of Christianity is that it offers a story which is the story of the whole world. It is public truth."[5] And since this story is universal history, it is the clue or light for understanding everything in creation. This is an astonishing claim but consistent with the Bible's own witness.

Newbigin's emphasis on the historical nature of the narrative is also important for challenging the Greek rationalism that remains very powerful today. For many the "absolute truth" of Scripture is found in unchanging ideas that stand above history. Those theological ideas are found embedded in Scripture and may be extracted from the story to express the Christian faith in confessions or theologies. In this view, the storied nature of the Bible is incidental; the unchanging theological truths stated propositionally are the heart of the matter. Propositions are a stronger statement of truth.

Newbigin challenges this ancient pagan notion rooted in Plato and Aristotle. More than once, *Drama of Scripture*, a book that I coauthored with Craig Bartholomew, has been critiqued for finding truth in a story, which is seen as a weaker or postmodern form of truth.[6] Theological propositions and systems supposedly carry more substance and weight. But this is simply capitulation

4. Richard Bauckham, *Bible and Mission: Christian Witness in a Postmodern World* (Grand Rapids: Baker, 2003), 4–5; N. T. Wright, *The New Testament and the People of God* (Minneapolis: Fortress, 1992), 135.

5. Wright, *New Testament and the People of God*, 41–42.

6. Craig G. Bartholomew and Michael W. Goheen, *The Drama of Scripture: Finding Our Place in the Biblical Story*, 2nd ed. (Grand Rapids: Baker Academic, 2014).

to the pagan Greek tradition revived in the Enlightenment. The biblical story shows us that truth is rooted in historical events, in God's mighty acts in history, which are leading toward the goal of cosmic renewal. This is the way the Bible reveals truth to us, and we are invited to accept the way God has revealed himself and his purpose and then to find our place in that story.

Newbigin distinguishes between Eastern and Western religions in the way they understand ultimate and comprehensive truth. Again this brings us to the heart of the matter. The great divide between religions is where comprehensive and ultimate truth can be found. Eastern religions find it in some unchanging principle that stands behind the diversity of creation (e.g., Brahman). Western religions, shaped in one way or another by the Old Testament, including the Christian faith, find it in a story that is leading to a goal for universal history. If we want to understand the Christian faith, we must attend to God's mighty acts in history, especially in Jesus Christ, and see the Bible as a narrative of those mighty deeds that are leading the whole world to a renewed creation.

Recovering the comprehensive scope of the biblical story as a cosmic narrative is one of the most important tasks for the church today. It provides the basis for understanding the gospel in its cosmic scope as the climactic moment of the story. This provides the proper context for the climactic events in Jesus Christ. It provides the proper context for understanding the breadth of the church's mission in the midst of the world. And, importantly for the syncretistic church of the West, it is the only bulwark that can protect the gospel from being accommodated to the cultural story: if the Bible is broken up into theological or devotional bits, it will be absorbed into a more comprehensive cultural story, and it will be that story rather than the Bible that shapes our lives.

Finally, Newbigin's insistence on the Bible as one story enables us to rightly understand the Christian faith in terms of its true "logic": cosmic, communal, and personal. Since the time of the Reformation, the individual has increasingly been moved to the center stage in the Christian faith. While this has had some benefits and opened up insight into Scripture, in this year when I write, on the occasion of the five hundredth anniversary of the Reformation, we have to acknowledge that there is a desperate need for a Copernican revolution. The individual is not at the center of the biblical story! This individualism feeds the narcissism and the consumerism of the West. "For me, for me—it's all about me!" For Newbigin the Bible is a story of *cosmic* history with Christ at the center. It is from him, to him, by him, and ultimately for him. The story is *communal*: at its center is a community he has chosen to embody and enact his reconciling purpose for the world.

Individuals are extended a *personal* invitation into that community and called to play their role in God's story. Surely this is the very structure of thought we find in the apostle Paul, for example, in Colossians 1 and Ephesians 1. This challenges the spiritual narcissism and consumerism that is rampant in the Christian faith of the West. And—this must be clear—it does not lessen the importance of individual response, nor does it diminish the blessing each of us may enjoy as we are "included in Christ when we hear the message of truth, the gospel of our salvation. When we believed . . ." (Eph. 1:13).[7] Rather, it sets each person where they belong—finding their place in the cosmic work of Christ (vv. 9–10), "to the praise of his glory" (vv. 12, 14), and in the community created by his work.

The Centrality of Election in the Biblical Story

It may seem initially surprising that Newbigin makes election so central to his understanding of the Christian faith. But the way he elaborates this central biblical theme is important in clarifying our understanding of the Christian faith in at least two ways. First, it reminds us of the nature of salvation. Salvation is not the rescue of one individual after another with each one set in their own personal relationship with God. This is often held as an unexamined assumption. Rather, creation has a harmony, unity, and integrity that have been ruptured in the fall. Salvation is the restoration of the coherence and shalom of human life in the context of the creation. Humans are not created as discrete individuals, nor will they be redeemed as such. God's redemptive work travels along the channels he cuts at creation. People live related to God, to each other in many different kinds of relationships, to the nonhuman creation, and in a certain unity within themselves. All of this is shattered in Adam and Eve's rebellion. Salvation is the healing of the lost shalom, the reconciliation of what was alienated, the knitting back together of separated fragments. If that is God's cosmic purpose, then there must be a nucleus of people who are already restored in all these ways as the starting point for God's work, and then they may be the place where others are incorporated into that reconciled community. Election means a reconciled and reconciling community. In this light, election is a central biblical doctrine. And it sheds light on the mission of the church.

But election also shows us the importance of Israel in the biblical story. How easy it is to forget the longest part of the biblical story or reduce it, say, to

---

7. The original verse is in the second person: "And you also were included in Christ when you heard the message of truth, the gospel of your salvation. When you believed . . ."

promise. Newbigin chooses the word "election" almost as a label for the Old Testament and the history of Israel. It places the mission of Israel to embody God's universal purposes at the center of the story. This is important for a missional reading of Scripture but also sets the proper context for the work of Jesus Christ and the continuing mission of the church to the nations. The biblical story is about the election of Israel—the "three Israels":[8] God chooses Israel to reveal and accomplish his redemptive purpose; the story narrows to Jesus, who is chosen to himself bear the vocation of Israel and who fulfills that purpose; Jesus gathers and sends the nucleus of the true Israel, chosen to continue the mission of Jesus amid all nations.

A Missionary Encounter with Western Culture

Newbigin is right to see that one of the biggest dangers facing the Western church is its acceptance of the relegation of the gospel and the church's mission to the private sphere. This goes against everything that the gospel is and the vocation the church has been given to embody the public truth of the gospel. It is no small issue. The notion of a missionary encounter sets before us an understanding of the very nature of the Christian faith as a clash of equally comprehensive and equally religious stories. The gospel is not about religious doctrine but headline news that God's rule over all things has broken into history. That must clash with any cultural public doctrine that does not submit to Christ's lordship, which can be found in every culture.

The terminology of missionary encounter keeps us from carving out a small space within culture into which the gospel is made to fit. And it does not allow us to think of Western culture as innocuous; it is religious at its core, shaped by idolatry and the spiritual powers. Newbigin warns that we have been fooled by myths—the myth of a Christian culture and the myth of a neutral culture, whether secular or pluralistic—and it is a timely warning for the church today. There is no friendly "Christian-like" culture in the West, nor is there a neutral secular culture based on objective science, nor is there a pluralistic culture that holds the ring impartially for all religions to live in peace. Newbigin claims that Western culture is the most powerful, the most pervasive, the most dangerous, and the most resistant culture to

8. Newbigin has this intriguing reference to "the three Israels" in an outline on canon and mission. It is one item of a list of important interpretive clues for reading the biblical story. See Lesslie Newbigin, "Canon and Mission," unpublished notes, Newbigin Archives, University of Birmingham (n.d.), 2. See also comments above in chap. 1 in the section "God's Purpose and the Logic of Election."

the gospel, and this is a salient warning and apt challenge to the church to not allow the gospel to be accommodated to it. A missionary encounter is the only faithful posture the church may take. This gets to the very nature of the Christian faith and a conscious habit of the heart that the church in the West must cultivate.

A Missionary Encounter with Global Economic Modernity and Consumerism

Perhaps one of the most neglected aspects of Newbigin's thought is his focus in the last decade of his life on the danger of global capitalism and consumerism. Newbigin's interpreters have rightly attended to what he has said about the modern scientific worldview flowing from the Enlightenment and especially his interest in epistemology. When they have turned to his comments on the cultural changes in the late twentieth century, changes that continue into the early twenty-first century, it has usually been in terms of postmodernity. But for Newbigin the biggest threat facing the church at the end of the twentieth century (and now certainly in the twenty-first century) is not postmodernity; it is economic globalization and a consumer culture.[9] Newbigin's references to postmodernity are few, but not so with global capitalism, economic modernity, and consumerism.[10] He says, "The crucial question is going to be whether the Christian church can recover its confidence in the gospel in order to be able to challenge with confidence the enormous power of this ideology which now rules us. We are dealing here

9. Richard Bauckham holds a similar conviction: "The reality of our world is not the end of grand narratives, but the increasing dominance of the narrative of economic globalization" (Bauckham, *Bible and Mission*, 94). Interestingly, he interacts with Newbigin throughout this chapter.

10. See, e.g., Lesslie Newbigin, "New Birth into a Living Hope" (keynote address, European Area Council of the World Alliance of Reformed Churches meeting, Edinburgh, Scotland, August 28, 1995), 2–3, 9; Lesslie Newbigin, "Whose Justice?" *Ecumenical Review* 44 (July 1992): 309; Lesslie Newbigin, "Gospel and Culture" (unpublished speech, Denmark, November 1995), 11–12; Lesslie Newbigin, "A Missionary's Dream," *Ecumenical Review* 43, no. 1 (January 1991): 5–6; Lesslie Newbigin, "The Gospel as Public Truth: Swanwick Opening Statement" (unpublished address, 1992), 5–6; Lesslie Newbigin, "Modernity in Context," in *Modern, Postmodern and Christian*, ed. John Reid, Lesslie Newbigin, and David Pullinger, Lausanne Occasional Paper 27 (Carberry, Scotland: Handsel, 1996), 8; Lesslie Newbigin, "The End of History," *Gospel and Our Culture (U. K.)* 13 (Summer 1992): 1–2; Lesslie Newbigin, ". . . and Culture," in *Signs amid the Rubble: The Purposes of God in Human History*, ed. Geoffrey Wainwright (Grand Rapids: Eerdmans, 2003), 119–20. For essays that seek to expose the religious and idolatrous roots of globalization, see Michael W. Goheen and Erin G. Glanville, eds., *The Gospel and Globalization: Exploring the Religious Roots of Globalization* (Vancouver: Regent College Press and Geneva Society, 2009).

with an idol, the idol of the free market, and idols do not respond to moral persuasion. They are cast out only by the living God, and it is only the power of the gospel in the last analysis which can dethrone idols."[11]

I was alerted to Newbigin's views while listening to him preach at Beeson Divinity School in the early 1990s. Initially I was taken aback by the passion and intensity with which he spoke about the global free market and economic idolatry as a demonic power. But the danger of global capitalism may be gauged even more by Newbigin's hint that perhaps the economic policies of Margaret Thatcher in the 1980s were leading us to a "confessional situation." Here he is referring to a very specific kind of confession. The whole of the Christian faith is a matter of confessing the gospel over against idolatry, of course. But sometimes there are threats to our world that bring injustice on such a wide and deep scale that they require the church to take special action and make a counterconfession in response. This has been called a *status confessionis*. The Barmen Declaration (1934) was just such an act in the face of the threat of Nazism. A similar response has been made to apartheid in South Africa. Some have argued that global neoliberalism presents a threat on just this same scale and puts us into a *status confessionis*.[12] Newbigin notes that when Margaret Thatcher's economic policies were taking hold in the 1980s, the public good was being "swept contemptuously aside in favour of commitment to private gain. Market forces were to have final sovereignty over our lives." Newbigin believed we were moving into an era of blatant ideology that would require the church's mission to change. "We were dealing not with a political programme but with an idolatry. We were coming into a confessional situation."[13]

For Newbigin this is a global form of economic modernity that has its roots in the eighteenth-century Enlightenment. He believed that it was through the economic theory of Adam Smith and others that the Enlightenment would have its most far-reaching impact. The new Enlightenment economics would supposedly create unlimited economic growth and bring fulfillment and happiness. While the modern scientific worldview would take two forms in the twentieth century—communism in Russia and Eastern Europe, and liberalism in Western Europe and North America—the collapse of the communist

11. Newbigin, ". . . and Culture," 119.

12. Ulrich Duchrow, *Global Economy: A Confessional Issue for the Churches?* (Geneva: World Council of Churches, 1987); Timothy Gorringe, "The Principalities and Powers: A Framework for Thinking about Globalization," in *Globalization and the Good*, ed. Peter Heslam (Grand Rapids: Eerdmans, 2004), 85; Guillermo Hansen, "Neoliberal Globalization: A *Casus Confessionis*?," *Lutheran World Fellowship Documentation* 50 (December 2004): 163–78.

13. Lesslie Newbigin, *Unfinished Agenda: An Updated Autobiography* (Edinburgh: Saint Andrew Press, 1993), 250.

bloc would open the way for the global spread of the liberal economic form of modernity around the world in globalization. While Newbigin believed that the free market is a good way to balance supply and demand, he also recognized that when it is in the grip of the powerful idolatry of freedom, the market is an oppressive tyrant and an evil power that has final sovereignty over much of cultural life.

The free market as an idolatrous power is bringing terrible injustices, especially economically and ecologically, and the only story that seems to be able to withstand it is the Muslim story. Economic modernity and globalization are also producing a consumer society that is sweeping all of life into its current. Newbigin's challenge to take this threat seriously is one the church of the twenty-first century must take to heart.

I have a vivid memory in this regard. In 1994 I had just finished a tour of the civil rights museum in Birmingham, Alabama, with Newbigin and my family. I was standing beside my car with Newbigin, waiting for my wife to return. He shook his head as he tried to come to terms with what he had just witnessed—the complicity of Christians in the horror and cruelty of slavery. He asked with agony etched all over his face, "How could Christians have been so blind to their sin?" He continued, "I wonder what later generations will identify as our biggest idol to which we are oblivious." Immediately he offered an answer to his own query: "No doubt it will be our economic idolatry and our blindness to consumerism. It will be our lives immersed in mindless consumption in a world where there is so much poverty and hunger."

The Church as Distinctive Community and the Calling of the Laity

In the face of the powerful threat of Western culture, Newbigin stressed two aspects of the church's mission: the church as a distinctive community and the calling of the laity in the public life of culture. Both of these are important for the church today if the gospel is ever to be recognized as public truth. Newbigin's call to the church to be a hermeneutic of the gospel is especially pointed. In the list of what that might look like, he stresses aspects of the Bible's teaching over against the idols of the day. Following his example of making a list of what a distinctive community might look like can be a valuable way to challenge the church, especially leaders. I have done this often, making a list of what a distinctive community today might look like—for example, as we live in the midst of a consumer society; as we read, preach, and hear the books of Colossians, 1 Peter, and James; as we form academic institutions; and so on. More often than any other request I receive after I finish speaking, I am asked for these lists. Creating lists of this sort seems to trigger a few things, in my experience. It sparks the imagination to think about the church as a distinctive or contrast community. For many, that notion is simply not familiar territory. It also challenges leaders and others to think contextually. Too much preaching and teaching or Bible reading, for example, is quite abstract. We often think of doctrine and ethics in terms of timeless principles abstractly divorced from their original context and quite separate from our cultural idols. For example, we call people to be patient without considering the cultural forces that form us in the way of immediate gratification. We challenge people to live generously without considering the way a consumer society seduces us to find satisfaction in accumulating consumer goods. We exhort people to live selflessly without considering the way our culture constantly puts the self at the center. We invite people to live in wisdom without taking account of its difficulty in a world of proliferating knowledge spawned by information technology. And the list could go on. Making the kind of list Newbigin made challenges us to think contextually about the religious beliefs and structures of our culture and to set our calling in that setting. And that is why preaching or teaching any book of the Bible, for example, can become more alive and relevant if it is in dialogue in this way with our cultural story.

To elaborate: We may preach Psalm 63, for example, and invite people to live their lives *coram Deo*, in the presence of God, without considering the pressures of a secular culture that forms us to live our lives apart from God. It is not just a secular ethos that makes it difficult for us to walk in continual fellowship with God. Rather, the very structures and institutions of our culture are inherently atheistic. Craig Gay examines the way Western politics, technology, and economics, for example, teach us to live as if God doesn't exist. They are molding us into the pattern of practical atheism that is built right into the very cultural structures we inhabit.[14] It is this kind of cultural analysis that will help us as we seek to understand what it means to be a distinctive people living in the biblical story. The stress on being a distinctive people will push us to engage idolatrous cultural structures that oppose faithfulness and ask how those structures are challenged by a biblical view of the world.

Let me provide another concrete example of how this may work. In August 2018 I spoke to pastors and church planters in Brazil on the book of James at a conference to celebrate the five hundredth anniversary of the

14. Craig M. Gay, *The Way of the (Modern) World: Or, Why It's Tempting to Live as if God Doesn't Exist* (Grand Rapids: Eerdmans, 1998).

Reformation. Inspired by Newbigin, I soaked in James for months and asked how he challenges us to think about the church as a hermeneutic of the gospel. Behind what I said were Richard Bauckham's words about the book of James:

> What is needed is for the Christian community to develop as a counter-cultural alternative to the dominant culture, in its own life together both distinctive and outgoing, shaping its members' lives, both within and without the community's own life, in ways that witness to Jesus Christ, in critical solidarity with all that is good in dominant society and in prophetic critique of all that is corrupting and destructive. James can inform the life of such a counter-cultural community because its aim is precisely the formation and nurturing of the Christian community as a counter-cultural embodiment of God's values and commandments. . . . The aim [in reading James today] must be to hear within our own context the distinctive voice of the text with a view to the distinctive community it aims to construct.[15]

Here is a small sample of my list of how James aims to construct a distinctive community in the twenty-first century to be a hermeneutic of the gospel. The point is to set James's teaching in today's context, especially the structural idolatry of our culture that stands opposed to his exhortation.

- A community who single-mindedly wills one thing in a world of aimless consumption and hedonism (James 1:5–8; 4:8)
- A community committed to obedience and submission to God's law of freedom in a world of autonomous freedom and antinomian grace (1:22–25; 2:8–11)
- A community in solidarity with the poor and vulnerable in a world with a growing disparity of wealth (2:1–7)
- A community that uses their tongues well in a world of cheap words, many words, destructive words, unaccountable words (3:1–12; cf. 1:26)
- A community of self-giving wisdom in a world of envy and selfish ambition (3:13–18)
- A community of wholehearted devotion to God in a world of syncretism and compromised living (4:4–5)
- A community of joy (1:2) *and* lament (4:9) in a world of pain and idolatry
- A community that lives in God's presence and rests in his sovereign purpose in a world of practical atheism and the "eclipse of God" (4:13–17)

---

15. Richard Bauckham, *James: Wisdom of James, Disciple of Jesus the Sage*, New Testament Readings (London and New York: Routledge, 1999), 174–75.

If we are to communicate the gospel as public truth, we will also need to take the calling of the laity in public life seriously, along with its implications for congregations. This is also an important emphasis for our day. Ian Barns has rightly pointed out the importance of this area of Newbigin's thought:

> For Newbigin it was lay Christians, in the context of their daily occupations and professions, that played a crucial role in communicating the public truth of the gospel in our culture. Because of this he was particularly concerned for the effective and ongoing equipping and support of lay Christians in their daily lives. Notwithstanding the various impressive "Christians at work" initiatives around the world, I don't think that this challenge has really been taken on board by pastors, theologians, Christian educators and Christian leaders in the professions. . . . Many Christians in professional occupations are godly, honest, and caring people in their personal dealings with others, but they default to being technocratic humanists at a cognitive level. Given the enormous societal upheavals that are about to befall the planet, the human community will desperately need Christian community organisers, food producers, doctors, engineers, peacemakers, counsellors, inventors (to name just a few) inspired by the love of Christ and the public vision of God's peaceable universal kingdom.[16]

I can say with joy that in Phoenix I see the Surge network of churches that have begun to take this challenge seriously. About forty churches work together to provide a curriculum and discipleship program to train over three hundred people a year to work out what it means to live in light of the gospel and the biblical story in their particular callings. This concern for vocation combined with another of Newbigin's concerns—the unity of the church— has enabled this initiative to be quite effective and to have an influence on the public life of the city. But even in Phoenix there is a long way to go. And so, given that most places are much further behind, this surely remains a significant challenge for our day.

Theology and Theological Education

Few would disagree that there is a crisis in theological education today and that this is not a new problem. The urgency of the issue is that missionary churches need well-trained missionary leaders. Recently, a growing chorus

---

16. Ian Barns, "Some Reflections on Lesslie Newbigin's Challenge to Bear Witness to the Gospel as 'Public Truth,'" Fellowship of Saint Thomas, "Lesslie Newbigin Centenary," www .fost.org.uk/bigincont.htm.

of voices has argued that mission may play an important role in the renewal of education today. Yet what is surprising is how few of those who advocate this are returning to the missionary leaders and thinkers of the 1960s, '70s, and '80s. During that period there was rich reflection on the nature and practice of theological education in view of the rapidly growing church in the Southern Hemisphere. There was little interest in transporting the university model of theological education to those churches, and so there was some deep thinking about what kind of theological education would meet their needs.

The theological reflection of this time was primarily concerned with the so-called younger churches of the global South and East. Yet Newbigin rightly posed the question of whether the issue was "that the theological schools of the Third World needed to be brought up to the 'best' western standards. It was the question whether these standards really are the best; whether the models of ministerial formation accepted in Europe and North America are really the right ones for the Third World—*or even for the areas where they have been developed.*"[17]

Discussion of theological education focused on four main areas: structures, pedagogy, evaluation, and curriculum. While Newbigin did not become deeply immersed in the discussions, he did wade in a few times. And his comments arose out of a long history of reflection on theological education. Where his legacy may be most important is in the area of curriculum, specifically his constant challenge to rethink the various theological disciplines. On this his challenge was twofold. On the one hand, there was not enough awareness of how much the cultural assumptions of the West were shaping theological studies. The problem was not that the Western church had a Western theology; that is the way it should be. Rather, the problem is a lack of awareness of the contextual nature of theology and an assumption that one's theology, formed in a particular culture, is universal—a *theologia perennis*. When this happens, there is little critique, and the church is vulnerable to embracing the idols of the culture. On the other hand, Newbigin also challenged the church to see that the centrality of mission in the biblical story had little formative power on the theological disciplines. The main patterns of theological education were formed when mission had ceased to exist as a living reality in the minds of many Christians. In what follows, we'll briefly consider Newbigin's take on the primary disciplines within theological education.

17. Lesslie Newbigin, "Theological Education in a World Perspective," *Churchman* 93, no. 2 (1979): 105–15 (my emphasis).

Biblical Studies

Newbigin believes that much Western scholarship within the realm of biblical studies has substituted one religious creed for another. "From the late 18th century onwards, the Bible came more and more into the hands of the scholars whose scholarship was shaped by the new perspectives of the Enlightenment. The Bible was read and interpreted from within another belief-system, another worldview. It was (to the scholarly world) no longer Holy Scripture, but a corpus of ancient writings to be understood and assessed in the light of a different creed. It no longer stood in judgement on culture but was itself judged by new cultural standards."[18] Newbigin did not reject historical-critical method or that there was much fruit arising out of this scholarship. Rather, he rejected its dominance and captivity to another creed that crippled church leadership. The renewed interest today in theological hermeneutics is something that Newbigin would have strongly encouraged. The church and mission must be the primary dialogue partner for biblical scholarship.

But Newbigin would also want to encourage what he calls a "missionary hermeneutic" for the sake of the church. He believed Scripture "is from Genesis to Revelation the essential missionary text."[19] And so he speaks of a "proposed marriage" between the "canon of scripture" and the "whole mission committed to the Church." It seems to be a marriage "made in heaven," he says, "but at present partners are rarely linked together and appear to be still awaiting introduction." Yet "canon and mission are interdependent and should be inseparable," and "if the marriage takes place and is consummated there will be progeny essential to the future life of the Church."[20] Today we might say that the introduction of mission to biblical studies has been made; a missional hermeneutic has begun to develop in earnest. But we are still a long way from an enduring marriage. And so the formulation of a missionary hermeneutic in biblical scholarship remains an important task for the present.

Systematic Theology

Newbigin also inquired as to whether we had developed a "missiologically adequate systematic theology."[21] Such a theology would certainly be

18. Lesslie Newbigin, "The Bible: Good News for Secularised People" (keynote address, Europe and Middle East Regional Conference, Eisenach, Germany, April 1991), Newbigin Archives, University of Birmingham, 1.

19. Newbigin, "Canon and Mission," 1.

20. Newbigin, "Canon and Mission," 1.

21. Newbigin, "Canon and Mission," 2.

contextual.[22] Theology is a fresh task in each generation because the cultural context is constantly changing. Theology has the negative role of exposing and expelling the idolatry that perverts the faith. It also has the positive task of expressing the faith in relationship to the relevant issues of the day so the church may fully and vividly take hold of the faith. Contextual theology is not a fad for Newbigin but the prerequisite of a living and faithful faith; it must be both rooted in Scripture and relevant to the cultural currents of the day.

> If the Church is going to meet and master the forces which are shaping the secular world of our time, she needs to put a far greater proportion of her strength behind the work of the theologians; she needs a theology which is not the mere product of changing moods and fashions but deeply based on Scripture, stated in terms in which the world lives, relevant to the forces which are actually shaping the lives of men. It is not sufficient for the Church to attend to tactics: she must attend first to truth.[23]

Newbigin is concerned that theology has been primarily focused on "a mutual struggle of rival interpretations of the Gospel" and not enough concerned about the cultural context.[24] Dialogue has been between theological traditions rather than between the gospel and religio-cultural context. This leads to either a "jellyfish" theology that is blown about on the cultural tides or a "fossil" theology that clings to old and irrelevant forms of theological expression. A good example of challenging a "rival interpretations" approach is when Newbigin was asked to speak to the Anglican-Reformed International Commission on the sacraments. In effect, his talk relativized the differences between the traditions when he argued that both share the same problematic approaches to the sacraments, rooted in Christendom. The real battle is not between Anglican and Reformed views of the sacraments but has to do with whether baptism and the Lord's Supper are nourishing a missionary congregation.[25]

Newbigin also offers some helpful structures for a missiologically adequate systematic theology. In chapter 2, we discussed how the eschatological, missional, communal, and individual contexts informed Newbigin's

22. Michael W. Goheen, "Theology in Context: Lesslie Newbigin's Contribution," *Christian Courier*, 2668 (July 9, 2001): 16–17.

23. Lesslie Newbigin, "Bishop Newbigin's Final Word," in *We Were Brought Together*, ed. David M. Taylor (Sydney: Australian Council for the World Council of Churches, 1960), 129.

24. Lesslie Newbigin, *Honest Religion for Secular Man* (Philadelphia: Westminster, 1966), 102.

25. Lesslie Newbigin, "How Should We Understand Sacraments and Ministry?" (paper for the Anglican-Reformed International Commission meeting, London, 1983), Newbigin Archives, University of Birmingham.

formulation of his pneumatology and doctrine of the sacraments. Pneumatology has often been shaped by an understanding of the application of Christ's work to individuals; the sacraments are understood in terms of the means of grace for individual salvation. Newbigin's formulation does not diminish the importance of these insights but places them in a broader framework. We might also think of the way he views the "logic" of the Christian faith in cosmic, communal, and personal terms. Many theological themes would be much better understood within this framework. For example, the atonement and the resurrection, understood in their cosmic and communal significance, would challenge typical individualistic approaches.[26] The *beneficia Christi* that often make up the whole of soteriology would be rightly placed in a more comprehensive soteriology. These frameworks offer much potential for revitalizing systematic theology in a way that nourishes the missionary church.

Church History

Newbigin's brief suggestions about church history are likewise filled with promise. He believed that church history had been taught in terms of doctrinal and polity conflicts within the life of the church. Instead, he calls us to approach church history in terms of a series of successive missionary encounters of the gospel with the various cultures of the world. In fact, it was in a talk that Newbigin once gave that my own understanding was changed, and I saw the value of this approach. He said something like this: "I wish someone had taught me in seminary that the christological and trinitarian controversies of the second and third centuries were not first and foremost matters of orthodoxy and heresy but examples of a contextual struggle in theology." He wasn't denying the faithfulness of Athanasius in contrast to Arius, saying both were equally contextual theologies. But both were struggling to contextualize the gospel in a Greek context. Athanasius offered a more faithful contextualization in keeping with Scripture, challenging the idolatrous Neoplatonic framework assumed by Arius and others. Church history is about exposing the contextual struggle of the gospel with the cultural currents of the day. This approach to church history has much to teach students, not just in terms of content—that is, the actual theological results—but also in terms of models. We may observe the way churches in other historical periods confessed and taught the gospel faithfully within their

26. I have taken this approach in Michael W. Goheen, *A Light to the Nations: The Missional Church and the Biblical Story* (Grand Rapids: Baker Academic, 2011), 101–19 (chap. 5, "The Death and Resurrection of Jesus and the Church's Missional Identity").

own cultural context. And so we learn both by good and by bad example how to walk in a way that is faithful.

Pastoral Theology

Newbigin has also offered insight for the development of a more missional pastoral theology. On the one hand, he rejects the theory-praxis dichotomy that underlies theological education and divides the subjects into theoretical disciplines (biblical studies, systematic theology, church history) and practical disciplines (pastoral and practical theology). This dichotomy is the product of the Enlightenment.[27] On the other hand, he believes that pastoral theology operates on a view of ministry that is not shaped by a missionary understanding of the church. Pastoral care is conceived in Christendom terms, assuming that each individual believer is a passive recipient of the means of grace. It is the duty of the minister to administer it. He acknowledges the partial truth in this; pastoral care must indeed employ the means of grace to build up believers. But there is more: pastoral care must also be for the discharge of the missionary task.[28]

Missiology

Finally, Newbigin also has much to offer the discipline of missiology. He describes his own experience as he takes up teaching missiology at Selly Oaks and determining where to begin and how to approach the discipline. He says he wants to root his missiology in an understanding of the church as missionary.[29] The text that he authored for the course on theology of mission was *The Open Secret*. There we see the way he sets the church's mission in the context of the narrative of God's mission. Mission is a central theme in the biblical story as a whole, and the people of God are missionary by their very nature. Mission is not formulated as one of the tasks of the church.

Beyond this important starting point Newbigin has offered two significant distinctions—between missionary dimension and missionary intention, and between mission and missions—that remain extremely helpful in approaching missiology. Both distinctions are attempting to protect an intentional witness of the church in evangelism and cross-cultural missions while

27. Lesslie Newbigin, *Proper Confidence: Faith, Doubt, and Certainty in Christian Discipleship* (Grand Rapids: Eerdmans, 1995), 38–39.

28. Lesslie Newbigin, *Household of God: Lectures on the Nature of the Church* (New York: Friendship Press, 1954), 166–67.

29. Newbigin, *Unfinished Agenda*, 229.

recognizing the comprehensive scope of the church's mission to bear witness to Christ's lordship over all of life.[30]

More could certainly be said about Newbigin's legacy in theology and theological education, but these brief comments show that he has much to offer in our present crisis in the way of missional theology and missional theological education.

An Unanxious Witness

N. T. Wright tells the story of a time in the 1980s when he entered the second term of the academic year fearful and exhausted, not wanting to face the tasks ahead. Newbigin was scheduled to preach in chapel that first day, and when he walked through the gateway of Worcester College, Oxford, Wright felt all those fears and exhaustions drop away. He knew he could tackle the new term with joy. He notes that others have expressed a similar experience when he has related that story.

I experienced this too but in a different way. I was entering Duke University Chapel with Newbigin just prior to his second Hickman lecture on the topic of scriptural authority. We had been discussing at a meal just prior some opposition he was receiving from liberal quarters on his view of Scripture and how he was being characterized as a fundamentalist. I confess I was mildly anxious as we walked in, knowing the lecture that was coming. Just before reaching the door, he momentarily reached for my hand and said, "There will be many who will oppose what I say." And then, as if in an act of resolve, he pushed my hand away and said, "But I must be faithful whatever the consequences and leave it in God's hand." I remember my own sense of anxiety and fear dropping away.[31]

What accounts for this? In my case at least it was the joyful and bold, yet humble, confidence that characterized Newbigin's approach to the faith. This

---

30. In my own missiological text—Michael W. Goheen, *Introduction to Mission Studies Today: Scripture, History, and Issues* (Downers Grove, IL: InterVarsity, 2014)—I start with mission in the biblical story (chap. 1) and three theological distinctions: between mission of God and mission of the church, missionary dimension and missionary intention, and mission and missions (chap. 2) as a foundation for missiology.

31. A postscript to the story: I sat in front of a pastor and conversed with him before the lecture. It was rather clear he did not like Newbigin's orthodox views that he had heard in the first lecture. At the end of the lecture, Newbigin received a lengthy standing ovation, something I am told is uncommon for that lecture series. I turned and saw this liberal pastor applauding, and so when it concluded I asked him why. His answer surprised me: "He just gave me the gospel back again to preach!"

is rooted in a shift that he describes in his own theology and experienced in the 1960s. He believed that his own theology was not as fully trinitarian as it should be. Some have discounted Newbigin's self-description here because his earlier writing appears to be fully trinitarian from the start. However, what changed was not simply a fuller theological formulation of the Trinity, although this may be true. It was his deepened confidence in the sovereign rule of the Father over all of history, ineluctably working out his purpose, and the conviction that the Spirit is the first and only effectual witness to Christ. This theme becomes far more prominent in his writing and, we can assume, in his own experience. Mission is not only following Christ and continuing his mission of life, word, and deed. It is following in Christ's way, with the same trust in the work of the Father throughout history and the same faith in the power of the Spirit working in his words and deeds.

This very real faith that it is God's mission stands against the powerful humanist tides that are sweeping the Western church into its currents today. There is a managerial ecclesiology that relies—in practice but not in theology—on planning, strategy, and the social sciences for the church's life. Just recently a pastor said to me that he believes this to be one of the biggest threats, even while being hidden, for American pastors today. Confessing in our theology that God is sovereignly working out his redemptive purposes in history and that the Spirit is the primary witness is much easier than taking this truth into our being so deeply that our ecclesial practice is reshaped.

This confidence in God's work, coupled with the conviction that central to our very being as the church is the call to bear faithful witness to Christ, led Newbigin to an unanxious witness that was full of joy, boldness, and trust. It also liberates us from fear and concern about results and frees us to be directed to the glory of God. Those who knew Newbigin can testify to this. And this also may offer an explanation of why he has had this calming effect on others. One just knew with Newbigin that mission is in God's hands, and our responsibility is quite simply to be faithful.

Index